A POPULAR DICTIONARY OF

Islam

A POPULAR DICTIONARY OF

Islam

IAN RICHARD NETTON

Curzon

First published by Curzon Press
15 The Quadrant, Richmond
Surrey, TW9 1BP

Revised edition 1997
Cover photograph by Sharon Hoogstraten
Cover design by Kim Bartko
Printed in the United States of America

British Library Cataloguing in Publication Data
A catalogue record for this book is available from the British Library

ISBN 0 7007 1046 9

For Deborah and Jonathan with much love

PREFACE AND ACKNOWLEDGEMENTS

Islam is one of the world's great religions. It has become a truism to acknowledge, also, that it is much more than merely a religion to be practised on a Friday in the Mosque. Islam embraces – or should embrace – the entirety of man's life. This may help to explain to the reader coming fresh to the subject why this *Dictionary* covers so many diverse topics ranging from famous battles to details of ritual purity. Not surprisingly, Islam has been surveyed by a huge number of books. A few, which may be of further use to the interested reader, are listed at the back of this *Dictionary* in the *Guide to Further Reading*. The quality of the books which deal with Islam, in both the West and the East, is also various, embracing the good and the bad, the profoundly bigoted and the devoutly sympathetic.

This *Popular Dictionary of Islam* aims to be an inexpensive, yet profusely cross-referenced, literary tool and source book which may be of use to layman, student and scholar alike, both Muslim and non-Muslim, surveying and introducing as it does diverse aspects of Islam's religion, ritual, theology, philosophy, law, history, art and architecture plus many others. Of course, the author is very much aware that the compilation of *any* dictionary, particularly of one which claims to be *popular*, is a highly subjective affair. Everyone has his or her own ideas about what is crucially important and the compiler is thus a hostage to his reader's interests, preferences and scholarly emphases. I hope that I have not omitted anything vital. I have tried to present the bare minimum of what is an immensely rich and vitally important subject. The approach has been, in so far as it is humanly possibly, objective and phenomenological which does not, however, preclude immense respect for all the subjects here treated. I am, of course, responsible for all errors of commission, omission, misinterpretations and misprints which may unwittingly have crept into the text. If readers will kindly notify me of these, I will do my best to rectify them in any future edition.

For the sake of completeness, and because of their Islamic *origins*, entries are included for subjects like **Bābism**, the **Bahā'īs** and the **Druze**. I am aware that some will dispute the right of such entries to appear in a Dictionary dealing with Islam.

It is a particular, and unusual if not unique, feature of this *Dictionary* that it contains an individual entry for *each one* of the 114 chapters (**sūras**) of the **Qur'ān**, listed under its Arabic title. These entries, however, while they *do* claim to give a brief *flavour* of the content of each Qur'ānic Chapter, do not in any way claim to provide an *exhaustive* summary or paraphrase of what is contained in that Chapter. Qur'ānic verses and Chapter numbers referred to in this *Dictionary* follow those of the Royal Cairo Edition of the Arabic text of the Qur'ān printed in *The Bounteous Koran*, ed. M. M. Khatib, (see *Guide to Further Reading* at the back of this volume for full bibliographical details). This bilingual Arabic-English edition of the Qur'ān was approved by Al-Azhar in 1984.

Finally, it is a pleasure to acknowledge some of the debts of gratitude which I have incurred in the writing and compilation of this *Dictionary*. My thanks and love go firstly to my wife and family for their patience and tolerance. I am grateful to Mrs Sheila Westcott for her exemplary typing of parts of this work; and to Miss Heather Eva, Director of the Inter-Library Loans Department of the University of Exeter Library for superb service: she never panicked even when I did! David Firth, a former student, kindly sent materials on Islamic banking, and al-Hajj Isma'il 'Abd al-Halim generously supplied me with information on the Islamic Conference Organisation. Dr Fadia Faqir, Dr Talib al-Saraf and the Cultural Section of the Saudi Arabian Embassy in London all gave freely and generously of their time to answer questions about Middle Eastern place names and the topography of various areas which I had not myself visited. I am also very grateful to my colleagues, Mr Brian

Pridham, Director of the Centre for Arab Gulf Studies in the University of Exeter, and Dr Charles Davies, Research Fellow in that Centre, for much valuable information and help. It has been a pleasure every year to invite Dr Richard Hitchcock, Head of the Department of Spanish and Reader in Hispano-Arabic Studies in the University of Exeter, to lecture to my first year undergraduate students on Islamic Spain: a few of the ideas gleaned from these lectures are incorporated in this *Dictionary*. My final thanks go to Dr Lynn Williams, also of the Department of Spanish at Exeter University, for his encouragement and provision of useful and fascinating information which I have incorporated in this *Dictionary*.

Ian Richard Netton
University of Exeter
June 1991

ABBREVIATIONS

AD	:	(*Anno Domini*) Christian era
AH	:	(*Anno Hegirae*) Muslim era
Ar.	:	Arabic
c.	:	(*circa*) about
edn	:	edition
ff.	:	following
fl.	:	(*floruit*) he/she lived
Fr.	:	French
Guj.	:	Gujarati
ibid.	:	(*ibidem*) in same book etc.
masc.	:	masculine
Pers.	:	Persian
pl.	:	plural
q.v.	:	(*quod vide*) which see
r.	:	(*raka'āt*) units of Muslim prayer
reg.	:	(*regnabat*) he/she ruled
sing.	:	singular
Span.	:	Spanish
s.v.	:	(*sub verbo*) under the word
Turk.	:	Turkish
Ur.	:	Urdu
v.	:	Qur'ānic verse
vv.	:	Qur'ānic verses

HOW TO USE THIS DICTIONARY

The Arabic word or name constitutes the major entry but this is heavily cross-referenced from the English. Cross references within entries are printed in **Bold** (*sic*) type, and the letters q.v. also appear after all but the most common like **Muḥammad**, **Qur'ān**, **Sūra** etc. The order of entries in this *Dictionary* is strictly alphabetical, except 'al-' is ignored *at the beginning* of an entry. In all cases the Arabic letters *'ayn* and *hamza* (transliterated as ' and ' respectively) are ignored for purposes of alphabetization.

The Arabic word for a Qur'ānic chapter, *Sūra*, is written as *sūra* normally, but as *sūrat* when it is in a genitive construction. To find, for example, the entries for **Sūrat al-Naḥl** or **Sūrat al-A'rāf** the reader should look under **al-Naḥl** and **al-A'rāf** respectively, and *not* under **Sūra**. (Forms such as **Sūrat al-Kāfirūn** are reproduced as in *The Bounteous Qur'ān*).

The transliteration of Arabic words follows a consistent pattern. However, I have written 'Abd Allāh, 'Abd al-Raḥmān, but I have sometimes preferred Āyatullāh, 'Ubaydullāh, Bahā'ullāh, Ruḥullāh, Ni'matullāh etc. The words Persia and Iran are used interchangeably.

With regard to *dating*, the Islamic year is given first, then the Christian, e.g. 36/656 = AH36/AD656 (*See* **Calendar** entry in this *Dictionary*). A similar procedure is followed in references to whole centuries, e.g. 'in the 3rd/9th century' means 'in the third century of the Islamic era which is equivalent to the ninth century of the Christian era'. Where there is any lack of precision, this is reflected in the dates given, e.g. 'in 566/1170-1' means 'in the Islamic year 566, part of which falls in the Christian year 1170 and part in 1171'.

A POPULAR DICTIONARY OF ISLAM

'Abasa (Ar.) The title of the 80th **sūra** of the **Qur'ān**; it means literally 'He frowned'. The *sūra* belongs to the Meccan period and contains 42 verses. Its title reflects the Prophet **Muḥammad**'s impatience on being interrupted by a blind man while the former was expounding the Qur'ān. The *sūra* goes on to stress the honourable, high and pure nature of the Qur'ān before concluding with a survey of some of the gifts which God has bestowed upon man and a warning about the Last Judgement. (*See* **al-Ḥisāb**; **Yawm al-Qiyāma**.)

al-'Abbās b. 'Abd al-Muṭṭalib (died *c.* 32/653) Merchant uncle of **Muḥammad** who married Maymūna, the sister of al-'Abbās' wife, in 7/629. Al-'Abbās fought Muḥammad at the Battle of Badr: he was captured but later released. He became a Muslim and joined the Prophet Muḥammad in the final assault on **Mecca** (q.v.) in 8/630. Because of this Muḥammad called al-'Abbās the last of the **Muhājirūn** (q.v.). He gave his name to the dynasty of the **'Abbāsids** (q.v.). (*See* **Badr, Battle of**.)

'Abbāsids Major dynasty in mediaeval Islam which flourished between 132/750–656/1258 in **Baghdād** (q.v.), and survived as a shadow caliphate in **Cairo** (q.v.) from 659/1261 until 923/1517. The dynasty took its name from the Prophet **Muḥammad**'s uncle, **al-'Abbās b. 'Abd al-Muṭṭalib** (q.v.). The seat of the 'Abbāsid empire was established at Baghdād by the 'Abbāsid caliph al-Manṣūr in the 2nd/8th century. A great cultural efflorescence took place under the 'Abbāsids between the 2nd/8th–5th/11th centuries. Politically the power of the dynasty declined after the **Būyids** (q.v.) entered Baghdād in 334/945. The last 'Abbāsid caliph in Baghdād, al-Musta'ṣim (*reg.* 640/1242–656/1258), was murdered by the **Mongols** (q.v.) when they sacked that city in 656/1258. (*See* **Hāshimiyya**; **Umayyads**; **Zāb, Battle of the Greater**.)

'Abd (Ar.) [pl. *'ibād* or *'abīd*] Male slave, servant (of God), man, human being. In the plural *'abīd* is often used to designate 'slaves', while *'ibād* is used for 'servants (of God)'. *Al-'Ibād* means 'mankind'. However, the **Qur'ān** does use the plural *'ibād* for slaves: *see* v.32 of **Sūrat al-Nūr** (q.v.). *'Abd* often forms part of a proper name, e.g. 'Abd al-Raḥmān (= Servant of the Merciful God). Slavery was common throughout Islamic history and the institution was governed by a variety of rules established by Islamic jurisprudence. Modern Islam is in favour of the abolition of slavery. (*See* **al-Rabb**; **al-Raḥmān**.)

Abdāl (Ar.) [sing. *badal*] The word means literally 'substitutes' or 'replacements'. It acquired a technical meaning in **taṣawwuf** (q.v.) and was used to designate a rank in the **ṣūfī** (q.v.) hierarchy of saints. The *abdāl* are so-called because each is replaced by another on his death throughout the course of history. Authorities differ over the number of *abdāl*: some maintain that there are forty, others seventy. (*See* **Walī**.)

'Abd al-Ḥamīd II (1258/1842–1336/1918) The 36th Ottoman sultan, he acceded to the throne in 1293/1876. During his reign Turkey fought wars with Russia and Greece. After the Young Turk Revolution (1326/1908), 'Abd al-Ḥamīd was deposed in 1327/1909 and sent into exile. (*See* **Ottomans**.)

'Abd al-Jabbār (323-4/935–415/1025) His full name was 'Abd al-Jabbār b. Aḥmad b. 'Abd al-Jabbār al-Hamadhānī al-Asadābādī. He espoused the theology of the **Mu'tazila** (q.v.) and was a notable exponent of their views. Legally he belonged at first to the Shāfi'ī School of Islamic law. He held the post of Chief Judge in Rayy which was near modern Tehran. When his protector in Rayy died, he was deposed and little is known about the latter part of his life. His most important work of Theology was the huge *Summa* (*al-Mughnī*). (*See* **Qāḍī**; **Shāfi'īs**.)

'Abd Allāh b. 'Abd al-Muṭṭalib (AD 545?–570?) Father of the Prophet **Muḥammad**. He belonged to the clan of **Hāshim** (q.v.) of the tribe of **Quraysh** (q.v.). His mother, who came from the clan of **Makhzūm** (q.v.), was called Fāṭima bint 'Amr. His wife's name was **Āmina bint Wahb** (q.v.); she came from the clan of the Zuhra. 'Abd Allāh died before the birth of Muḥammad. The **Qur'ān** in v.6 of **Sūrat al-Ḍuḥā** (q.v.) makes a direct reference to Muḥammad as an orphan. (*See* **'Abd al-Muṭṭalib b. Hāshim**.)

'Abd Allāh b. al-'Abbās *See* **Ibn 'Abbās**.

'Abd Allāh b. Muḥammad Son of the Prophet **Muḥammad** and **Khadīja bint Khuwaylid** (q.v.); he died while very young. He was born before AD 619 and hardly anything is known about him. (*See* **Ibrāhīm** (3); **al-Qāsim**.)

'Abd al-Malik b. Marwān (26/646-7–86/705) The 5th caliph of the dynasty of the **Umayyads** (q.v.). He ruled over the Islamic empire from 65/685–86/705. In the first part of his reign he had to deal with the anti-caliph 'Abd Allāh b. al-Zubayr: the latter was eventually defeated and killed by 'Abd al-Malik's great general, al-Ḥajjāj, in 73/692. Revolts by the **Khārijites** (q.v.) constituted a further problem. During the rule of 'Abd al-Malik, the garrison of Wāsiṭ was built in Iraq, an Islamic gold coinage was issued and the Dome of the Rock (**Qubbat al-Ṣakhra** (q.v.)) was built in **Jerusalem** (q.v.). (*See* **al-Aqṣā, al-Masjid**.)

'Abd al-Muṭṭalib b. Hāshim The grandfather, on the paternal side, of the Prophet **Muḥammad**, and father of Muḥammad's father **'Abd Allāh** (q.v.). He became head of the clan of **Hāshim** (q.v.) and was Muḥammad's first guardian after his father's death. One of 'Abd al-Muṭṭalib's wives was Fāṭima bint 'Amr: 'Abd Allāh was her son. 'Abd al-Muṭṭalib became a properous merchant and was the digger of a number of wells; he discovered and restored the Well of **Zamzam** (q.v.). It is difficult to give precise dates for 'Abd al-Muṭṭalib's life beyond stating that he flourished in the 6th century AD.

'Abd al-Qays Important Arab tribe in pre-Islam and the early Islamic period, involved in many of the major political and religious events of those days. In the main they opposed the **Khārijites** (q.v.) though some did support, and indeed head, a few of the Khārijite movements. The tribe of 'Abd al-Qays supported the Prophet **Muḥammad, 'Umar b. al-Khaṭṭāb** (q.v.), **'Uthmān b. 'Affān** (q.v.) for the first part of his rule, and **'Alī b. Abī Ṭālib** (q.v.). However, they were by no means uncritical supporters of the succeeding **Umayyads** (q.v.). Before conversion to Islam the tribe was initially pagan and then Christian, probably of the Nestorian variety. The tribe of 'Abd al-Qays was called after an ancestor of that name: it meant 'the servant of al-Qays' (a god or idol).

'Abd al-Raḥmān III b. Muḥammad b. 'Abd Allāh (*c.* 276/889–350/961) Generally considered to be the greatest of the Umayyad Andalusian caliphs. He ruled from 300/912–350/961. 'Abd al-Raḥmān consolidated the unity of **Cordova** (q.v.) and waged war against the Christian rulers of Spain, not always successfully. As a result of his reign Cordova became one of the great capitals of the Arab-Islamic West.

'Abd al-'Uzzā Name of ancestor of the Prophet **Muḥammad**; 'Abd al-'Uzzā was one of the four sons of **Quṣayy** (q.v.) (who lived in the 5th century AD), and a brother of **'Abd Manāf** (q.v.)

'Abd al-'Uzzā b. 'Abd al-Muṭṭalib (died *c.* 3/624) Uncle of the Prophet **Muḥammad** who vehemently opposed the Prophet. He was called by the name Abū Lahab meaning 'Father of Flame' because he was so good-looking. He may be said to have been one of the catalysts which led to the **hijra** (q.v.) of Muḥammad from **Mecca** (q.v.) to **Medina** (q.v.): when the Prophet Muḥammad's uncle **Abū Ṭālib** (q.v.), who had been head of the clan of **Hāshim** (q.v.), died, Abū Lahab assumed the headship, and the protection of the clan of Hāshim was later withdrawn from Muḥammad. The tension between Muḥammad and Abū Lahab is reflected in **Sūrat al-Masad** (q.v.) of the **Qur'ān**. Abū Lahab died soon after the Battle of Badr. His children converted to Islam. (*See* **'Abd al-Muṭṭalib b. Hāshim**; **Badr, Battle of**)

'Abd Manāf Father of **Hāshim** (q.v.) and ancestor of the Prophet **Muḥammad**. 'Abd Manāf was a son of **Quṣayy** (q.v.). His name in Arabic means literally 'servant of Manāf' and he was so-called because he was promised to the pre-Islamic deity **Manāf** (q.v.) by his mother. 'Abd Manāf gave his name to the clan grouping in the tribe of **Quraysh** (q.v.) called the 'Abd Manāf.

'Abd Shams Ancestor of the Prophet **Muḥammad**, son of **'Abd Manāf** (q.v.) and father of **Umayya**. 'Abd Shams gave his name to a major clan of the tribe of **Quraysh** (q.v.). The **Umayya** (q.v.) family was descended from him, as was the 3rd caliph **'Uthmān b. 'Affān** (q.v.)

'Abduh, Muḥammad (1265/1849–1323/1905) One of the most famous of the 13th/19th century reformers. Born in the Egyptian Delta, he studied at the **al-Azhar** (q.v.) in **Cairo** (q.v.) and later, in Paris, having been exiled to that city. Here he formed brief links with **al-Afghānī** (q.v.) After returning to Egypt, 'Abduh became the Chief Muftī. Because of his commitment to the use of reason, he employed and developed the principle of **talfīq** (q.v.) in jurisprudence. He was also committed to the **Salafiyya** (q.v.) movement. (*See* **Ijtihād**; **Muftī**.)

Ablaq (Ar.) Literally 'piebald'. The word is used as a technical term in Islamic architecture to designate stone, marble or brick decoration in which two colours or tones (often one light and one dark) are used alternately in courses by way of contrast. *Ablaq* or striped masonry may be seen on much of the Mamlūk architecture of **Cairo** (q.v.). (*See* the various entries listed under **Art and Architecture, Islamic**; *see also* **Mamlūks**.)

Ablution, Ritual *See* **Ghusl**; **Mīḍa'a**; **Tayammum**; **Wuḍū'**.

Abraha Christian ruler or governor of Abyssinian origins who flourished in South Arabia in the mid-6th century AD. He is famous among the Islamic chroniclers for having led an unsuccessful assault on the city of **Mecca** (q.v.) in *c*. AD 570: the incident is covered in **Sūrat al-Fīl** (q.v.) of the **Qur'ān**. The presence of one or more elephants in Abraha's entourage led to the year AD 570 (the year of the Prophet **Muḥammad**'s birth) being called 'The Year of the Elephant'. The facts of Abraha's life became much embellished with legend. (*See* **Elephant, The Year of the**)

Abraham *See* **Ibrāhīm**.

Abrogation *See* **Nāsikh and Mansūkh**.

Abubacer *See* **Ibn Ṭufayl**.

Abū Bakr (*c*. AD 573–13/634) Father of **'Ā'isha bint Abī Bakr** (q.v.), and the 1st **khalīfa** (q.v.) to rule over the Islamic community, after the death of the Prophet **Muḥammad** in 11/632. His rule lasted for slightly more than two years. He belonged to one of the clans of the tribe of **Quraysh** (q.v.) called **Taym** (q.v.). Abū Bakr was one of the first to convert to Islam and made the **hijra** (q.v.) with **Muḥammad** from **Mecca** (q.v.) to **Medina** (q.v.). His first task on becoming *khalīfa* was to put down the **Ridda** (q.v.) insurgency. The Arab conquests also began during his rule. Abū Bakr had a reputation as a noted genealogist. His honesty also earned him the Arabic title **al-Ṣiddīq** (q.v.). (*See* **Rāshidūn**.)

Abū Dā'ūd (202/817–275/889) His full name was Sulaymān b. al-Ash'ath Abū Dā'ūd al-Sijistānī. He ranks as one of the six chief compilers of Islamic tradition (**ḥadīth** (q.v.)) in Sunnī Islam. His most important work was *The Book of Traditions* (*Kitāb al-Sunan*). He adopted a more critical approach in his collection of traditions than many others of his age and before him.

Abū Ḥanīfa (*c.* 80/699–150/767) His full name was Abū Ḥanīfa al-Nu'mān b. Thābit. He gave his name to the Ḥanafī School of Islamic law which was really founded by his disciples rather than Abū Ḥanīfa himself. He was one of the most important jurists and theologians of early mediaeval Islam, living in **al-Kūfa** (q.v.) and becoming the most distinguished member of the law school there. Towards the end of his life he was imprisoned in **Baghdād** (q.v.) where he died. His views on jurisprudence were collected and recorded by his disciples. (*See* **Ḥanafīs**.)

Abū Hurayra (died *c.* 58/678) Name of one of **Muḥammad**'s companions. His reputation is mainly based, however, on the huge number of traditions which he is said to have narrated. Because of this large quantity suspicion has frequently dogged his name. Yet in his lifetime he was known as a pious man and, later, **al-Bukhārī** (q.v.), **Muslim b. al-Ḥajjāj** (q.v.) and **Aḥmad b. Ḥanbal** (q.v.) had no hesitation in incorporating his traditions in their collections. (*See* **Ḥadīth**; **Ṣaḥāba**.)

Abū Jahl (*c.* AD 570–2/624) A member of the **Makhzūm** (q.v.) clan of the tribe of **Quraysh** (q.v.) and a fierce opponent of the Prophet **Muḥammad** while the latter was still in **Mecca** (q.v.) before the **hijra** (q.v.). After that event Abū Jahl was killed fighting against Muḥammad at the Battle of Badr. (*See* **Badr, Battle of**; **Sumayya bint Khubbāṭ**.)

Abū Lahab *See* **'Abd al-'Uzzā b. 'Abd al-Muṭṭalib**.

Abū 'l-Hudhayl al-'Allāf (born between 135/752-3 and 131/748-9; died between 226/840-1 and 235/849-50) Leading

Mu'tazilite theologian and metaphysician from **al-Baṣra** (q.v.). His thought was imbued with Aristotelian concepts and terminology. He stands at the beginning of the formal development of **kalām** (q.v.) and had a profound impact on the thought both of his own age and that of succeeding generations through his disciples, whether or not they agreed with him. (*See* **Aristotelianism, Islamic; Mu'tazila.**)

Abū 'l-Qāsim *See* **Muḥammad** (1); **al-Qāsim.**

Abū Sufyān (died *c.* 32/653) A member of the **'Abd Shams** (q.v.) of the tribe of **Quraysh** (q.v.). His fuller name was Abū Sufyān b. Ḥarb b. Umayya. The Prophet **Muḥammad** married his daughter **Umm Ḥabība** (q.v.). Abū Sufyān was prominent in the opposition to Muḥammad and fought against the Prophet, for example, at the Battle of Uḥud. However, in 8/630, when Muḥammad led the final march on **Mecca** (q.v.), Abū Sufyān accepted him and embraced Islam. His son **Mu'āwiya** (q.v.) was the first ruler of the **Umayyads** (q.v.). (*See* **Uḥud, Battle of**)

Abū Ṭālib (died *c.* AD 619) Uncle of the Prophet **Muḥammad** whose guardian he became on the death of **'Abd al-Muṭṭalib b. Hāshim** (q.v.). Muḥammad is said to have gone on trading expeditions with him. As head of the clan of **Hāshim** (q.v.) he was able to give Muḥammad some protection while the latter was in **Mecca** (q.v.). The succession of Abū Ṭālib by **Abū Lahab** (q.v.) as clan chief had grave repercussions for Muḥammad. Abū Ṭālib was also the father of the 4th **khalīfa** (q.v.), **'Alī b. Abī Ṭālib** (q.v.).

Abū 'Ubayda b. al-Jarrāḥ (*c.* AD 581-18/639) Early Muslim general. He fought at the Battle of Uḥud and, after **Muḥammad**'s death, he won the Battle of Yarmūk against the Byzantines in 16/637. He died of plague in Syria. Abū 'Ubayda was one of the ten companions of the Prophet Muḥammad who was promised Paradise. (*See* **al-'Ashara al-Mubashshara; Uḥud, Battle of the; Yarmuk, Battle of**)

Abyssinia *See* **Ethiopia**.

Accident (as philosophical term) *See* **'Araḍ**.

Acquisition (as theological term) *See* **Kasb**.

'Ād The tribe of 'Ād were pre-Islamic South Arabian giants who built monuments on mountains tops. Their wealth led to much arrogance. There are several references to them in the **Qur'ān**. The latter tells, for example, how **Hūd** (q.v.) was sent to warn them: they rejected him and were killed by a terrible wind. Later Arabic literature embroidered the story of 'Ād with much legend. (*See* **Sūrat Fuṣṣilat**; **Sūrat Hūd**.)

Adab (Ar.) [pl. *ādāb*] Word with a wide variety of meanings ranging from 'culture' and 'good-manners' to 'belles-lettres'. The basic Arabic root indicates the possession of refinement or good habits bequeathed down the ages. One of the most notable exponents of *adab* in its sense of belles-lettres was **al-Jāḥiẓ** (q.v.).

Ādam The first prophet and God's **khalīfa** (q.v.) on earth, referred to many times in the **Qur'ān**. After Ādam's creation, God ordered the angels to bow down to Ādam: all obeyed except **Iblīs** (q.v.). Ādam and Eve (**Ḥawwā'** (q.v.)) were tempted by Iblīs in the Garden where they tasted the Tree and were therefore sent down to earth by God. (*See* vv.19–25 of **Sūrat al-A'rāf**.) Arabic literature and legend have considerably elaborated the basic Qur'ānic portrait of Ādam. He also has a special role in the cosmology of the **Ismā'īlīs** (q.v.), being the first of seven **nāṭiqs** (q.v.). For all Muslims throughout history Ādam has had a special significance and symbolism. (*See* **al-Janna**.)

'Adhāb al-Qabr (Ar.) The Punishment of the Grave. According to Muslim tradition, the soul is reunited with the body in the grave after death, and the dead person is then interrogated by two angels **Munkar** and **Nakīr** (q.v.). If the dead person is able to answer the questions correctly and state that **Muḥammad** is his Prophet and Islam is his religion, a window in the grave will be opened looking onto Paradise. The infidels who do not answer correctly will be beaten until the Day of Judgement. Muslims in mediaeval times were warned against treating the Punishment of the Grave as an allegory. (*See* **al-Ḥisāb**; **al-Janna**; **Rūmān**.)

Adhān (Ar.) The call to prayer. This is made five times a day to the Muslim faithful by the **Mu'adhdhin** (q.v.). The call consists of seven main parts, with some slight variation in the number of repetitions of each part according to **madhhab** (q.v.). There are also slight differences between the calls to prayer of the Sunnīs and the Shī'ites. The *adhān* may be chanted to many different tunes and considerable variations will be heard from city to city and country to country. (*See* **Masjid**; **Ṣalāt**; **Shī'ism**; **Sunnī**.)

al-'Ādiyāt (Ar.) The title of the 100th **sūra** of the **Qur'ān**; it means here 'The War Horses' or 'Chargers'. The *sūra* belongs to the Meccan period and contains 11 verses. The title is drawn from the 1st verse which contains an oath 'By the war horses' and which, with the succeeding four verses, evokes the early Arabs' predilection for raiding each other. Man is also reminded that he will be resurrected and judged on the Day of Judgement. (*See* **al-Ḥisāb**.)

'Adn (Ar.) Eden. One of the names used for Paradise in the **Qur'ān**. *See* v.12 of the **Sūrat al-Ṣaff** (q.v.). (*See also* **al-Janna**.)

Adultery *See* **Zinā'**.

Aesop *See* **Luqmān** (1); **Luqmān** (2).

al-Afghānī, Jamāl al-Dīn (1254/1838-9–1314/1897) Despite his name, and his own claims, al-Afghānī was born and raised in

Iran. He was one of the most influential figures in the attempt to reinterpret Islam in the 13th/19th century. His travels to India and Afghanistan gave him a vehement dislike of British imperialism. He was expelled from **Istanbul** (q.v.) and, later, from **Cairo** (q.v.) where he gained political notoriety, making several anti-British speeches. Returning to India he associated with, and then wrote against, the followers of Sayyid Aḥmad **Khān** (q.v.). Later, in Paris, he published with Muḥammad **'Abduh** (q.v.), his most famous follower, a pan-Islamic newspaper in Arabic called *The Strongest Link* (*al-'Urwa al-Wuthqā*), and also wrote a famous rebuttal of the anti-Islamic polemic of Ernest Renan. Al-Afghānī ended his days in Istanbul where he first gained, and then lost, the confidence of the sultan **'Abd al-Ḥamīd II** (q.v.). Al-Afghānī died from cancer of the chin. (*See* **Salafiyya**.)

Afrād (Ar.) [sing. *fard*] Technical term in a variety of fields including that of **ḥadīth** (q.v.) criticism. It means literally 'single (ones)', 'unique (ones)'. In the study of *ḥadīth* the *afrād* are those traditions where the second link in the **isnād** (q.v.) contains no more than a single name of a *tābi'* (one who did not know the Prophet **Muḥammad** directly but knew one of the Prophet's companions). The terms *fard/afrād* also have technical meanings in such areas as poetry, astronomy and theology. (*See* **Ṣaḥāba**; **Tābi'ūn**.)

Afterlife *See* **al-Ākhira**; **al-Ma'ād**.

Āghā Khān (Ar./Turk./Pers.) The word *Agha* was used in Turkish to indicate a 'chief' or 'head'; it could also indicate eunuchs in government service. The word was also used in Persian with similar meanings but often spelled *Āqā*. *Khān* was a Turkic and Persian word which meant 'chief' or 'lord'. The combination of the two words into a single title was adopted by the Imāms of the **Nizārīs** (q.v.), a branch of the **Ismā'īlīs** (q.v.). The title was bestowed by the Shāh of Persia in 1233-4/1818.

Aghlabids Islamic dynasty which flourished in North Africa between 184/800–296/909. The dynasty, which ruled from **Qayrawān** (q.v.) took its name from its founder Ibrāhīm b. al-Aghlab (*reg*. 184/800–197/812). Ibrāhīm was made Prince (*Amīr*) of Ifrīqiya, in return for an annual tribute, by the 'Abbāsid caliph **Hārūn al-Rashīd** (q.v.). Aghlabid control eventually extended as far as Malta and Sicily. The Aghlabids were finally overthrown in North Africa by the **Fāṭimids** (q.v.). (*See* **'Abbāsids**.)

Āgra Major Indian city on the River Yamunā (Jumna) and capital of many Mughal rulers who beautified it with much fine architecture. The most famous example is the **Tāj Maḥal** (q.v.) built by **Shāh Jahān** (q.v.). (*See* **Mughals**.)

al-Aḥkām al-Khamsa (Ar.) The five qualifications, i.e. the way in which Islamic law and ethics have traditionally divided human behaviour. The five categories of behaviour are those which are regarded as obligatory, recommended, indifferent or morally neutral, reprehensible and forbidden.

Ahl al-'Adl wa 'l-Tawḥīd (Ar.) Literally, 'the People of Justice and Unity'. This was a title assumed and preferred by the **Mu'tazila** (q.v.).

Ahl al-Dhimma *See* **Dhimmī**.

Ahl al-Kahf (Ar.) The People of the Cave. (*See* **Aṣḥāb al-Kahf**; **Sūrat al-Kahf**.)

Ahl al-Kisā' *See* **Fāṭima**.

Ahl al-Kitāb (Ar.) The People of the Book. The name initially referred to the Jews and the Christians whose scriptures like the Torah and the Gospel were completed in Muslim belief by the Islamic revelation of the **Qur'ān**. The term was later broadened to cover adherents of other religions like Zoroastrianism. Differences on the same subject between the Qur'ān and, for example, the Gospels are accounted for by the doctrine of corruption (**taḥrīf** (q.v.)) according to which Christians are believed to have corrupted or distorted the original Gospel text. Qur'ānic references to the People of the Book are a mixture of the friendly and the hostile. In early Islamic history the People of the Book had a protected status provided that they paid the poll tax (**jizya** (q.v.)). (*See* **Dhimmī**.)

Ahl al-Sunna wa 'l-Jamā'a (Ar.) Literally, 'the People of Custom and Community'. This was a title by which the Sunnīs were known. (*See* **Sunna**; **Sunnī**.)

Ahl-i Ḥaqq (Pers.) Literally, 'People of the True One', i.e. People of God. The phrase is used to refer to a religious group in Western Persia. The dogmas of their religion are highly syncretic as well as mysterious. Although they appear to have points in common with the **Ismā'īlīs** (q.v.), they revere *twelve* Imāms. (*See* **Imām**; **Ithnā 'Asharīs**.)

Aḥmad al-Badawī *See* **al-Badawī, al-Sayyid Aḥmad**.

Aḥmad b. Ḥanbal **(164/780–241/855)** One of the most distinguished mediaeval jurists and theologians in Islam. He founded the Ḥanbalī School of Islamic Law. Because he refused to agree that the **Qur'ān** was created (as opposed to the mainstream view that it was uncreated), he was imprisoned and persecuted during the Mu'tazilite inquisition (**miḥna** (q.v.)). He became an inspiration for **Ibn Taymiyya** (q.v.) after him and, indeed, for the later Wahhābī movement as well. Aḥmad b. Ḥanbal's most important work was his tradition collection called the *Musnad*. (*See* **Ḥadīth**; **Ḥanbalīs**; **Istawā**; **Mu'tazila**; **Wahhābīs**.)

Aḥmadiyya (1) A religious movement founded in 1306/1889 by Mīrzā Ghulām Aḥmad of Qādiyān (1251/1835–1326/1908).

The Aḥmadiyya have often been persecuted by other Muslims since Ghulām Aḥmad made a number of claims including being a recipient of revelation, the Promised Messiah, the **Mahdī** (q.v.) and an avatar of Krishna. Aḥmadīs believe that Jesus escaped from death on a cross and went to Srinagar where he died and was buried. The Aḥmadiyya are split into two main groups: (i) Qādiyānīs, who hold that Ghulām Aḥmad was a prophet (**nabī** (q.v.)), and (ii) Lahoris, a smaller group, who believe their founder to have been a 'Renewer' (Mujaddid) only. The headquarters of the Aḥmadiyya today is at Rabwah, Pakistan. (*See* **'Īsā**.)

Aḥmadiyya (2) The name of a major **ṣūfī** (q.v.) order, established initially in Egypt, which is called after the ṣūfī saint, Aḥmad al-Badawī. To prevent confusion with other orders and religious groups, it is probably better to refer to the order as the Badawiyya. Independent branches of the order spread all over the Middle East. (*See* **al-Badawī, al-Sayyid Aḥmad**; **Taṣawwuf**.)

al-Aḥqāf (Ar.) The title of the 46th **sūra** of the **Qur'ān**; it means literally 'The Sand Dunes'. The *sūra* belongs to the Meccan period and has 35 verses. It takes its name from the 21st verse which refers to a place called al-Aḥqāf where **Hūd** (q.v.) and the tribe of **'Ād** (q.v.) used to live. The latter part of the *sūra* is full of warnings about what happened to disbelievers in ancient times like the people of 'Ād.

Aḥwāl (Ar.) [sing. *ḥāl*] Literally the word means 'states'. It acquired the technical meaning in **taṣawwuf** (q.v.) of spiritual states which were not, however, permanent but which contained an element of illumination or ecstasy and were achieved only with the help of God. These spiritual states could constitute part of one's progress along the **ṣūfī** (q.v.) path. The term was widely used in ṣūfī writings. (*See* **Basṭ**; **Maqāmāt**; **Qabḍ**.)

al-Aḥzāb (Ar.) The title of the 33rd **sūra** of the **Qur'ān**; the name means literally 'The Parties' or 'The Groups' but is usually translated as 'The Confederate Clans' or 'The Confederate Tribes'. The *sūra* belongs to the Medinan period and has 73 verses. The clans or tribes of the title were those which banded together with the Meccans to besiege **Medina** (q.v.) in 5/627 at the siege and Battle of al-Khandaq. The latter part of the *sūra* also refers to the Prophet **Muḥammad**'s wives, and provides a considerable amount of ethical instruction for Muslims. (*See* **al-Khandaq, Siege and Battle of**; **Khātam al-Nabiyyīn**.)

'Ā'isha bint Abī Bakr (*c.* AD 614–58/678) Third wife of the Prophet **Muḥammad**. Her mother belonged to the Kināna tribe; her father **Abū Bakr** (q.v.) (Muḥammad's successor), was from the clan of **Taym** (q.v.) of the **Quraysh** (q.v.) tribe. She became Muḥammad's favourite wife and it was in her bedchamber that the Prophet died and was buried. During Muḥammad's lifetime, while returning from an expedition with him in 5/627, 'Ā'isha became the victim of malicious gossip. The **Qur'ān** refers to this in **Sūrat al-Nūr** (q.v.). 'Ā'isha fought unsuccessfully against **'Alī b. Abī Ṭālib** (q.v.) at the Battle of the Camel in 36/656. (*See* **Camel, Battle of the**)

'Ajā'ib (Ar.) [sing. *'ajība*] A notable literary genre in mediaeval Arabic literature. The word means literally 'wonders', 'marvels', 'miracles' or 'curiosities'. *'Ajā'ib* could embrace a whole variety of phenomena ranging from aspects of nature and severe weather through to great buildings. Two useful examples of the genre appear in the travel narrative (**Riḥla** (q.v.)) of the 8th/14th century Muslim traveller **Ibn Baṭṭūṭa** (q.v.): he describes the great but decaying lighthouse at **Alexandria** (q.v.), and also the terror of his fellow voyagers on beholding at sea what they later take to be the giant mythical bird called the *rukhkh*. It may also be noted that *The Thousand and One Nights* is full of *'Ajā'ib* tales.

Ajal (Ar.) Literally 'appointed time', 'moment of death', or 'lifespan'. The **Qur'ān** teaches that no one dies unless God allows: it is He who determines man's term of life; (*see* v.145 of **Sūrat Āl 'Imrān** (q.v.)). Terrestrial and celestial phenomena also have their fixed *ajal* (*see* v.3 of **Sūrat al-Aḥqāf** (q.v.)) until the Day of Judgement. Early Muslim theologians spent much time discussing *ajal* and the problems which they believed surrounded the concept. (*See* **al-Ḥisāb**.)

Ajnādayn, Battle of Major battle fought in Southern Palestine between the invading Arab armies and the Byzantine forces, in 13/634. The Byzantine forces were commanded by the Byzantine Emperor Heraclius' brother, Theodore. The Arabs were led by **Khālid b. al-Walīd** (q.v.). The Byzantines were defeated by the Arabs, a result which had significant consequences for the further rapid success of the Arab conquests and the Islamization of the region.

Akbar (949/1542–1014/1605) Mughal emperor who ruled from 972/1564, the son of **Humāyūn** (q.v.) and grandson of **Bābur** (q.v.). Akbar was the real architect of the Mughal empire adding a huge number of regions to his domains. He was also a thinker, religious innovator (like the Egyptian pharaoh Akhenaten before him), and educationalist as well as a notable administrator who successfully reorganized his government. He encouraged an experimental form of architecture which mixed Hindu and Muslim styles. His most famous monument was the city of Fatḥpūr-Sikrī, 23 miles from **Āgra** (q.v.) which he built, occupied briefly and then abandoned because of water problems. The deserted city is now a tourist attraction. (*See* **Mughals**.)

Akhbār (Ar.) [sing. *khabar*] News, messages, information, annals. In **ḥadīth** (q.v.) terminology *khabar* has the technical sense of 'report'.

al-Ākhira (Ar.) Literally, 'the last'. Together with its fuller form **al-Dār al-Ākhira**, (meaning 'the last abode', 'the everlasting abode'), the phrase is used to designate the afterlife in its various aspects. It occurs in the **Qur'ān**, for example, in v.32 of **Sūrat al-An'ām** and elsewhere. Islam also uses other Arabic words like **al-Ma'ād** (q.v.) (meaning literally 'the return', 'the place to which one goes back') as synonyms for **al-Ākhira**. (*See* **al-Janna**; **al-Nār**.)

Akhlāq (Ar.) [sing. *khulq* or *khuluq*] Morals, character of person. In Arabic the phrase *'Ilm al-Akhlāq* indicates ethics or morals. Islam developed its ethics from the **Qur'ān** and the **Ḥadīth** (q.v.), but its philosophical ethics may be said to have derived from the Greeks and to have been developed initially by the Islamic philosophers. (*See* **Falsafa**.)

al-A'lā (Ar.) The title of the 87th **sūra** of the **Qur'ān**; the name, which refers to God, means 'The Highest' and occurs in the 1st verse. The *sūra* belongs to the Meccan period and has 19 verses. The early part of the *sūra* provides a brief list of God's mercies to man and then instructs the Prophet **Muḥammad** to exhort sinners. It warns that the rogue who ignores all exhortation will burn in Hell fire. (*See* **al-Nār**.)

Alamūt The word is formed from two Daylami words meaning 'the teaching' (or, possibly, 'the nest') 'of the eagle'. It is the name of a castle, whose ruins still exist, in the Elburz mountains South of the Caspian Sea. It became the headquarters of the **Assassins** (q.v.), an extremist branch of the **Ismā'īlīs** (q.v.), under the Assassins' founder and leader **Ḥasan-i Ṣabbāḥ** (q.v.) in 483/1090. The castle of Alamūt fell to the **Mongols** (q.v.) in the 7th/13th century.

al-'Alaq (Ar.) The title of the 96th **sūra** of the **Qur'ān**; it means 'The Blood Clot'. The *sūra* belongs to the Meccan period and has 19 verses. The title is drawn from the 2nd verse which refers to God's creation of man from clotted blood. The *sūra* has a particular place in Muslim affections since it was the very first to be revealed by the angel **Jibrīl** (q.v.) to the Prophet **Muḥammad** on **Ḥirā'** (q.v.) in AD 610.

'Alawīs *See* **Nuṣayrīs**.

Alborak *See* **al-Burāq**.

Alcohol *See* **Khamr**; **Nabīdh**.

Aleppo Important city in Syria. In Arabic it is called Ḥalab. The site of the city was settled long before the rise of Islam. During the period of the **Umayyads** (q.v.) Aleppo had little importance. However, as the later capital of the **Ḥamdānids** (q.v.) it achieved an initial fame before being stormed and devastated by the Byzantines in 351/962. Aleppo later came under the rule of the **Mamlūks** (q.v.) and then the **Ottomans** (q.v.). Today Aleppo ranks as the second major city in Syria after **Damascus** (q.v.).

Alevis *See* **Nuṣayrīs**.

Alexandria Major city in Egypt with the Arabic name of al-Iskandariyya. It was founded by, and named after, Alexander the Great (called *al-Iskandar* in Arabic). In antiquity it was famous for its lighthouse which was numbered among the seven wonders of the ancient world. This lighthouse survived into Islamic times for several centuries and was seen and described, for example, by the 8th/14th century Muslim traveller **Ibn Baṭṭūṭa** (q.v.). Alexandria was captured by the Arabs in 21/642. Thereafter its fortunes were often those of Egypt itself. The commercial importance of Alexandria cannot be overemphasized: it was a major seaport through which many commodities, including its own cloth, passed down the ages. (*See* **'Ajā'ib**; **Ḥarrān**.)

Alhambra (Span.) Literally, 'The Red'. It is a Spanish word formed from the second of two Arabic words *al-Qal'a al-Ḥamrā'* together meaning 'The Red Fortress'. In fact, the Alhambra at **Granada** (q.v.) in Spain is a complex of many buildings rather than one, though the name *was* originally given to a single fortress on the site in the 3rd/9th century. The Alhambra as we know it today was built by the Naṣrid dynasty. It ranks as one of the great glories of Muslim architecture in Spain. Most of it was erected in the 8th/14th century. (*See* **al-Andalus**.)

'Alī al-Hādī (*c.* 212/827-214/829–254/868) Tenth Shī'ite Imām. His full name was Abū 'l-Ḥasan 'Alī b. Muḥammad. He was also called 'The Pure One' (*al-Naqī*). Born in **Medina** (q.v.), he assumed the imāmate at the age of seven when his father died. The 'Abbāsid caliph **al-Mutawakkil** (q.v.) placed him under house arrest in **Sāmarrā** (q.v.) in 233/848 and al-Hādī remained here for twenty years before his death. He and his son, the eleventh Shī'ite Imām **Ḥasan al-'Askarī** (q.v.), are buried in Sāmarrā. (*See* **'Abbāsids**; **Imām**; **Ithnā 'Asharīs**.)

'Alī al-Riḍā (*c.* 148/765–203/818) Eighth Shī'ite Imām. His full name was Abū 'l-Ḥasan 'Alī b. Mūsā. He lived at a time of great upheaval in the 'Abbāsid empire with a civil war between the two sons of **Hārūn al-Rashīd** (q.v.). The victor, **al-Ma'mūn** (q.v.) nominated al-Riḍā as his successor. However, two years later al-Riḍā suddenly died and it is alleged that he was poisoned by al-Ma'mūn. 'Ali al-Riḍā is buried at Mashhad, site of the ancient Ṭūs. (*See* **'Abbāsids**; **Imām**; **Ithnā 'Asharīs**; **Muḥammad al-Taqī**.)

'Alī b. Abī Ṭālib (*c.* AD 598–40/661) 'Alī was the First Shī'ite **Imām** (q.v.) and also the 4th **khalīfa** (q.v.) who ruled over the Islamic community from 35/656–40/661. He belonged to the clan of **Hāshim** (q.v.) in the tribe of **Quraysh** (q.v.). 'Alī was the Prophet **Muḥammad**'s cousin and he became his son-in-law as well by marrying the Prophet's daughter **Fāṭima** (q.v.). Their children were **al-Ḥasan b. 'Alī** (q.v.) and **al-Ḥusayn b. 'Alī** (q.v.). 'Alī defeated **'Ā'isha bint Abī Bakr** (q.v.), **Ṭalḥa b. 'Ubaydullāh al-Taymī** (q.v.) and **al-Zubayr b. al-'Awwām** (q.v.) at the Battle of the Camel in 36/656. However, he was later unsuccessful when he met **Mu'āwiya** (q.v.), the governor of Syria, at the Battle of Ṣiffīn in 37/657. 'Alī was assassinated in **al-**

Kūfa (q.v.) in 40/661 by Ibn Muljam. (*See* **Abū Ṭālib**; **Camel, Battle of the**; **al-Najaf**; **Shī'ism**; **Ṣiffīn, Battle of**)

Aligarh Major city in Uttar Pradesh, formerly called Koel (or Koil). The word Aligarh means 'high fortress'. The city became famous in Islamic circles for its university. This had its origins in the Muhammadan Anglo-Oriental College, founded in the last quarter of the 13th/19th century by Sir Sayyid Aḥmad Khān and open to Hindus as well as Muslims. The College achieved university status in 1338/1920. Aligarh, in its earlier incarnation as Koel, was visited by **Ibn Baṭṭūṭa** (q.v.) in 743/1342. (*See* **Khān, Sayyid Aḥmad**.)

Āl 'Imrān (Ar.) The title of the 3rd **sūra** of the **Qur'ān**; it means 'The Family of 'Imrān'. The *sūra* belongs to the Medinan period and has 200 verses. The title is drawn from v.33 which makes reference to **Ādam** (q.v.), **Nūḥ** (q.v.), **Ibrāhīm** (q.v.) and Āl 'Imrān. Muslims identify the 'Imrān in this verse as the father of **Mūsā** (q.v.). However, 'Imrān was also the name borne by the father of **Maryam** (q.v.). **Sūrat Āl 'Imrān** begins with three of the **Mysterious Letters of the Qur'ān** (q.v.) and deals with a variety of subjects including the oneness of God, the story of **'Īsā** (q.v.) and the Battle of Uḥud. (*See* **Ibrāhīm** (1); **Shirk**; **Uḥud, Battle of**)

'Alī Zayn 'l-'Ābidīn (36/658–94/712 or 95/713) Fourth Shī'ite Imām. His full name was Abū Muḥammad 'Alī b. al-Ḥusayn. As his name indicates his father was **al-Ḥusayn b. 'Alī** (q.v.). After the Battle of Karbalā', he lived an isolated pious life and avoided political involvement. Shī'ite historians believe he was poisoned by the ruling Umayyad caliph. He was buried in **Medina** (q.v.). (*See* **Ithnā 'Asharīs**; **Karbalā', Battle of**; **Umayyads**.)

Allāh (Ar.) This word for the Deity is formed from the Arabic *al-Ilāh* which means literally 'The God'. The name Allāh is for

Muslims the supreme name. Allāh is the eternal and uncreated Creator of the universe and all mankind. The **Qur'ān** views Him from both a transcendent and an immanent perspective: on the one hand, there is absolutely nothing like him (*see* v.11 of **Sūrat al-Shūrā**); on the other, He is closer to man than the jugular vein in his neck (*see* v.16 of **Sūrat Qāf**).

Allāhu Akbar *See* **Takbīr**.

Almohads Anglicized form of *al-Muwaḥḥidūn* (Ar.) meaning literally 'The Unitarians'. (The Almohads are to be distinguished from the **Wahhābīs** (q.v.) who also liked the name *al-Muwaḥḥidūn*). The Almohad dynasty flourished in Morocco and Spain from 524/1130–667/1269. Their inspiration was the reformist Berber scholar Ibn Tūmart (470/1077-474/1081–524/1130). The dynasty, with its reforming zeal and piety, filled the vacuum left by the declining **Almoravids** (q.v.) in the Muslim West. However, the Almohads were defeated by the Christian kings at the Battle of Las Navas de Tolosa in 609/1212. They were followed in Morocco by the Marīnids. (*See* **Las Navas de Tolosa, Battle of**)

Almoravids Anglicized form of *al-Murābiṭūn* (Ar.) meaning literally 'those who line up together (in defence of the faith)'. On another level of meaning *al-Murābiṭūn* meant those who were connected with a **ribāṭ** (q.v.), an Arabic word indicating 'a fortress', 'a frontier post', 'a ṣūfī house' and even 'a military formation. The Almoravid dynasty flourished from 448/1056–541/1147. It was a Berber movement which gained power in both North Africa and Spain before being supplanted by the **Almohads** (q.v.). (*See* **Ṣūfī**; **Taṣawwuf**.)

Almsgiving *See* **Ṣadaqa**; **Zakāt**.

Alyasa' The Elisha of the **Qur'ān** specifically mentioned in v.86 of **Sūrat al-An'ām** (q.v.). He appears as part of a long list of prophets which includes **Ismā'īl** (q.v.), **Yūnus** (q.v.) and **Lūṭ** (q.v.). Alyasa', like these other three, is named as having been specially preferred by God over other men.

Amal (Ar.) Hope. This is also the name adopted by an Ithnā 'Asharī party or group in the Lebanon, founded in 1394/1974 by the Iranian Shī'ite Imām Mūsā al-Ṣadr who disappeared in 1398/1978. Amal has continued to provide a vocal focus for Shī'ite aspirations and hopes in the Lebanon. (*See* **Fundamentalism, Islamic**; **Ithnā 'Asharīs**.)

Ambiguities (Qur'ānic) *See* **Mutashābihāt**.

Ameer Ali *See* **Amīr 'Alī, Sayyid**.

al-Amīn (Ar.) 'The Trustworthy'. This was a pre-revelation epithet borne by the Prophet **Muḥammad** when he was younger. The title provides some indication of the respect in which Muḥammad was held, even before the revelation of the **Qur'ān**.

Amīn, Qāsim (*c.* 1279-80/1863–1325-6/1908) Egyptian writer and partisan of Arab women's rights. He studied law and later established contact with **al-Afghānī** (q.v.) and **'Abduh** (q.v.). His ideas on the rights of women were expressed in two books: *The Liberation of the Woman* and *The New Woman*. He favoured, among other things, the abolition of the veil. (*See* **Ḥijāb**.)

Āmina bint Wahb (died *c.* AD 576) The mother of the Prophet **Muḥammad**. Through her father she belonged to the Zuhra clan of the tribe of **Quraysh** (q.v.). She married **'Abd Allāh b. 'Abd al-Muṭṭalib** (q.v.) who died before the birth of the Prophet. Āmina herself died when the Prophet was six years old. The period when she was pregnant with Muḥammad, and the latter's birth, have given rise to many miraculous stories.

Amīr 'Alī, Sayyid (1265/1849–1346-7/1928) Important Indian author, jurist and reformer. He learned Arabic at a college near

Calcutta and studied law in England where he was called to the bar. Although from a Shī'ite family, Amīr 'Alī worked within a framework of Sunnī thought. He was part of the modernist Islamic movement in India which had been inaugurated there by Sayyid Aḥmad Khān and was continued by others like **Iqbāl** (q.v.). Amīr 'Alī wished to interpret Islam to the West and to this end he wrote his most famous work whose final title was *The Spirit of Islam*. Amīr 'Alī believed, furthermore, that in the ancient Islamic juristic principle of **ijmā'** (q.v.) lay the foundations of democracy. His writings have gained a favourable reception in both the East and the West. (*See* **Khān, Sayyid Aḥmad**.)

Amīr al-Mu'minīn (Ar.) A title which has been variously translated as 'Commander of the Faithful', 'Prince of the Believers' and 'Prince of the Faithful', among others. The phrase should really be translated in the light of the historical period under discussion: it acquired greater strength with the passage of time rather like the title **khalīfa** (q.v.) itself. At first **Amīr al-Mu'minīn** meant someone given military leadership. The title was then assumed by the 2nd *khalīfa* **'Umar b. al-Khaṭṭāb** (q.v.) but with few connotations of real power. From his time onwards, however, it became a title reserved for a caliph alone. It was sometimes used by the sultans in the early period of the **Ottomans** (q.v.). By contrast, the **Almoravids** (q.v.) preferred to use the title *Amīr al-Muslimīn* which meant 'Leader (or Prince) of the Muslims'.

'Amr b. al-'Āṣ (died *c.* 42/663) He belonged to the clan of Sahm of the tribe of **Quraysh** (q.v.). He embraced Islam before **Muḥammad**'s capture of **Mecca** (q.v.) and was sent by the Prophet to Oman. Later he was sent by **Abū Bakr** (q.v.) to Palestine. He fought at several battles but he is primarily renowned as the conqueror of Egypt between 19/640–21/642. 'Amr was the founder of **al-Fusṭāṭ** (q.v.) (now swallowed up by **Cairo** (q.v.)) where he built a fine mosque bearing his name.

This was the first mosque in Egypt. The mosque standing on the site today was extensively renovated in 1397/1977. (*See* **Manāra**; **Masjid**.)

al-Amr bi 'l-Ma'rūf wa 'l-Nahy 'an al-Munkar (Ar.) Classical Arabic phrase meaning 'Commanding the good and forbidding the evil'. This was one of the five key principles of the **Mu'tazila** (q.v.). The phrase has a clear Qur'ānic foundation as may be seen from v.104 of **Sūrat Āl 'Imrān** (q.v.) and elsewhere. (*See* **al-Wa'd wa 'l-Wa'īd**.)

'An (Ar.) Technical term used in **ḥadīth** (q.v.) to denote 'on the authority of'. It formed part of the chain of authorities, called the **isnād** (q.v.), in the *ḥadīth*. An example might run as follows: 'He informed me *on the authority of* (*'an*) Sulaymān . . .'

Analogy *See* **Qiyās**.

al-An'ām (Ar.) The title of the 6th **sūra** of the **Qur'ān**; it means 'The Cattle'. The *sūra* belongs to the Meccan period and contains 165 verses. Its title comes from the references to cattle and pagan practice in vv.136, 138–139. The *sūra* begins by praising God as the Creator of the Heavens and the earth; He has given every man his **ajal** (q.v.). There is much in the *sūra* about God's attributes and also many of the Islamic prophets. (*See* **Alyasa'**.)

al-Anbiyā' (Ar.) The title of the 21st **sūra** of the **Qur'ān**; it means 'The Prophets'. The *sūra* belongs to the Meccan period and has 112 verses. It is so-called because of the references to many of the great prophets revered by Islam. These include **Mūsā** (q.v.) and **Hārūn** (q.v.), who were given the Torah; **Ibrāhīm** (q.v.), whom pagans attempt to burn to death (*see* vv.68–69); and **Dāwūd** (q.v.) and **Sulaymān** (q.v.). (*See* **Dhū 'l-Kifl**; **Idrīs**; **Jibrīl**.)

al-Andalus This Arabic word probably derived from a word for Atlantis, rather than from Vandalicia (Land of the Vandals) as often thought. Mediaeval Islam used the term to designate Spain and Portugal together. Al-Andalus was successfully invaded by the advancing Arabs in 91/710–92/711. (*See* **'Abd al-Raḥmān III**.)

Andalusia *See* **al-Andalus.**

al-Anfāl (Ar.) The title of the 8th **sūra** of the **Qur'ān**; it means 'The Spoils'. The *sūra* belongs to the Medinan period and has 75 verses. Its title is taken from the 1st verse which refers to questions which will be asked about the spoils gained at the Battle of Badr. The verse indicates that there was some quarrelling among the Muslims over the division of the spoils after the Battle. (*See* **Badr, Battle of; Fitna.**)

Angel Incorporeal being created from light to render absolute praise, service, and obedience to God. The angels often serve as God's messengers or envoys. The word used in Arabic for angel is *malak* (or *mal'ak*) [pl. *malā'ika*]. The Arabic language does not differentiate between angels and archangels. However, see the entry **Archangel** in this *Dictionary* for the names of some of the great Islamic angels. Each person has two recording or guardian angels who record his or her good and bad deeds. (*See* **Kirām al-Kātibīn; al-Zabāniyya.**)

al-'Ankabūt (Ar.) The title of the 29th **sūra** of the **Qur'ān**; it means 'The Spider'. The *sūra* belongs to the Meccan period and has 69 verses. Its name derives from the 41st verse where it is stated that those who take helpers or protectors (*awliyā'*) apart from God do no better than the spider when it builds itself what is always the weakest of houses. The *surā* begins with three of the **Mysterious Letters of the Qur'ān** (q.v.). After insisting that evil doers will not escape God's wrath and judgement, the *sūra* mentions many of the prophets like **Ibrāhīm** (q.v.), who tried to turn men away from idol worship; **Lūṭ** (q.v.), who similarly attempted to persuade his people away from abomination; and

Shu'ayb (q.v.), who was sent to **Madyan** (q.v.). The illiteracy of **Muḥammad** the Prophet is stressed in v.48.

Ankara, Battle of Important battle fought near Ankara in Anatolia between the Ottoman sultan Bāyazīd I (*reg.* 791/1389–805/1403) and **Tīmūr -i Lang** (q.v.), in 804/1402. Tīmūr defeated Bāyazīd and took him prisoner. (*See* **Ottomans**.)

Anniversary *See* **Mawlid**.

al-Anṣār (Ar.) The Helpers. This is the epithet given to the Medinese who helped **Muḥammad**. Many of the *Anṣār* fought on Muḥammad's side as early as the Battle of Badr, and constituted, with the **Muhājirūn** (q.v.), the principal support for his power base in **Medina** (q.v.) before the return of the Prophet to **Mecca** (q.v.) when he captured that city. (*See* **al-Aws**; **Badr, Battle of**)

Anthropomorphism *See* **Tashbīh**.

Anti-Christ *See* **al-Dajjāl**.

Anṭūn, Faraḥ (1290-1/1874–1340-1/1922) Notable Lebanese writer and journalist who spent most of his life in **Cairo** (q.v.) and New York. He was much influenced by Western thought and later fell out with **'Abduh** (q.v.) and **Riḍā** (q.v.). His novels have a small but significant part in the history of Arabic fiction.

Apostasy *See* **Ilḥād**; **Irtidād**; **Ridda**.

Apostasy War *See* **Ridda**.

Apostate *See* **Irtidād**.

Apostle See **Rasūl**.

Appointed Time *See* **Ajal**.

al-'Aqaba There are a number of places which go by this name. The two most important are a major Jordanian seaport, and a place between **Minā** (q.v.) and **Mecca** (q.v.). The latter became notable in early Islamic history because of the meetings held there between the Prophet **Muḥammad** and groups of Medinese (before the **Hijra** (q.v.)) in AD 621 and 622, at which certain pledges were made to Muḥammad. Al-'Aqaba is one of the sites for the ritual stone-throwing which takes place during the **Ḥajj** (q.v.). (*See* **al-Jamra**.)

'Aqīda (Ar.) [pl. *'aqā'id*] Doctrine, dogma, faith, belief, creed. The term was used in early Islam to indicate credal formulations epitomized, for example, by that attributed to **Abū Ḥanīfa** (q.v.). The term *'aqīda* is often used more loosely today, as the above definitions show. (*See* **Dīn**; **Īmān**.)

'Aqrabā', Battle of Important and extremely bloody battle fought on the borders of Yamāma between **Musaylima** (q.v.), aided by many members of the Banū Ḥanīfa, and **Khālid b. al-Walīd** (q.v.) leading the Muslim forces, in 12/633. Musaylima was defeated and killed in this battle, thus putting an end to his attempt to be accepted as a rival, or even an equal, of the Prophet **Muḥammad**. There is a story that he earlier wrote to Muḥammad describing both the Prophet and himself as 'Messengers of God': Muḥammad is said to have responded by addressing Musaylima as 'the Liar'.

al-Aqṣā, al-Masjid (Ar.) Literally, 'The Furthest Mosque' or 'The Furthest Sanctuary'. This is the name given to one of Islam's holiest mosques, traditionally regarded as having been built by **'Abd al-Malik b. Marwān** (q.v.), which stands on the Temple Square in **Jerusalem** (q.v.). The name of the mosque, *al-Masjid al Aqṣā*, derives from v.1 of **Sūrat al-Isrā'** (q.v.) in the **Qur'ān**. (*See* **al-Burāq**; **Isrā'**; **Mi'rāj**; **Qubbat al-Ṣakhra**.)

Arabesque Decoration involving leaf or other vegetal shapes designed in a coherent pattern. It is a common feature in Islamic Art. (*See* **Art and Architecture, Islamic**)

'Araḍ (Ar.) [pl. *a'rāḍ*] Technical term in Islamic philosophy meaning 'accident', derived from Aristotelian metaphysical terminology. It is an Arabic translation of the Greek *sumbebēkós*. Mediaeval Islamic philosophy was swift to absorb the vocabulary of substance and accidents from the writings of Aristotle. *'Araḍ* later assumed a special significance in mediaeval Islamic theology with the rise of the theory of **Atomism** (q.v.) or 'Occasionalism'. (*See* **Aristotelianism, Islamic**; **Falsafa**; **Jawhar**.)

al-A'rāf (Ar.) The title of the 7th **sūra** of the **Qur'ān**; the word is frequently translated as 'The Ramparts', 'The Heights' or 'The Battlements'. The *sūra* belongs mainly to the Meccan period and has 206 verses. The title refers to an apparently intermediate place or state (*see* vv.46–48), not in Paradise or Hell, inhabited by those whose good and bad deeds are equal. One tradition has it that they too will eventually enter Paradise. The word *al-A'rāf* should not be translated as 'Purgatory' since the latter word is too imbued with a Catholic Christian theology of purgation and suffering. It may be noted that the men on 'The Ramparts' have also been identified as angels, prophets or apostles. The rest of this *sūra* includes major references to important Islamic prophets like **Hūd** (q.v.), **Ṣāliḥ** (q.v.), **Shu'ayb** (q.v.), and **Mūsā** (q.v.), as well as to the rebellion of **Iblīs** (q.v.) and the temptation of **Ādam** (q.v.). (*See* **Barzakh**; **Fir'awn**; **Hārūn**; **al-Ḥisāb**; **Istawā**; **al-Janna**; **al-Nār**.)

'Arafa or **'Arafāt** Plain about 13 miles from **Mecca** (q.v.) which is a major focal point for the **Ḥajj** (q.v.). On the ninth day of the Islamic month of Dhū 'l-Ḥijja, pilgrims make a solemn 'standing' (**wuqūf** (q.v.)) at 'Arafa and a special sermon is preached. If the *wuqūf* at 'Arafa is omitted, the entire pilgrimage is considered to be invalid. Legend derives the name 'Arafa or 'Arafāt from the encounter and mutual recognition between **Ādam** (q.v.) and Eve at this place after they were expelled from Paradise and initially separated. The Arabic verb meaning 'to recognize one another' or 'to become acquainted with one another' is *ta'ārafa*. (*See* **Ḥawwā'**; **al-Janna**.)

Archangel There is no separate word in Arabic by which to distinguish the greater angels, known in the West as Archangels, from the lesser ordinary angels. The same Arabic word *malak* or *mal'ak* [pl. *malā'ika*], deriving from a verb meaning 'to send as an envoy or messenger', serves for both. However, Islam certainly does have its great angels and the reader is referred in this *Dictionary* in particular to the following entries: **Isrāfīl**, **'Izrā'īl**, **Jibrīl**, **Mīkā'īl**, **Munkar** and **Nakīr**. Others are mentioned as well. The greatest of all the Islamic angels, of course, is **Jibrīl** since he was the vehicle of the revelation of the **Qur'ān** from God to **Muḥammad**. (*See* **Angel**.)

Aristotelianism, Islamic The thought and concepts of Aristotle played a significant and diverse role in the development of Islamic philosophy. In particular, the latter absorbed much of the technical metaphysical terminology of Aristotle. It should be stressed here, however, that the Aristotelian thought which the Arab and Islamic writers knew and absorbed was not always something which Aristotle would have accepted as his own. A prime example of this lies in a work known to the early Arabs, the so-called *Theology of Aristotle* (*Theologia Aristotelis*) which was, in fact, a Neoplatonic compilation based on parts of the *Enneads* of Plotinus (AD 204-5–270). (*See* **'Araḍ**; **Falsafa**; **Ibn Rushd**; **Jawhar**; **Neoplatonism, Islamic**; **Platonism, Islamic**)

Arkān (Ar.) [sing. *rukn*] Literally, 'supports', 'basic elements'. The word is used in Arabic to refer to the five pillars of Islam. These are, in alphabetical order: **Ḥajj** (q.v.) (=Pilgrimage to Mecca); **Ṣalāt** (q.v.) (=The Prayer Ritual); **Ṣawm** (q.v.) (=Fasting during Ramaḍān); **Shahāda** (q.v.) (=The Profession of Faith); and **Zakāt** (q.v.) (=Almsgiving). A sixth pillar, **Jihād** (q.v.) (=Holy War) is added to the above five by some groups, e.g. the **Ibāḍīs** (q.v.). (*See* **Mecca**; **Ramaḍān**.)

al-Arqam (*c*. AD 594–*c*. 53/673–55/675) One of the earliest converts to Islam and companions of **Muḥammad**. His full name was Abū 'Abd Allāh al-Arqam b. Abī 'l-Arqam. He was a member of the **Makhzūm** (q.v.) clan of the tribe of **Quraysh** (q.v.). His primary significance in Islamic history is that it was to his house in **Mecca** (q.v.) that Muḥammad went from AD 614 for the purposes of early preaching, teaching and worship.

'Arsh (Ar.) Throne. The word acquired considerable mystical and symbolic overtones and significance among some groups in mediaeval Islam, especially the **Ismā'īlīs** (q.v.). In the **Qur'ān**, God is portrayed as being on a throne (*see* e.g., v.54 of **Sūrat al-A'rāf** (q.v.)). It was this kind of phrase which engendered and sustained the debate in mediaeval Islam about anthropomorphism and the attributes of God. (*See* **Istawā**; **Ṣifāt Allāh**; **Tashbīh**.)

Art and Architecture, Islamic Scholars have debated at length over those features which make a piece of art or architecture specifically Islamic. Its relation to, or infusion by, Islam as a religion must be one, albeit simplistic, answer. Further information about diverse aspects of Islamic Art and Architecture will be gleaned from the following entries among many others in this *Dictionary*: **'Abd al-Malik b. Marwān**; **Ablaq**; **al-Aqṣā, al-Masjid**; **Arabesque**; **Delhi**; **Dikka**; **Ḥammām**; **Hilāl**; **Iṣfahān**; **Īwān**; **al-Kūfa**; **Masjid**; **al-Masjid al-Ḥarām**; **Mīḍa'a**; **Miḥrāb**; **Minbar**; **Muqarnaṣ**; **Qubba**; **Qubbat al-Ṣakhra**; **Quṭb Mīnār**; **Sabīl**; **Ṣaḥn**; **Sāmarrā**; **Ṣawma'a**; **Shīrāz**; **Sinān Pasha**; **Tāj Maḥal**. For further material the interested reader is directed to Ettinghausen & Grabar, *The Art and Architecture of Islam: 650–1250*. (See back of this *Dictionary* for full bibliographical details.)

'Aṣabiyya (Ar.) Group solidarity, kinship ethos. The term was popularized by the great late-mediaeval Arab historian **Ibn Khaldūn** (q.v.).

Asad Clan of the tribe of **Quraysh** (q.v.), to which **Khadīja bint Khuwaylid** (q.v.) (**Muḥammad**'s first wife), and **Waraqa b. Nawfal** (q.v.) (Khadīja's cousin), belonged.

Ascension of Muḥammad *See* **Mi'rāj**; *see also* **al-Aqṣā, al-Masjid; al-Burāq; Isrā'; Qubbat al-Ṣakhra; Sūrat al-Isrā'.**

Asceticism *See* **Zuhd.**

Aṣḥāb al-Kahf (Ar.) The Companions of the Cave. This is the Qur'ānic title frequently given to a gang of youths who fall asleep in a cave, and awake many years later, who are described in the **sūra** of the **Qur'ān** named after the episode, **Sūrat al-Kahf** (q.v.); (*see* vv.9–26). The story is paralleled in the Christian tradition by that of the Seven Sleepers of Ephesus.

Aṣḥāb al-Kisā' *See* **Fāṭima.**

al-'Ashara al-Mubashshara (Ar.) Literally, 'The Ten who have been brought good news'. Tradition portrays the Prophet **Muḥammad** promising Paradise to ten of his followers. The names on the received lists vary but they usually include the **Rāshidūn** (q.v.).

al-Ash'arī, Abū 'l-Ḥasan 'Alī b. Ismā'īl (260/873-4–324/935-6) Although he was one of mediaeval Islam's most famous theologians, not very much is known about his life. He was born in **al-Baṣra** (q.v.) and died in **Baghdād** (q.v.). Originally a member of the **Mu'tazila** (q.v.), he abandoned their doctrines in 300/912-3. This is said to have been the result of a vision in which he saw the Prophet **Muḥammad**. He later used Mu'tazilite logic to defend his new Sunnī beliefs. Doctrinally, he believed that the anthropomorphic expressions about God in the **Qur'ān** were simply to be accepted without, however, stating how (*bilā kayf*). One of his longest works was entitled *The Treatises of the Islamic Sects* (*Maqālāt al-Islāmiyyīn*). (*See* **Istawā; Sunnī.**)

'Āshūrā' The tenth day of the Muslim month of **al-Muḥarram** (q.v.). The Prophet **Muḥammad** used to fast on this day and so it is still regarded as a holy day in **Sunnī** (q.v.) Islam. Some Muslims still mark it by fasting. For **Shī'ite** (q.v.) Islam the day is regarded as sacred primarily because it is the anniversary of the martyrdom of **al-Ḥusayn b. 'Alī** (q.v.) at the Battle of Karbalā'. (*See* **Karbalā', Battle of**)

al-Asmā' al-Ḥusnā (Ar.) The most beautiful names. The reference is to the ninety-nine most beautiful names of God. (*See* **Subḥa**.)

al-'Aṣr (Ar.) The title of the 103rd **sūra** of the **Qur'ān**; the name means literally 'The Time', 'The Afternoon' or 'The Afternoon Prayer' and occurs in the 1st verse as part of an oath. The *sūra* belongs to the Meccan period; it is extremely short and has only 3 verses. After beginning with the phrase 'By the time!' (*Wa 'l-'Aṣr*), the *sūra* goes on to insist that man will be lost unless he is among the believers and doers of good. The *sūra* thus makes the important theological point that salvation is dependent on faith *and* works. (*See* **al-'Aṣr, Ṣalāt.**)

al-'Aṣr, Ṣalāt (Ar.). The Afternoon Prayer. (*See* **Ṣalāt**.)

Assassins Mediaeval extremist sect of **Nizārīs** (q.v.), a branch of the **Ismā'īlīs** (q.v.), who indulged in political assassination. They were founded by **Ḥasan-i Ṣabbāḥ** (q.v.) and had their base in the castle of **Alamūt** (q.v.). Their Arabic name, from which the English word 'Assassin' is derived, was *ḥashīshiyyīn*, (literally 'ḥashīsh users'); this was probably a term of abuse levelled at the group rather than a reflection of their actual habits. Among the notable victims of the Assassins were the crusader, the Marquis Conrad of Montferrat, who was the King of the Latin Kingdom of Jerusalem (killed 588/1192); and the Persian *wazīr* of the Saljūqs, Niẓām al-Mulk (killed 485/1092). (*See* **Jerusalem**; **Saljūqs**; **Wazīr**.)

Atatürk, Muṣṭafā Kemāl (1298-9/1881–1357/1938) The founder of the modern state of Turkey in 1342/1923 and first President of that secularized Republic. His name *Atatürk* means 'Father of the Turks'. The secularization of Turkey meant the abolition of the sultanate and the caliphate, as well as the **ṣūfī** (q.v.) orders, **Qur'ān** schools and **Sharī'a** (q.v.) courts. It was no longer stated in the Constitution that Islam was the state religion. Atatürk blamed Islam for the long decline of the **Ottomans** (q.v.) and their empire. (*See* **Khalīfa**; **Sulṭān**; **Taṣawwuf**.)

Atomism Also called Occasionalism. This was a theory in mediaeval Islamic theology according to which absolutely everything (except God) was made up of atoms and perishable accidents (*a'rāḍ*). The theory stressed the continuous intervention by God in the affairs of the world and humanity. It was embraced (though interpreted in its detail in different ways) by many mediaeval Islamic theologians including the Mu'tazilite **Abū 'l-Hudhayl al-'Allāf** (q.v.) and the Ash'arite theologian **al-Bāqillānī** (q.v.). (*See* **'Araḍ**; **al-Ash'arī**; **Kalām**; **Mu'tazila**.)

'Aṭṭār, Farīd al-Dīn (died *c.* 627/1230) One of the great mystical poets of mediaeval Persia. Tradition has it that he met his death at the hands of the **Mongols** (q.v.) in Nishāpūr. The work for which he is best known is the famous *Speech of the Birds* (*Manṭiq al-Ṭayr*): in a Bunyanesque fashion this describes how the birds of the earth, led by the hoopoe bird – and after a long discussion which in fact occupies most of the work – decide to set out on a great pilgrimage to visit the court of the great King of Birds, the Sīmurgh. Only thirty birds survive the journey but they meet the Object of their quest and, in a final act of **fanā'** (q.v.) and **baqā'** (q.v.) become one with the Sīmurgh. This Persian poem is one of the finest allegories of a major theme in **taṣawwuf** (q.v.) in the whole of Islamic literature.

Attributes of God *See* **Ṣifāt Allāh**.

Aurangzeb (1026/1617–1118/1707) Mughal emperor who ruled in India from 1068/1658 until his death in 1118/1707. He was one of the sons of the famous **Shāh Jahān** (q.v.) and Mumtāz Maḥal for whom the **Tāj Maḥal** (q.v.) was built. When Shāh Jahān fell ill, Aurangzeb later interned his father and finally emerged successful in the war of succession with his three brothers. Aurangzeb's immensely long reign was spent fighting a large number of wars which constituted a backcloth against which the gradual decline of the Mughal empire started. He was particularly interested in the Islamization of his empire. (*See* **Mughals**.)

Avempace *See* **Ibn Bājja**.

Averroes *See* **Ibn Rushd**.

Avicebron *See* **Ibn Gabirol**.

Avicenna *See* **Ibn Sīnā**.

Awā'il (Ar.) [sing. *awwal*] Literary genre in mediaeval Arabic literature. The singular word means literally 'first' and the plural was used to indicate literature which dealt with people, events, ideas, etc. who or which were first.

Awaited Imām *See* **Muḥammad al-Qā'im.**

Awliyā' *See* **Walī**.

al-Aws Major Arab tribe of **Medina** (q.v.) which constituted an important section of the **Anṣār** (q.v.) after the arrival of the Prophet **Muḥammad** in Medina. The name of al-Aws is mentioned in the 'Constitution of Medina'. The principal enemy of al-Aws in Medina was the tribe of **al-Khazraj** (q.v.).

al-Awzā'ī (died *c.* 157/774) Important early jurist of the Syrian law school. His full name was Abū 'Amr 'Abd al-Raḥmān b.

'Amr al-Awzā'ī. He was probably born in **Damascus** (q.v.) but died in Beirut and he is buried near that city. His tomb has been at various times a focal point for pilgrimage. Al-Awzā'ī's works on law did not survive but he is often quoted by other jurists. In his jurisprudence al-Awzā'ī placed considerable emphasis on the role of tradition. (*See* **Fiqh**.)

Āya (Ar.) [pl. *āyāt*] Verse, especially a verse of the **Qur'ān**. The word has the additional meaning of 'sign' or 'miracle' and the Qur'ān contains many references to the signs of God: for example, 'We will show them Our signs (*āyātinā*) on the horizons and in their own selves' (v.53 of **Sūrat Fuṣṣilat** (q.v.)). (*See* **Āyat al-Kursī**; **Sūra**.)

Āyat al-Kursī (Ar.) The Throne Verse: one of the most famous and beloved of the verses of the **Qur'ān**, frequently recited as a protection against harm or evil. It is v.255 of **Sūrat al-Baqara** (q.v.) and may be translated as follows: 'God, there is no God but He, the Living, the Eternal. He is not subject to either slumber or sleep. He owns what is in the Heavens and what is on earth. Who can intercede with Him except with His permission? He knows what is in front of them and behind them. They glean nothing of His knowledge except what He wishes. His *throne* encompasses the Heavens and the earth and He is not burdened by sustaining both in existence. He is the Most High, the Great' [my translation].

Āyat al-Nūr *See* **Sūrat al-Nūr**.)

Āyat al-Rajm (Ar.) The Verse of the Stoning. Tradition maintains that this was a Qur'ānic verse although it was not - and is not - included in the final compilation. It prescribed stoning as a penalty for fornication. (*See* **Ḥadd**; **Qur'ān**; **Zinā'**.)

Ayatollah *See* **Āyatullāh**.

Āyatullāh (Ar./Pers.) Literally, 'The Sign of God'. The word is often popularly spelled 'Ayatollah' in English. It is a 20th century title of high esteem bestowed by popular acclaim, and the Āyatullāh peer group, in Iran on other Shī'ite scholars who have achieved eminence, usually in the fields of Islamic jurisprudence or Islamic theology. After the 1979 Iranian Revolution there was a considerable increase in the number of people calling themselves Āyatullāhs. However, a very small number - perhaps fewer than ten at one time - also bear the pre-eminent higher title of *Āyatullāh al-'Uẓmā* (meaning 'The Greatest Sign of God'). Of these the best known was the spiritual leader of Iran, the Āyatullāh **Khumaynī** (q.v.) (=Khomeini). These latter Grand Āyatullāhs are the **Marāji' al-Taqlīd** (q.v.) (Sources of Imitation). The rank below that of ordinary Āyatullāh is that of **Ḥujjat 'l-Islām** (q.v.). The majority of Āyatullāhs live in Iran but one of the most distinguished Āyatullāhs, whom some would regard as the supreme Āyatullāh of all, is the venerable Abū 'l-Qāsim al-Khū'ī (born 1317/1899) who lives in Iraq. (*See* **Mujtahid**; **Shī'ism**.)

Aynabakhti, Battle of *See* **Lepanto, Battle of.**

'Ayn al-Quḍāt al-Hamadhānī *See* **al-Hamadhānī, 'Ayn al-Quḍāt**.

'Ayn Jālūt, Battle of The Battle of the Well of Goliath. This was one of the most significant and important battles ever to be fought on Middle Eastern soil, equivalent in impact and consequences to the Battles of Hastings or Waterloo for England. The village of 'Ayn Jālūt is situated in Palestine. It was here, in 658/1260, that the Mamlūk army of Egypt decisively defeated the invading **Mongols** (q.v.) and prevented their further advance into Egypt and the rest of North Africa. (*See* **Mamlūks**.)

Ayyūb (Ar.) The Job of the **Qur'ān**, specifically mentioned in four **sūras** of the sacred text: (1) v.163 of **Sūrat al-Nisā'** (q.v.); (2) v.84 of **Sūrat al-An'ām** (q.v.); (3) vv.83–84 of **Sūrat al-Anbiyā'** (q.v.); (4) vv.41–44 of **Sūrat Ṣād** (q.v.). In the first two references Ayyūb is listed among a number of other prophets; while in the third, mention is made of the trials to which Ayyūb was subjected by God who later released him from those trials. v.44 of **Sūrat Ṣād** refers to an oath which Ayyūb had made to strike his wife because of some fault of hers.

Ayyūbids Important dynasty in mediaeval Islam which flourished between 564/1169 and *c*. 648/1250 in Egypt. There were also Ayyūbid branches in **Damascus** (q.v.), **Aleppo** (q.v.), Diyārbakr and the Yemen. The name of the dynasty derived from a Kurd named Ayyūb (died 578/1182–3), father of the famous **Ṣalāḥ al-Dīn** (q.v.). The Ayyūbids in Egypt were succeeded by the **Mamlūks** (q.v.). (*See* **Ḥaṭṭīn, Battle of**)

Āzar The pagan father of the prophet **Ibrāhīm** (q.v.). The **Qur'ān** mentions him by name in v.74 of **Sūrat al-An'ām** (q.v.). Here Ibrāhīm asks his father if he is going to take idols as gods. Elsewhere in the Qur'ān (**Sūrat al-Tawba** (q.v.)) Ibrāhīm is forbidden to pray for his obdurate father (who is not here in vv.113–114 named) since it is clear that the father will persist in idol worship. It may be noted that some commentators believe that the word Āzar, which is a non-Arabic word, is a term of abuse or disgust, rather than the proper name of Ibrāhīm's father.

Azd Name of two ancient Arab tribes, one in Western Arabia ('Asīr) and one in Oman. The former group became Muslim in 10/631; Islam also entered Oman early and several of the leaders of the **Ibāḍīs** (q.v.) were from the tribe of Azd.

al-Azhar (Ar.) Literally, 'The Brilliant' or 'The Radiant'. The full name is *al-Jāmi' al-Azhar* (The Radiant Mosque). This is the title borne by Islam's most famous University and Mosque, founded by the **Fāṭimids** (q.v.) in **Cairo** (q.v.), after their conquest of Egypt in 358/969. It was founded originally as a beacon for Ismā'īlī doctrine and scholarship but it became a bastion of **Sunnī** (q.v.) orthodoxy with the takeover by the **Ayyūbids** (q.v.) in Egypt. (*See* **Ismā'īlīs**; **Riwāq**; **al-Zaytūna**.)

Azrael *See* **'Izrā'īl**.

Baba, Bābā (Turk./Pers.) Father. The word became popular as a surname among some **ṣūfī** (q.v.) preachers, and shaykhs of such orders as the famous syncretic ṣūfī order of **Bektāshiyya** (q.v.). In the latter the head of a **tekkē** (q.v.) bore the title of *bābā*. The best known of all *bābā*s in secular usage was 'Alī Bābā in *The Thousand and One Nights*. The main difference between Turkish and Persian usage of the word was that in Turkey the word followed a person's name but in Persia it came before. (*See* **Shaykh**.)

Bābism Movement named after the *Bāb* (literally 'Door') (i.e. to the Hidden Imām), a title assumed by Mirzā 'Alī Muḥammad (1235/1819–1266/1850) of **Shīrāz** (q.v.) in 1260/1844, who was finally executed for his beliefs. The Bābī sect later gave rise to the **Bahā'īs** (q.v.). (*See* **Imām**; **Muḥammad al-Qā'im**.)

Bābur (888/1483–937/1530) Warrior ruler who founded the Mughal dynasty in India. His full name was Ẓāhir al-Dīn Muḥammad Bābur. He ruled from 932/1526 until 937/1530. Bābur was directly descended from the famous **Tīmūr-i Lang** (q.v.) on his father's side, and from Čingiz Khān (=Genghis Khan) on his mother's. It was left to Bābur's eldest son **Humāyūn** (q.v.) to consolidate Bābur's initial victories in Hindūstān. Bābur was aided in his conquests by the use of muskets and a rudimentary mortar. (*See* **Mughals**.)

al-Badawī, al-Sayyid Aḥmad (*c.* 596/1199-1200–675/1276) Famous Egyptian Muslim saint. Born in **Fez** (q.v.), he made the pilgrimage to **Mecca** (q.v.) as a child. Later he visited Iraq but returned to Ṭanṭā in Egypt where he lived an ascetic life and died. Al-Badawī achieved the very high **ṣūfī** (q.v.) rank of **al-Quṭb** (q.v.), 'The Pole'. Many miracles are ascribed to him and his tomb in the mosque at Ṭanṭā receives many pilgrims. The ṣūfī order of the Aḥmadiyya, which is called after him, is immensely popular in Egypt. The **Mawlid** (q.v.) of al-Sayyid Aḥmad al-Badawī is celebrated every year in Ṭanṭā with much festivity, ceremony and procession. The **dhikr** (q.v.) is performed on the roofs of houses and many infants and young boys are circumcised during the *mawlid*. This is perhaps the most famous of all the *mawlids* to take place in Egypt and is of great antiquity. (*See* **Aḥmadiyya** (2); **Khitān**; **Taṣawwuf**.)

Badawiyya *See* **Aḥmadiyya** (2); **al-Badawī, al-Sayyid Aḥmad**.

Badr, Battle of The first major battle fought between **Muḥammad** supported by the Medinans, and the Meccans in 2/624 at Badr, to the South-West of **Medina** (q.v.). The Meccan forces, commanded by **Abū Jahl** (q.v.), were defeated and about seventy Meccans, with Abū Jahl among them, were killed. The **Qur'ān** indicates that angels fought on Muḥammad's side at the Battle of Badr (*see* vv.9, 12 of **Sūrat al-Anfāl** (q.v.)). The Muslim success in the battle gave immense prestige to the infant Islamic community in Medina and dealt a major blow to the pride of the Meccans.

Baghdād Major city in the Middle East, and capital of modern Iraq from 1339–40/1921. It was founded in 145/762 near the River Tigris by the 'Abbāsid caliph al-Manṣūr under the name *Madīnat al-Salām* meaning 'City of Peace'. The city became the centre of the 'Abbāsid caliphate until 656/1258 and was also occupied for substantial periods by the **Būyids** (q.v.) and the **Saljūqs** (q.v.) during this time. Baghdād was sacked by the **Mongols** (q.v.) in 656/1258 but later achieved some prominence again in the pre-modern period under the **Ottomans** (q.v.) in the 11th/17th century. Baghdād was heavily bombed in the 1991 Gulf War. (*See* **'Abbāsids**; **Hārūn al-Rashīd**; **Kāẓimayn**.)

Bahā'īs Members of new religion, deriving from **Bābism** (q.v.), founded by **Bahā'ullāh** (q.v.), and propagated by the latter's son 'Abd al-Bahā'. Bahā'īs believe in an utterly transcendent God who has, none the less, manifested Himself through a continuing chain of prophets who include many of the great figures familiar to adherents of the three major monotheistic religions of Judaism, Christianity and Islam. The *Bāb* and Bahā'ullāh also have prophetic rank. The Bahā'īs believe that all the religions which have prophets possess an intrinsic truth. Because the Bahā'īs, technically speaking, are an offshoot of an offshoot of an offshoot of the **Ithnā 'Asharīs** (q.v.) they have often been regarded as gravely heretical by Muslims, and sometimes subjected to persecution and execution.

Bahā'ullāh (1233/1817–1309/1892) Founder of the **Bahā'īs** (q.v.). Born into an aristocratic family in Tehran, he became an early disciple of the *Bāb*, though he never actually met him. While in prison in Tehran he underwent a profound mystical experience. In 1279/1863 Bahā'ullāh announced himself as 'The Man whom God shall reveal', in fulfilment of a prophecy by the *Bāb*; and later he openly announced his mission in Edirne. He is buried in Haifa in Israel. (*See* **Bābism**.)

Baḥīrā Name of a Christian monk and hermit encountered by **Muḥammad** while on a trading expedition to Syria with his uncle **Abū Ṭālib** (q.v.); Muḥammad at the time was aged about twelve. Baḥīrā recognized the seal of prophethood on Muḥammad and he forecast great things for the Prophet.

al-Balad (Ar.) The title of the 90th **sūra** of the **Qur'ān**; the name here most likely means 'The City' (i.e. the city of **Mecca** (q.v.)) or possibly just 'The Land'. The word *al-balad* from which the *sūra* derives its name occurs in both the 1st and 2nd verses. The *sūra* belongs to the Meccan period and has 20 verses. The *sūra* underlines the idea that man has been born to a life of hardship and that he has a choice, either to follow the difficult path of charity and generosity or, in his arrogance and disbelief, forget his fellow man. The *sūra* ends with a warning about Hell fire. (*See* **al-Nār**.)

al-Balādhurī (3rd/9th century) A notable Arab historian. Born, most likely, in **Baghdād** (q.v.), he studied in a variety of centres of Islamic learning. His two most important historical works were his *Muslim Conquests* and *The Genealogies of the Nobles*. Both works are extremely valuable for the early history of Islam and the Arabs.

Balkh Major city of mediaeval Islam which has today been reduced to the size of a village. It is situated in what is now Afghanistan.

Balqis *See* **Bilqīs**.

Banī Isrā'īl, Sūrat *See* **Sūrat al-Isrā'**.

Banking, Islamic *See* **Islamic Banking**.

al-Bannā', Ḥasan (1323-4/1906–1368/1949) Founder of the **Ikhwān al-Muslimūn** (q.v.) better known in Europe as the Muslim Brotherhood. He exhibited an early interest in **taṣawwuf** (q.v.) and joined a **ṭarīqa** (q.v.) at the age of fourteen. His studies led him to believe that Islam in its present state was in dire need of revival and that this should be undertaken through adherence to the **Qur'ān** and **Ḥadīth** (q.v.). He began preaching his views and became a school teacher, first in the Egyptian Canal Zone and later in **Cairo** (q.v.). He incurred the hostility of the Egyptian government on many occasions. He was assassinated in 1368/1949. (*See also* **Ikhwān**.)

Baqā' (Ar.) Remaining, subsistence, abiding, survival, immortality. As a technical term in **taṣawwuf** (q.v.) the word *baqā'* is used to indicate a stage in the mystical experience after **fanā'** (q.v.) in which the mystic 'abides' or 'subsists' in God. *Baqā'*, which takes place after death, does not entail a total loss of individuality. The mediaeval writers realized that the concept was a difficult one to grasp and they therefore wrote parables, like that of **'Aṭṭār** (q.v.) entitled *The Speech of the Birds*, to illustrate exactly what they meant.

al-Baqara (Ar.) The title of the 2nd **sūra** of the **Qur'ān**; the word means 'The Cow' and is drawn from the story of the cow which occurs in vv.67–71. This was the first Medinan *surā* to be revealed. With 286 verses it is also the longest *sūra* in the Qur'ān. After beginning with three of the **Mysterious Letters of the Qur'ān** (q.v.), the *sūra* goes on to deal, *inter alia*, with the creation of **Ādam** (q.v.), the rebellion of **Iblīs** (q.v.), **Mūsā** (q.v.) (including the story of the cow), **Hārūt and Mārūt** (q.v.), **Ibrāhīm** (q.v.), the change of the **qibla** (q.v.) from **Jerusalem** (q.v.) to **Mecca** (q.v.), the prohibition on eating pork, fasting in **Ramaḍān** (q.v.), pilgrimage, divorce and the prohibition of **ribā** (q.v.). (*See* **Āyat al-Kursī**; **Compulsion**; **Fir'awn**; **Gambling**; **Ḥajj**; **Ibrāhīm** (1); **'Idda**; **Jibrīl**; **Ṭalāq**.)

al-Bāqillānī (died 403/1013) Distinguished mediaeval Ash'arite theologian, proponent of **Atomism** (q.v.) and Mālikī jurist and judge. He lived mainly in **Baghdād** (q.v.) and gained a considerable reputation in lecturing and debate. He wrote works on the **Qur'ān**, the imāmate, miracles and theological problems. (*See* **al-Ash'arī**; **Imām**; **Mālikīs**.)

Baraka (Ar.) Blessing. It is a quality possessed especially by holy men in Islam, who can impart it to others. *Baraka* may also be attached to places and objects. It should never be translated as 'grace' in view of the Christian theological connotations of that latter word. In popular Islam, *baraka* may be gained by visiting the tombs of saints. (*See* **Marabout**; **Shafā'a**; **Wahhābīs**; **Walī**; **Ziyāra**.)

Bareilly *See* **Barēlwīs**.

Barēlwīs Indian Muslim sect with a particular veneration for the Prophet **Muḥammad**. The word *Barēlwī* (or *Barēlvī*) in Urdu is an adjective deriving from the city of Bareilly (Barēlī) in Uttar Pradesh, seat of an academy whose tradition predated that of Deoband. Indeed, the Barēlwīs are often compared and contrasted with the **Deobandis** (q.v.). Like the latter they were **Ḥanafīs** (q.v.) but they were closely linked to a type of **taṣawwuf** (q.v.) which stressed shrine and tomb, **shaykh** (q.v.) and **pīr** (q.v.), and intercession. They adhered to a formidable belief in hierarchy whether of their own **'ulamā'** (q.v.) or their saints together with the Prophet **Muḥammad**. The leading figure of the Barēlwīs in the 13th/19th century was Mawlānā Aḥmad Riẓā Khān Barēlwī (1272-3/1856–1339-40/1921). (*See* **Shafā'a**; **Taṣawwuf**; **Walī**.)

Barmakids The Barmecides. In Arabic, this family of scribes and ministers, who served important **'Abbāsids** (q.v.) like the caliph **Hārūn al-Rashīd** (q.v.), was known as *al-Barāmika* or *Āl Barmak*. Having served their masters faithfully for many years, the Barmakids were suddenly overthrown by Hārūn in 187/803. Many reasons have been advanced by historians to account for this sudden reversal in their fortunes. The attractive account of the relationship between Ja'far al-Barmakī and Hārūn's sister 'Abbāsa, recounted in the histories of both **al-Mas'ūdī** (q.v.) and **al-Ṭabarī** (q.v.) must however, be discounted. The most likely reason for their precipitate downfall appears to have been the caliph's increased perception of the family's growing political, and especially economic, power.

Barmecides *See* **Barmakids**.

Barzakh (Ar./Pers.) Literally, 'obstacle', 'hindrance', 'barrier', 'partition', 'isthmus'. In Islam the word came to indicate an intermediate area between Hell and Heaven, or the place/state between this earthly life and the hereafter. It should not be translated, however, as 'Purgatory' because, as in the case of **al-A'rāf** (q.v.), *barzakh* is not associated with purgation of sin. The word is mentioned three times in the **Qur'ān** (in v.100 of **Sūrat**

al-Mu'minūn (q.v.), v.53 of **Sūrat al-Furqān** (q.v.) and v.20 of **Sūrat al-Raḥmān** (q.v.)), and also acquired a specialist meaning in the philosophy of such Islamic mystical philosophers as **al-Suhrawardī** (q.v.). Here it may be translated as 'isthmus': one such isthmus, associated with the heavenly spheres, was emanated by each of the lights in that philosopher's hierarchy of lights. (*See* **al-Ākhira**; **al-Janna**; **al-Nār**.)

Basin *See* **Ḥawḍ**.

Basmala (Ar.) The invocation, or utterance of the common Islamic invocation, ***Bism**ⁱ **'llāh al-Raḥmān al-Raḥīm*** which means 'In the name of Allāh, the Merciful, the Compassionate'. These words occur at the beginning of every **sūra** of the **Qur'ān** except the 9th, **Sūrat al-Tawba** (q.v.).

al-Baṣra Major city and river port in Southern Iraq, as well known in mediaeval Islamic times as it is today. It was famous for the varied and international nature of its trade and culture. Al-Baṣra was, *inter alia*, the birthplace of Arabic philology, one of the homes of the **Mu'tazila** (q.v.) theological movement, the birthplace also of the great belletrist **al-Jāḥiẓ** (q.v.) and the probable home of the philosophical **Ikhwān al-Ṣafā'** (q.v.). Baṣra was heavily bombed in the 1991 Gulf War. (*See* **al-Kūfa**; **Qubba**.)

Basṭ (Ar.) Literally, 'expansion', 'extension'. This is used as a technical term in **taṣawwuf** (q.v.). *Basṭ* is a joyful and happy spiritual state (*ḥāl*) granted to the **ṣūfī** (q.v.) by God. *See* v.245 of **Sūrat al-Baqara** (q.v.) in the **Qur'ān**. (*See also* **Aḥwāl**; **Maqāmāt**; **Qabḍ**.)

al-Basṭāmī, Abū Yazīd *See* **al-Bisṭāmī, Abū Yazīd**.

Ba'th (Ar.) (1) Resurrection; (2) Sending: (1) Pre-Islamic Arabia believed that the souls of the dead lived on in some kind of shadowy existence beyond the grave. However, there was no concept of any resurrection of the body. The **Qur'ān** later taught that there would be a resurrection of both bodies and souls, something at which many of the pagan Arabs scoffed. Many Islamic philosophers held, contrary to the teaching of the Qur'ān, that only souls would be resurrected. The Qur'ān contains much information about the Day of Resurrection (called in Arabic *Yawm al-Ba'th* or **Yawm al-Qiyāma** (q.v.)) as well as its terrors and judgements. (2) The word *ba'th* also has a technical theological sense indicating the sending out of prophets by God. (*See* **al-Ḥisāb**.)

Bāṭin (Ar.) Esoteric, inner. Its opposite in Islam and, in particular, in the theology of the **Ismā'īlīs** (q.v.) is **Ẓāhir** (q.v.). That which is *bāṭin* belongs to an inner or secret dimension of Islam. (*See* **Tafsīr**.)

Bāṭiniyya *See* **Ismā'īlīs**.

Bāyazīd al-Bisṭāmī *See* **al-Bisṭāmī, Abū Yazīd**.

al-Bayḍāwī, 'Abd Allāh b. 'Umar Nāṣir al-Dīn (died *c.* 691/1291 but other dates are given) One of the most famous and popular exegetes of the **Qur'ān**. Persian by birth and Shāfi'ī by **madhhab** (q.v.), he became Chief Judge in **Shīrāz** (q.v.). He is famous for his Qur'ānic commentary entitled *The Lights of Revelation* (*Anwār al-Tanzīl*). This owed much to the commentary of **al-Zamakhsharī** (q.v.) but al-Bayḍāwī tried to purge the latter of its **Mu'tazilite** (q.v.) content. (*See* **Qāḍī**; **Shāfi'īs**.)

Bayram *See* **Qurbān**.

Bayt al-Ḥikma (Ar.) The House of Wisdom. Philosophy and translation academy in **Baghdād** (q.v.) founded by the 'Abbāsid caliph **al-Ma'mūn** (q.v.) in 216–7/832. (*See* **'Abbāsids**).

al-Bayyina (Ar.) The title of the 98th **sūra** of the **Qur'ān**; the word, which means 'The Clear Proof', occurs in the 1st verse. As the 2nd verse shows, this 'Clear Proof' may be either a divine messenger or sacred pages. The *sūra* belongs to the Medinan period and has 8 verses. It notes at the beginning the request by the People of the Book (**Ahl al-Kitāb** (q.v.)) and the polytheists for a 'clear proof'. The disbelievers in both groups will dwell in Hell fire (**Jahannam** (q.v.)) for ever. By contrast, believers and the doers of good deeds will be rewarded in the gardens of Eden (**'Adn** (q.v.)).

Beatific Vision *See* **Ru'yat Allāh**.

Beautiful Names of God There are ninety-nine known in Arabic as **al-Asmā' al-Ḥusnā**.

Bektāshiyya Highly syncretic Turkish **ṣūfī** (q.v.) order whose beliefs and practices include elements drawn from Christianity. It is named after the 7th/13th century ṣūfī Ḥājjī Bektāsh. The order gained political influence under the **Ottomans** (q.v.) but was suppressed by **Atatürk** (q.v.). The main centre of the Bektāshiyya today is in Albania. (*See* **Baba**; **Dede**; **Taṣawwuf**.)

Belief *See* **'Aqīda**; **Dīn**; **Īmān**.

Bequest, Religious *See* **Waqf**.

Bid'a (Ar.) Literally, 'innovation'. Its proper opposite is **sunna** (q.v.). However, in popular speech *bid'a* has come to indicate 'heresy' although, if one is to be absolutely correct, it is in fact distinct from heresy, since not all innovation (*bid'a*) may be bad or hostile to Islam, according to Islamic law. (*See* **Ilḥād**; **Irtidād**.)

Bilā Kayf (Ar.) Literally, the phrase means 'without (asking) how'. It was put forward as a solution in mediaeval times to the great debate about the attributes of God (**Ṣifāt Allāh** (q.v.)). According to this Muslims were obliged to believe that God did indeed have real attributes like hands and a face, since these were mentioned in the **Qur'ān**. Such attributes were to be accepted without asking *how* they existed. Adherents of this position included **al-Ash'arī** (q.v.) and **Aḥmad b. Ḥanbal** (q.v.). (*See* **Istawā**; **Mu'tazila**; **Ru'yat Allāh**.)

Bilāl b. Rabāḥ (died *c.* 20/641 but other dates are given) First **mu'adhdhin** (q.v.) appointed by the Prophet **Muḥammad**, who also served the Prophet in a variety of other ways. An Abyssinian slave, he was freed by **Abū Bakr** (q.v.). He made the **Hijra** (q.v.) with Muḥammad to **Medina** (q.v.) and later, when the Prophet conquered **Mecca** (q.v.), he gave the call to prayer from the top of the **Ka'ba** (q.v.). During the conquests, after Muḥammad's death, Bilāl joined the campaign to Syria.

Bilqīs Pre-Islamic queen of Sheba (a place variously spelled in Arabic). She is not mentioned by name in the **Qur'ān** but the exegetes identify her with the queen in **Sūrat al-Naml** (q.v.) who visits **Sulaymān** (q.v.) and surrenders with Sulaymān to the one true God. (*See* **Sūrat Sabā'**.)

Bīmāristān (Pers./Ar.) Hospital; also a lunatic asylum in modern usage. The word derives from two Persian words: *bīmār* (sick) and *-istān* (place). Tradition credits the Umayyad caliph Walīd I (*reg.* 86/705–96/715) with having built the first *bīmāristān* in Islam. The medical traditions of the philosophico-medical centre and town of **Gondēshāpūr** (q.v.) were continued in the hospital founded in **Baghdād** (q.v.) by **Hārūn al-Rashīd** (q.v.). (*See* **Umayyads**.)

Birthday *See* **Mawlid**.

Bishr b. al-Mu'tamir (died 210/825–226/840) Leading Mu'tazilite and founding father of the **Baghdād** (q.v.) school of the **Mu'tazila** (q.v.). His early studies were done in **al-Baṣra** (q.v.) and he suffered imprisonment under **Hārūn al-Rashīd** (q.v.). He was interested in questions of responsibility, free will and epistemology. He was patronized by the **Barmakids** (q.v.) and the great historian **al-Mas'ūdī** (q.v.) records his presence at, and contribution to, a noted seminar and discussion on the subject of passionate love (*'ishq*) held by Yaḥyā b. Khālid al-Barmakī. (*See* **Qadar**; **Qadariyya**.)

al-Bisṭāmī, Abū Yazīd (died 261/874 or 264/877–8) One of the most famous of all the mediaeval ṣūfīs and notorious utterer of such ecstatic phrases (*shaṭaḥāt*) as 'Glory be to me! How great is my majesty!'. He spent most of his life in Bisṭām where he died. If he wrote anything, nothing has survived. However, his multitudinous sayings became well-known. (*See* **al-Ḥallāj**; **Ṣūfī**; **Taṣawwuf**.)

Black Stone *See* **al-Ḥajar al-Aswad**; **Ka'ba**.

Blood money *See* **Diya**.

Body *See under* **Ba'th**.

Bohorās (Guj.) The word *bohorā* indicates 'merchant' and is derived from the Gujarati *vohōrvū*, 'to engage in trade'. The word *bohorā* in India has been used to denote some Hindus as well as **Sunnī** (q.v.) Muslims and **Ismā'īlīs** (q.v.). The latter are the spiritual heirs of those who supported al-Musta'lī (*reg*. 487/1094–495/1101) as Fāṭimid caliph in Egypt on the death of **al-Mustanṣir** (q.v.) in 487/1094. The Ismā'īlī Bohorās, who do not follow the **Āghā Khān** (q.v.), later split into two further groups called Sulaymānīs and Dā'ūdīs. (*See* **Fāṭimids**; **Khojas**; **Nizārīs**.)

Bokhara *See* **Bukhārā**.

Books, Judgement with *See* **al-Ḥisāb**.

Brethren of Purity *See* **Ikhwān al-Ṣafā'**.

Bridge *See* **Ṣirāṭ al-Jaḥīm**.

Bukhārā (Bokhara) City now situated in the Republic of Uzbekistān, which became a centre of rule by the Samānid dynasty in the 3rd/9th–10th centuries. It is often mentioned in the same breath as **Samarqand** (q.v.) because of the wealth of its magnificent Islamic artistic and architectural remains.

al-Bukhārī, Muḥammad b. Ismā'īl (194/810–256/870) Very famous compiler of **ḥadīth** (q.v.) whose collection, entitled the *Ṣaḥīḥ* meaning the *Sound*, *True* or *Authentic*, was culled from a huge corpus of about 600,000 traditions. Al-Bukhārī's *Ṣaḥīḥ* is often esteemed by Muslims as second only to the **Qur'ān** itself. During his lifetime he travelled throughout much of the Islamic world in search of traditions. Al-Bukhārī took particular care over which traditions he incorporated into his collection and arranged his material mainly according to the subjects with which they dealt. (*See* **Muslim b. al-Ḥajjāj**; **Riḥla**; **Ṣaḥīḥ**.)

al-Burāq The name of the mount on which **Muḥammad**, in the company of the angel **Jibrīl** (q.v.) made his famous **isrā'** (q.v.) or night nourney from **Mecca** (q.v.) to **Jerusalem** (q.v.), and thence the **mi'rāj** (q.v.) to Paradise, before returning in the same way; the journey was accomplished all in one night. In appearance, al-Burāq resembled a kind of small winged horse and is sometimes portrayed with a human face, for example, in Indian pictures of this celestial mount, and some produced in Harāt. The night journey is referred to in the **Qur'ān** at the beginning of **Sūrat al-Isrā'** (q.v.); however, al-Burāq is neither mentioned by name nor even referred to and we depend for details about this famous creature on the **tafsīr** (q.v.) and **ḥadīth** (q.v.) literature. (*See* **al-Aqṣā, al-Masjid**; **Qubbat al-Ṣakhra**.)

Burhāniyya Popular **ṣūfī** (q.v.) order in Egypt, especially in **Cairo** (q.v.), and elsewhere, also called the Dasūqiyya. It derives its names from its founder Burhān al-Dīn Ibrāhīm b. Abī 'l-Majd

'Abd al-'Azīz al-Dasūqī (*c.* 644/1246–687/1288 but other dates are given). The present-day order in Egypt characterizes itself as Shādhilī as well as Dasūqī and Burhānī. (*See* **al-Ḥusayn b. 'Alī; Shādhiliyya; Taṣawwuf.**)

Burqa *See* **Burqu'.**

Burqu' (Ar.) [pl. *barāqi'*]; **Burqa'** (Pers.) Long veil for women which covers most of the body except for the eyes. (*See* **Chādor; Ḥijāb.**)

Bursa The most important city of the **Ottomans** (q.v.) in the 8th/14th century. The city was much improved by the Ottoman sultan Bāyazīd I (*reg.* 791/1389–805/1403) but it was burned by the army of **Tīmūr-i Lang** (q.v.) after the latter defeated Bāyazīd at the Battle of Ankara in 804/1402. Bursa had a particular importance in international trade, especially the silk trade. It contains some superb specimens of early Ottoman architecture. (*See* **Ankara, Battle of**)

al-Burūj (Ar.) The title of the 85th **sūra** of the **Qur'ān**; it means 'The Constellations' or 'The Signs of the Zodiac'. The *sūra* belongs to the Meccan period and contains 22 verses. The title is drawn from the oath in the 1st verse. The early part of the *sūra* makes reference to 'the people of the pit' who have been variously identified. (One account sees them as Christian victims of the Jewish ruler **Dhū Nuwās** (q.v.)). The *sūra* goes on to warn that those who persecute the believers and do not repent will burn in Hell fire (**Jahannam** (q.v.)). Reference is made at the end to the people of **Thamūd** (q.v.) and also to the Qur'ān being a *lawḥ maḥfūẓ*. (*See* **al-Lawḥ al-Maḥfūẓ.**)

Buwayhids *See* **Būyids.**

Būyids Major dynasty in mediaeval Islamic history which flourished in Persia and Iraq between 320/932 and 454/1062.

Ethnically they were Daylamites; religiously they were Shī'ite, possibly of the Zaydī persuasion. Whatever their own beliefs, however, they exercised a considerable tolerance towards other branches of Islam. The Būyids entered **Baghdād** (q.v.) in 334/945 and held sway there until the advent of the **Saljūqs** (q.v.) in 447/1055. (*See* **Shī'ism**; **Zaydīs**.)

Cain and Abel *See* **Qābīl and Hābīl.**

Cairo Capital of Egypt and major Middle Eastern city. It is known in classical Arabic as **al-Qāhira** meaning 'The Victorious', but also, more colloquially, as *Maṣr*, a word which also means 'Egypt' itself as well as the city of Cairo. Today Cairo is one of the most over-populated but also dynamic and vibrant cities in the world. In a sense, it is several cities in one, ranging from the *qarāfa*, or cemetery behind the Muqaṭṭam Hills to the modern suburb of Zamālik. Cairo was founded as a capital for the **Fāṭimids** (q.v.) in 358/969, and this and succeeding dynasties, especially the **Mamlūks** (q.v.), all left their architectural mark upon the city. Indeed, Cairo is a treasure house of mosques and monuments. These include not only great Islamic buildings like **al-Azhar** (q.v.) Mosque University but relics of other cultures like the Coptic, with its churches and artefacts in the Coptic Museum, and the Pharaonic: many of the remains of the latter culture are to be viewed in the great Cairo Museum as well as just outside Cairo, where, in the shape of the Pyramids and the Sphinx, the visitor is vividly reminded of Egypt's ancient, imperial and splendid past. Perhaps the best guide to the Islamic monuments of Cairo is the work by Parker, Sabin and Williams entitled *Islamic Monuments in Cairo: A Practical Guide* (see back of this *Dictionary* for full bibliographical details).

Calendar The Islamic calendar is lunar rather than solar. It formally began with the **Hijra** (q.v.) of the Propher **Muḥammad** from **Mecca** (q.v.) to **Medina** (q.v.). This took place in AD 622 which became the first year of the Muslim lunar calendar.

Because of the *Hijra* Islamic dates are therefore termed in Arabic *hijrī* dates and written in English with AH (=*Anno Hegirae*) as a prefix or suffix in place of AD. Users of the *Dictionary* will note that, wherever possible, both AH and AD dates are given, the former always appearing first.

Caliph *See* **Khalīfa**.

Caliphate *See under* **Khalīfa**.

Call to Prayer *See* **Adhān**.

Camel, Battle of the Battle fought near **al-Baṣra** (q.v.) between **'Ā'isha bint Abī Bakr** (q.v.), **Ṭalḥa b. 'Ubaydullāh al-Taymī** (q.v.) and **al-Zubayr b. al-'Awwām** (q.v.) on the one hand, and the forces of **'Alī b. Abī Ṭālib** (q.v.) on the other. It took place in 36/656. The forces of 'Ā'isha were defeated; Ṭalḥa and, later, al-Zubayr, were killed and 'Ā'isha was taken prisoner though accorded enormous reverence as a wife of the Prophet **Muḥammad**, and later sent back to **Medina** (q.v.). The battle was so-called because of the camel which 'Ā'isha rode during it.

Cami (Turk.) =Arabic *Jāmi'*, a large, often central, mosque. (*See* **Masjid**).

Camphor *See* **Kāfūr**.

Carmathians *See* **Qarāmiṭa**.

Case Law *See* **Taqlīd**.

Čelebī (Turk.) Author, reader, wise man. Honorific term borne by a variety of types of people generally up to the 12th/18th century. These included royalty, aristocrats, writers and **ṣūfī** (q.v.) shaykhs. In some cases it has been used in modern times. Scholars have disputed over the etymology of the word. (*See* **Shaykh**; **Taṣawwuf**.)

Chādor (Pers.) Large black cloak and veil which envelops the woman's entire body, worn in Iran and elsewhere. (*See* **Burqu'**; **Ḥijāb**.)

Chapter (of the Qur'ān) *See* **Sūra**.

Chistiyya *See* **Čishtiyya**.

Circumambulation (of the Ka'ba) *See* **Ṭawāf**.

Circumcision *See* **Khitān**.

Čishtiyya or Chistiyya Major **ṣūfī** (q.v.) order founded in India by Mu'īn al-Dīn Ḥasan Čishtī (*c.* 537/1142–633/1236), after whom it is called. The order in India was early influenced by the writings of Shihāb al-Dīn Abū Ḥafs al-Suhrawardī, and, like **Ibn al-'Arabī** (q.v.), it adhered to the doctrine of 'Unity (or Oneness) of Being' (***Waḥdat al-Wujūd***). Its attitudes were both ascetic and pacific and it also placed much emphasis on the recitation of the *ṣūfī* **dhikr** (q.v.), among other mystical and ascetical practices. The order became divided into a number of major branches, notably the Ṣābiriyya and the Niẓāmiyya. Despite the adoption of the above-mentioned al-Suhrawardī's writings, the order is not, in fact, part of the **Suhrawardiyya** (q.v.). (*See* **al-Suhrawardī**; **Taṣawwuf**.)

Cistern *See* **Ḥawḍ**.

Civil War *See* **Fitna**; **Ridda**.

Cleanliness, Ritual *See* **Ṭahāra**.

Commander of the Faithful *See* **Amīr al-Mu'minīn**; **Khalīfa**.

Community, Islamic *See* **Umma**.

Companions of the Cave *See* **Aṣḥāb al-Kahf**; **Sūrat al-Kahf**.

Companions of the Prophet Muḥammad *See* **Ṣaḥāba**.

Compassionate, The *See* **al-Raḥīm**.

Compensation *See* **Diya**.

Compulsion It is one of the basic principles of Islam that one's religion should be freely adopted, and this point is enshrined in the **Qur'ān**. In v.256 of **Sūrat al Baqara** (q.v.) the Qur'ān states: 'There is no compulsion in religion' (*lā ikrāha fī 'l-dīn*). This is underlined in a slightly different form in v.6 of **Sūrat al-Kāfirūn** (q.v.): 'For you your religion and for me [my] religion' (*lakum dīnukum wa lī dīn*).

Consensus of opinion (as legal term) *See* **Ijmā'**.

Constantinople *See* **Istanbul**.

Constitution of Medina *See* **Medina**.

Cordova Called in Arabic Qurṭuba, Cordova was one of the great cities of mediaeval Islamic Spain. Throughout its Islamic history it was often the focus of invading armies or other factions. It became the capital of **al-Andalus** (q.v.) in *c.* 99/717, was sacked in 403–4/1013, captured by the **Almoravids** (q.v.) in 484/1091 and occupied by the Christian Ferdinand III of Castile (and later Leon) in 633/1236. The period up to the end of the 4th/10th century saw the appearance of a distinctive form of Moorish art in Spain. This is epitomized in the Great Mosque of Cordova, the building of which was commenced by 'Abd al-Raḥmān I (*reg.* 138/756–172/788) (who founded the Umayyad Emirate of Cordova), and continued by his successors. (*See* **Umayyads**.)

Corruption, Textual *See* **al-Injīl**; **Taḥrīf**.

Creed *See* **'Aqīda**; **Dīn**; **Īmān**.

Crescent *See* **Hilāl**.

Crusades A series of conflicts which took place in mediaeval times, often on Middle Eastern soil, between Christian Europe and the Muslim East. Known in Arabic as *al-Ḥurūb al-Ṣalībiyya*, meaning 'The Wars of the Cross', they were, perhaps, of greater significance for the European West, and later Western historians, than for the Muslim East where far greater threats loomed like the invasions of the **Mongols** (q.v.). Although such cities as **Jerusalem** (q.v.) and Acre were at various times captured by the Christians, the latter never succeeded in taking more than small pieces of territory, temporarily, from Islam. While *some* of the Christian invaders *were* inspired by genuine religious motives, others (often second sons who would not inherit in their European homelands) were driven by the lure of booty, power and prestige. It is interesting that such travellers as the 6th/12th century Spanish Muslim Ibn Jubayr describe the passage of Muslims aboard Christian ships in the Mediterranean, as well as the continuation of Muslim-Christian trade, while their respective armies were at war on the land. The first Crusade, preached at Clermont by Pope Urban II in 488/1095 resulted in the Christian capture of Jerusalem in 492/1099. By the 8th/14th century the great age of the Crusades had almost finished. The final religious verdict on them must be that while for Islam the Crusades were an irritating hiccup in the fabric of Middle Eastern history, for Christian Europe they were a major historical and religious project, if not actual trauma. For an overall picture of the age of the Crusades, see Holt, *The Age of the Crusades: The Near East from the Eleventh Century to 1517* (see back of this *Dictionary* for full bibliographical details). (*See* **Ḥaṭṭīn, Battle of**; **Jihād**; **Ṣalāḥ al-Dīn**.)

Custody of Children *See* **Ḥaḍāna**.

Dā'ī (Ar.) [pl. *du'āt*] Caller (i.e. to Islam), propagandist, one who preaches a (sometimes esoteric) missionary movement, summons or call. In the usage of the **Ismā'īlīs** (q.v.) the *dā'ī* represented the **Imām** (q.v.). Other branches of Islam have used the term in various ways. (*See* **Da'wa; al-Ḥāmidī**.)

Ḍa'īf (Ar.) Weak. Used as a technical term in **ḥadīth** (q.v.) criticism to characterize the lack of strength and reliability of a tradition. Compare the terms **Ḥasan** (q.v.), **Ṣaḥīḥ** (q.v.) and **Saqīm** (q.v.). There are various grades of weak tradition.

al-Dajjāl (Ar.) The word derives from Syriac and means 'the Cheat' or 'the Charlatan'. It is often translated to signify an Islamic 'anti-Christ'. A huge amount of tradition has grown up around this eschatological figure. The bare bones of these indicate that he will arrive on earth during the last days of which he himself will be a major sign. He will preside over forty years (or forty days) of injustice and licence, after which **'Īsā** (q.v.) will destroy him and the entire world will convert to Islam. Al-Dajjāl is not mentioned by name in the **Qur'ān**.

Damascus Capital of modern Syria and major Middle Eastern city from early mediaeval times onwards. It is called in Arabic *Dimashq*. Under the caliph **Mu'āwiya** (q.v.) Damascus became the capital of the Arab empire and it flourished under the **Umayyads** (q.v.) until finally replaced as the Arabs' capital by 'Abbāsid **Baghdād** (q.v.). Despite this, Damascus was always an important city through Islamic history and was recognized as such by succeeding dynasties like the **Ayyūbids** (q.v.) and the **Mamlūks** (q.v.). Like **Cairo** (q.v.) Damascus is filled with historic mosques and other Islamic monuments. Perhaps the most famous and magnificent of these is the Great Umayyad Mosque of Damascus, built by the Umayyad caliph Walīd I early in the 1st/8th century. (*See* **'Abbāsids**.)

Daqyā'īl Name of little-known angel responsible in one account for the guardians of Hell. (*See* **'Izrā'īl; al-Nār; al-Zabāniyya**.)

Dār al-Ḥarb (Ar.) Literally, 'The Abode (or House) of War'. The phrase is used, especially in Islamic law, to designate non-Islamic regions or countries. (*See* **Dār al-Islām**; **Sharī'a**.)

Dār al-Islām (Ar.) Literally, 'The Abode (or House) of Islam'. The term is used, particularly in Islamic jurisprudence, to denote the totality of those regions or countries which are subject to Islamic law. It may be contrasted with **Dār al-Ḥarb** (q.v.). We may also note here a third area, *between Dār al-Ḥarb* and *Dār al-Islām* called *Dār al-Amān* (='The Abode of Safety'). (*See* **Sharī'a**.)

Dār al-Māl al-Islāmī (Ar.) [DMI] Literally, 'The House of Islamic Wealth'. This is the name borne by the largest Islamic financial institution in the world. The DMI is based in Geneva and in 1989 comprised 24 Islamic banks and companies. It was established in 1981 with the specific purpose of co-ordinating implementing and emphasizing **Islamic Banking** (q.v.) undertaken in accordance with **Sharī'a** (q.v.) law.

Darwīsh (Ar.) [pl. *darāwīsh*] Word of obscure origin, possibly from Persian from which it is commonly derived, usually translated into English as 'dervish'. The members of the **Mawlawiyya** (q.v.) order were known colloquially as 'the Whirling Dervishes'. (*See* **Ṣūfī**.)

Dasūqiyya *See* **Burhāniyya**.

Dating *See* **Calendar**.

Dā'ūd *See* **Dāwūd**.

David *See* **Dāwūd**.

Da'wa (Ar.) [pl. *da'awāt*] Call, propaganda, invitation, invocation, missionary movement, missionary call. (*See* **Dā'ī**; **Ismā'īlīs**.)

Dawsa (Ar.) Literally, 'treading' or 'trampling underfoot'. The term was used in **taṣawwuf** (q.v.) to refer to a ceremony which used to be enacted in **Cairo** (q.v.) in which the **Shaykh** (q.v.) of the Sa'dī order would ride a horse over several hundred members of the order without apparent injury to these adherents. The *dawsa* ceremony has been vividly described in E. W. Lane's book *An Account of the Manners and Customs of the Modern Eygptians* (see back of this *Dictionary* for full bibliographical details).

Dāwūd or **Dā'ūd** (Ar.) David. He is one of the prophets mentioned in the **Qur'ān**, sometimes in conjunction with **Sulaymān** (q.v.). David is specifically called one of God's *khalīfas* (*see* v.26 in **Sūrat Ṣād** (q.v.)) and he is also the recipient of a book of revelation, *The Psalms*, known by the Arabic word *Zabūr* (*see* v.163 of **Sūrat al-Nisā'** (q.v.)). The Qur'ān shows that David has been endowed with special gifts of justice and wisdom. In an extended Qur'ānic passage (vv.21 ff of **Sūrat Ṣād** (q.v.)) both qualities are displayed in full measure where David both gives judgement between two disputants and then, feeling guilt for a perceived sin of his own, asks God's forgiveness, which he receives. (*See* **Khalīfa**; **Nabī**.)

Decree *See* **Qaḍā'**.

Dede (Turk.) Father, ancestor, grandfather. This is a title of respect borne by **ṣūfī** (q.v.) leaders like the head **Baba** (q.v.) of the **Bektāshiyya** (q.v.). The term was also used by the **Mawlawiyya** (q.v.). One of the best-known collections of tales in Turkish, dating from the Middle Ages, is called *The Book of Dede Korkut*. It has been translated and edited by Geoffrey Lewis (see back of this *Dictionary* for full bibliographical details).

Delhi Major city in India, known in Muslim sources as Dihlī. It was the centre of early Muslim rule in India from 608/1211 and retained its importance down the centuries, being adopted by the British as the capital of British India in the early part of the 14th/

20th century, and by the Indians themselves, after Independence in 1366/1947, as the capital of a fully independent India. Delhi contains some of the earliest examples of Muslim Indian architecture including the first mosque to be built in India: this was Quṭb al-Dīn Aybak's Masjid Quwwat al-Islām which has a 6th/12th century inscription. In the corner of the mosque is the famous **Quṭb Mīnār** (q.v.). Examples of Mughal architecture in Delhi include the tomb of **Humāyūn** (q.v.), and the Red Fort (1048/1638). (*See* **Mughals**).

Deobandis Members of fundamentalist Indian Muslim group of reformers originally centred on an academy of theology started in a town called Deoband, in 1282/1867. The object of the academy was the training of future **'ulamā'** (q.v.) who would be devoted to the reform of Islam. Deobandis have a particular reverence for the figure of the Prophet **Muḥammad**, and at Deoband the teaching placed special emphasis on the study of **ḥadīth** (q.v.). The Deobandis were **Ḥanafīs** (q.v.) and practised **ijtihād** (q.v.). Many of their early *'ulamā'* held a variety of **ṣūfī** (q.v.) beliefs and performed practices such as the **dhikr** (q.v.). For them the highest state of mysticism was the most successful emulation of the Prophet Muḥammad. However, intercession with God via the saints was frowned upon as was pilgrimage to their tombs. Presumably because of their attempts to purge Islam of what were regarded as *ṣūfī* abuses, the Deobandis were later characterized by some as 'anti-*ṣūfī*' and contrasted as such with the **Barēlwīs** (q.v.). Deobandis today are not confined to the Indian sub-continent: there are groups, for example, in Britain, as there are of Barēlwīs. (*See* **Shafā'a**; **Taṣawwuf**.)

Deo Volente *See* **In Shā'a Allāh.**

Dervish *See* **Darwīsh**.

Destiny *See* **Qadar**.

Determination *See* **Jabr**; **Qadar**.

Devil *See* **Iblīs.**

Devotion *See* **'Ibāda.**

Dhanb (Ar.) [pl. *dhunūb*] Sin, crime. Despite the latter meaning the word technically denotes a minor sin or fault, rather than a major crime or offence (*ithm*). Sin has been variously categorized by the jurists: some, for example, developed a scheme of venial and mortal sins. Perhaps the best known sins are those which attracted the **ḥadd** (q.v.) penalties. The remedy for all sin in Islam is sincere repentance (**tawba** (q.v.)) to God who will always forgive the repentant sinner. Islamic moral theology, like the Christian, stresses the place of intention (**niyya** (q.v.)) in all actions. God will judge a man by his intentions, and a death-bed repentance or final good deed will bring a sinner to Paradise. (*See* **al-Janna**).

al-Dhāriyāt (Ar.) The title of the 51st **sūra** of the **Qur'ān**; the Arabic title indicates 'The Scattering Winds'. The *sūra* belongs to the Meccan period and has 60 verses. It takes its title from the 1st verse which begins with the oath 'By the scattering winds . . .' which are but one of the bounties of God. The *sūra* goes on to warn of the punishment which will befall the evildoers and the joys of Paradise which await the pious and those who do good. Later reference is made to **Mūsā** (q.v.) and the punishment of Pharaoh, and also to the punishments which befell **'Ād** (q.v.), **Thamūd** (q.v.) and the people of **Nūḥ**(q.v.). At the end of the *sūra* God stresses that both **jinn** (q.v.) and men were created for His worship. (*See* **Fir'awn; al-Janna.**)

Dhawq (Ar.) [pl. *adhwāq*] Literally, 'taste'. The word is used in a technical sense in **taṣawwuf** (q.v.) to indicate experience of (divine) truth or a certain refined sensitivity illuminated by the light of the Divine.

Dhikr (Ar.) or **Zikr** (in Egyptian Colloquial Arabic) Literally, 'remembrance', 'recollection', 'mention'. In **taṣawwuf** (q.v.) the word has acquired a technical sense of 'litany' in which the name of God, or formulae like 'God is Most Great' (*Allāhu Akbar*), are repeated over and over again in either a high or a low voice, often linked to bodily movement or breathing. The *dhikr* is often one of the most important activities of the **ṣūfī** (q.v.) and its central place has analogies with that of the Divine Office in Western Monasticism. (*See* **Ḥaḍra**; **Samā'**; **Takbīr**.)

Dhimma *See* **Dhimmī**.

Dhimmī (Ar.) The Arabic word indicates one whose life was regulated according to 'an agreement of protection' (*dhimma*). Such persons, known collectively as 'People of (the agreement of) Protection' (*Ahl al-Dhimma*), were free non-Muslims who lived in Muslim countries and were guaranteed freedom of worship and security by the state from any form of harassment, provided certain taxes were paid. A certain number of restrictions were also imposed whose severity varied over the ages. For example, the Fāṭimid caliph **al-Ḥākim Bi-Amr Allāh** (q.v.) imposed a number of draconian measures on his Christian subjects including the wearing of black belts (*zunnār*), the wearing of crosses as badges while in the baths and a prohibition on the Christian use of wine, even for religious purposes. Technically, the concept of *dhimma* was held to apply only to **Ahl al-Kitāb** (q.v.). (*See* **Fāṭimids**; **Jizya**; **Kharāj**.)

Dhū 'l-Faqār (Ar.) Literally, 'Possessor of notches'. This was the name borne by a famous sword owned in turn by a pagan called al-'Āṣ b. Munabbih (who was killed at the Battle of Badr), then by the Prophet **Muḥammad**, and after him by **'Alī b. Abī Ṭālib** (q.v.) and the caliphs of the **'Abbāsids** (q.v.). The words *Dhū 'l-Faqār* have been transmuted into Zulfikar in Pakistan and used as a proper name. (*See* **Badr, Battle of**)

Dhū 'l-Ḥijja (Ar.) The Month of Pilgrimage, which is the last month of the Muslim lunar calendar. (*See* **Calendar**; **Ḥajj**.)

Dhū 'l-Kifl (Ar.) One of the prophets mentioned by name in the **Qur'ān**: see v.85 of **Sūrat al-Anbiyā'** (q.v.) and v.48 of **Sūrat Ṣād** (q.v.). He has been variously identified with Ḥizqīl (=Ezekiel) and a Bishr, son of Ayyūb, but other identifications have been made as well.

Dhū 'l-Nūn (Ar.) (*c.* 180/796–*c.* 246/861) His full name was Abū 'l-Fayḍ Thawbān b. Ibrāhīm Dhū 'l-Nūn al-Miṣrī. An important Egyptian **ṣūfī** (q.v.), he edited the Commentary on the **Qur'ān** written by **Ja'far al-Ṣādiq** (q.v.). Dhū 'l-Nūn was imprisoned and persecuted by the **Mu'tazila** (q.v.) for his belief that the Qur'ān was uncreated. Dhū 'l-Nūn, whose Arabic name means 'the holder (*or* possessor) of the fish', gained a considerable reputation as an alchemist. Although none of his mystical writings have survived, he is credited with being the first to provide a systematic exposition of **taṣawwuf** (q.v.) and its doctrines. It may also be noted here that the prophet Jonah, called in Arabic **Yūnus** (q.v.), is also sometimes called Dhū 'l-Nūn for obvious reasons.

Dhū 'l-Qarnayn (Ar.) Literally, 'He with the Two Horns'. This is the name of an important figure who appears in vv.83–98 in **Sūrat al-Kahf** of the **Qur'ān**, and has been identified as Alexander the Great (*al-Iskandar*) by Muslim commentators and others. The reasons for endowing Alexander with the title *Dhū 'l-Qarnayn* are unclear and a number of possibilities have been mooted. The Qur'ān portrays Dhū 'l-Qarnayn as a recipient of earthly power from God and one who promises punishment for wickedness and reward for goodness. He travels to the West and the East and builds a barrier to protect people against **Gog and Magog** (q.v.) called in Arabic Ya'jūj and Ma'jūj.

Dhū Nūwās Pre-Islamic South Arabian king who adopted Judaism, ruled, traditionally for thirty-eight years, and persecuted the Christians of Najrān, notably in AD 524–5. He is of interest to Islam because of the reference in the **Qur'ān** to 'the people of the pit' (*aṣḥāb al-ukhdūd*) in **Sūrat al-Burūj** (q.v.).

Dhū Qār, Battle of Famous battle between most of the united clans of the tribe of Bakr b. Wā'il and a group of other Arabs and Persians, named after a watering hole near **al-Kūfa** (q.v.). It is impossible to date the battle accurately and much legend has collected round the descriptions. It probably occurred very early in the 7th century AD. The victory went to the Bakr b. Wā'il.

Difference *See* **Ikhtilāf**.

Dikka or **Dakka** (Ar.) Raised platform in a mosque, often positioned near the **Minbar** (q.v.). On Friday at the congregational worship the **mu'adhdhin** (q.v.) uses the *dikka* to give the final call to prayer. It is also used by one or more prayer 'leaders' (*muballighūn*) other than the principal **Imām** (q.v.) (who is directly in front of the **miḥrāb** (q.v.)) when a large crowd is present in the mosque: these lead the vocal responses and the *dikka* also enables their ritual gestures and prostrations to be seen by the whole congregation so that all can pray together in unison. Like the *minbar* and the *miḥrāb*, the *dikka* is often beautifully decorated. (*See* **Adhān**; **Masjid**; **Ṣalāt**; **Yawm al-Qiyāma**.)

Dimashq *See* **Damascus**.

Dīn (Ar.) [pl. *adyān*] Faith, religion, the area of that which concerns the spiritual. In Islamic writings, the *dīn* (of Islam) is often contrasted with *al-dunyā* (the world). The Day of Judgement is often called 'The Day of Faith' (*Yawm al-Dīn*); in the **Fātiḥa** (q.v.) God is described as 'Lord of the Day of Judgement' (*Malik Yawm al-Dīn*). (*See* **'Aqīda**; **al-Ḥisāb**; **Īmān**; **Yawm al-Qiyāma**.)

Ḍirār b. 'Amr (fl. late 2nd/8th–early 3rd/9th century) Leading early theologian who lived mainly in **al-Baṣra** (q.v.) and wrote a book on Aristotelian metaphysics. He was an upholder of – and, indeed, may have originated – the idea of **kasb** (q.v.) and he played an important role with his followers in the early development of **kalām** (q.v.) in all its varied forms. (*See* **Aristotelianism, Islamic**; **al-Ash'arī**; **Mu'tazila**.)

Direction of Prayer *See* **Miḥrāb**; **Qibla**.

Dissimulation (of religion) *See* **Taqiyya**.

Ditch, Siege and Battle of the *See* **al-Khandaq, Siege and Battle of**

Divorce *See* **Ṭalāq**.

Diya (Ar.) [pl. *diyāt*] Blood money, indemnity or compensation for injury or death. The **Qur'ān**, in v.45 of **Sūrat al-Mā'ida** (q.v.), draws attention to the Judaic law which is stated to have enjoined a life for a life, an eye for an eye, a nose for a nose, an ear for an ear, a tooth for a tooth, and retaliation for inflicted wounds. (The verse also indicates that the wronged party could forego what was due.) Islam continued the Arabs' substitution of money, or goods which could, for example, be camels, in place of any rigid application of a *lex talionis*. Today, in those areas where Islamic law prevails, modern practice defines the *diya* as a variable quantity of *money*. (*See* **Qiṣāṣ**.)

Doctrine *See* **'Aqīda**; **Arkān**; **Dīn**; **Islām**.

Dogma *See* **Aqīda**; **Arkān**; **Dīn**; **Islām**.

Dome (Mosque) *See* **Qubba**.

Dome of the Rock *See* **Qubbat al-Ṣakhra**.

Doseh *See* **Dawsa**.

Dowry *See* **Mahr**.

Druze Adherent of a religion which developed originally from the 5th/11th century **Ismā'īlīs** (q.v.) in Egypt. 'Druze' is an anglicized form of the Arabic word *durzī* [pl. *durūz*] which in turn derives from the last element of the proper name Muḥammad b. Ismā'īl al-Darazī. The latter, who must be accounted one of the founders of the Druzes, taught that the 6th Fāṭimid caliph, **al-Ḥākim Bi-Amr Allāh** (q.v.), was divine. Al-Ḥākim disappeared in mysterious circumstances in 411/1021, and the Druzes teach that he is not dead. Druze doctrine is highly complex and secretive but it is clear that the religion has been influenced both by Neoplatonism and Gnosticism. It is also élitist in its organization, dividing its members into initiates (*'uqqāl*, literally, 'intelligent') and ordinary members (*juhhāl*, literally, 'ignorant'). The Druzes, who are permitted to practise **taqiyya** (q.v.), have no links now with the Ismā'īlīs and are to be found today mainly in the Lebanon, Israel and Syria. (*See* **Fāṭimids**; **Neoplatonism, Islamic**)

al-Ḍuḥā (Ar.) The title of the 93rd **sūra** of the **Qur'ān**; it means 'The Forenoon'. The *sūra* belongs to the Meccan period and has 11 verses. Its title comes from the oath in the 1st verse 'By the forenoon'. The *sūra* begins by reassuring the Prophet **Muḥammad** (who is the 'you' in the 3rd verse) that he has not been abandoned by God (simply because there has been a hiatus in the Revelation). The *sūra* reminds Muḥammad of God's favour to him when the Prophet was orphaned and urges that other orphans should not be oppressed.

al-Dukhān (Ar.) The title of the 44th **sūra of the Qur'ān**; it means 'The Smoke'. The *sūra* belongs to the Meccan period and has 59 verses. Its title comes from v.10 which talks of a day when Heaven shall bring forth evident smoke, which will cover the people (v.11). The reference may either be eschatological or to later events in **Mecca** (q.v.). The *sūra* begins with two of the **Mysterious Letters of the Qur'ān** (q.v.) and continues with references to Pharaoh, the deliverance of the Children of Israel and the divine purpose behind creation. Mention is also made of the Tree of **al-Zaqqūm** (q.v.) and the pains of Hell, called here

al-Jaḥīm (q.v.), as well as the pleasures of Paradise. (*See* **Fir'awn; al-Janna.**)

Duldul (Ar.) The name of a grey mule belonging to the Prophet **Muḥammad**. It is unclear why Duldul was so-named: the Arabic word means 'porcupine'.

Durūz *See* **Druze.**

Eden *See* **'Adn; al-Janna.**

Eid *See* **'Īd.**

Elephant *See* **Sūrat al-Fīl.**

Elephant, The Year of the The year *c.* AD 570 in which **Abraha** (q.v.) made an unsuccessful attack on the city of **Mecca** (q.v.) and also the year in which the Prophet **Muḥammad** was born. The year is so-called because there were one or more elephants in Abraha's army. (*See* **Sūrat al-Fīl.**)

Elias *See* **Ilyās.**

Elijah *See* **Ilyās.**

Elisha *See* **Alyasa'.**

Emanation *See* **Fayḍ.**

Endowment, Religious *See* **Waqf.**

Enoch *See* **Idrīs.**

Envoy *See* **Rasūl.**

Eschatology *See* **al-Ḥisāb; Isrāfīl; al-Janna; Munkar and Nakīr; al-Nār; Ṣirāṭ al-Jaḥīm; Yawn al-Qiyāma.**

Eternity *See* **Khuld**.

Ethics *See* **Akhlāq**.

Ethiopia Called in Arabic writings al-Ḥabash or al-Ḥabasha. Although mainly a Christian country, Ethiopia is of particular interest in early Islamic history: some of **Muḥammad**'s followers migrated to Ethiopia in *c.* AD 615, and Muḥammad himself had contacts with the ruler, the Negus. Trade was responsible for such early Islamization as took place. Muslims in Ethiopia today may belong to any one of three major law schools, i.e. **Ḥanafīs** (q.v.), **Mālikīs** (q.v.) or **Shafi'īs** (q.v.). (*See* **Madhhab**.)

Eve *See* **Ḥawwā'**.

Exegesis (of the Qur'ān) *See* **Tafsīr**.

Exegetes (of the Qur'ān) *See* **Mufassir**.

Expected Imām *See* **Muḥammad al-Qā'im**.

Ezekiel *See* **Dhū 'l-Kifl**.

Ezra *See* **'Uzayr**.

Faḍā'il (Ar.) [sing. *faḍīla*] Excellences, merits, virtues. *Faḍā'il* literature is a genre in Arabic which vaunts the excellent qualities in things, people, places, and, indeed, sacred books: a branch of early *faḍā'il* literature, for example, concentrated on praising the numerous merits of the **Qur'ān**. Compare and contrast **'Ajā'ib**.

Faith *See* **'Aqīda; Dīn; Īmān**.

Faith Movement Indian reformist or renewal movement based on **ṣūfī** (q.v.) teachings and principles, founded by Mawlānā

Muḥammad Ilyās. The latter believed that Muslims should genuinely *feel* that they are Muslims and this involved a real study of the religion of Islam. The **dhikr** (q.v.) was used with a preference for individual prayer rather than communal recitation and the movement stressed the need for simplicity of life. One of the more unusual aspects of the movement's principles was that of donation of time for preaching. The Faith Movement started in 1345–6/1927 in Mewat, south of **Delhi** (q.v.), and has continued to expand. (*See* **Ilyās, Mawlānā Muḥammad**; **Taṣawwuf**.)

al-Fajr (Ar.) The title of the 89th **sūra** of the **Qur'ān**; it means 'The Dawn'. The *sūra* belongs to the Meccan period and has 30 verses. Its title comes from the oath in the 1st verse 'By the dawn'. The first verses remind man of the divine punishments inflicted on the tribe of **'Ād** (q.v.), **Iram of the Pillars** (q.v.), the tribe of **Thamūd** (q.v.) and Pharaoh. Man will remember God when he sees the terrors which precede the Last Judgement. (*See* **Fir'awn**; **al-Ḥisāb**; **Yawm al-Qiyāma**.)

al-Fajr, Ṣalāt (Ar.) The Dawn Prayer, the Morning Prayer. (*See* **Ṣalāt**.)

al-Falaq (Ar.) The title of the 113th **sūra** of the **Qur'ān**; it means 'The Dawn' or 'The Daybreak'. The *sūra* belongs to the Meccan period and has 5 verses. It is the penultimate *sūra* of the Qur'ān. Its title is drawn from the 1st verse where God is referred to as 'The Lord of the dawn' (*Rabb al-falaq*). The whole *sūra* is a plea for protection by God from a variety of evils including darkness, vicious women (or witches) and enviers.

Falsafa (Ar.) Philosophy. The word derives from the Greek *philosophía*. Perhaps the most notable legacy of Greek philosophy to Islamic was Aristotelian philosophical vocabulary and Greek logic. Islamic philosophy was much influenced by Aristotelianism, Neoplatonism and, to a lesser degree, Platonism, but it would certainly be untrue to say that Islamic philosophy is merely an amalgam or synthesis of other foreign philosophies. It may rightly claim to be a system of thought in its own right. Down the ages the Islamic philosophers were frequently suspected of heterodoxy and heresy. There are diverse philosophical entries in this *Dictionary* but see, in particular, **Aristotelianism, Islamic**; **al-Fārābī**; **Fayḍ**; **Ibn al-'Arabī**; **Ibn Rushd**; **Ibn Sīnā**; **Ikhwān al-Ṣafā'**; **al-Kindī**; **Neoplatonism, Islamic**; **Platonism, Islamic**; **al-Suhrawardī**.)

Fanā' (Ar.) Extinction, cessation, annihilation, passing away. As a technical term in **Taṣawwuf** (q.v.) the word *fanā'* is used to indicate a stage in the mystical experience before **baqā'** (q.v.) in which all the mystic's imperfections and earthly ties are annihilated or extinguished, and he is absorbed into the Deity losing consciousness of the self and those things which impede his spiritual perfection. To put it another way, *fanā'* means that the mystic 'dies to himself' so that he may be 'born in God' and 'God be born in him'. *Fanā'* does not, however, mean that the mystic's individuality is totally lost.

Faqīh (Ar.) [pl. *fuqahā'*] Jurist, jurisprudent, one who practises **fiqh** (q.v.), i.e. jurisprudence. In colloquial Egyptian usage the *fiqī* is a **Qur'ān** reciter or teacher.

al-Fārābī (*c*. 256-7/870–339/950) Abū Naṣr Muḥammad al-Fārābī was one of the greatest Islamic philosophers and a leading proponent of Islamic Neoplatonism. He became known as 'The Second Master' (i.e. after Aristotle). He made a major contribution to Islamic metaphysics with his development of the doctrine of essence and existence. His writings describe God through both negative and positive propositions and epithets, the negative being designed to stress God's utter transcendence. His most notable work was *The Book of the Opinions of the People of the Virtuous City*, the Arabic rendition of which is often abbreviated simply to *al-Madīna al-Fāḍila*. This work has rather less in common with Plato's *Republic* than has been claimed. Al-

Fārābī's great philosophical successor, **Ibn Sīnā** (q.v.), was much influenced by the thought of al-Fārābī, and this indebtedness was acknowledged by Ibn Sīnā in his autobiography. (*See* **Falsafa**; **Fayḍ**; **Neoplatonism, Islamic**; **Platonism, Islamic**.)

Farḍ (Ar.) [pl. *furūḍ*] Religious duty. Except among the **Ḥanafīs** (q.v.) *farḍ* and *wājib* (obligatory) are considered to be exactly the same. Islamic law makes a distinction between those duties incumbent upon individuals and those incumbent upon the entire community, which may be fulfilled by a representative number of persons from that community. An example of the first type of *farḍ* is the **ḥajj** (q.v.) and of the second, **jihād** (q.v.). (*See* **al-Aḥkām al-Khamsa**.)

Fasting *See* **Ramaḍān**; **Ṣawm**.

Fate *See* **Jabr**.

al-Fatḥ (Ar.) The title of the 48th **sūra** of the **Qur'ān**; it means 'The Victory'. The *sūra* belongs to the Medinan period and contains 29 verses. Its title comes from the 1st verse in which God tells **Muḥammad** that He has given him an evident victory (i.e. the Treaty of **al-Ḥudaybiyya** (q.v.) in 6/628 and/or the coming conquest of **Mecca** (q.v.) by Muḥammad in 8/630). The *sūra* was revealed around the time of al-Ḥudaybiyya and is dominated by the thought of this Treaty and the coming conquest of Mecca.

al-Fātiḥa (Ar.) The title of the 1st **sūra** of the **Qur'ān**; it means 'The Opening' in reference to its being the opening chapter of the sacred text. The *sūra* belongs to the Meccan period and has 7 verses. It constitutes both a hymn of praise to God (who is the Lord of all being as well as the Last Judgement and who is worshipped and prayed to for assistance) as well as a plea for guidance onto the right path (**al-Ṣirāṭ al-Mustaqīm** (q.v.)), a path for the virtuous rather than the wicked. The *Fātiḥa* is recited many times a day during the Muslim's daily prayers. (*See* **Ṣalāt**; **Yawm al-Dīn**.)

Fāṭima (*c*. AD 605–11/632–3) The daughter of the Prophet **Muḥammad** and **Khadīja bint Khuwaylid** (q.v.), sister of **Ruqayya** (q.v.), **Umm Kulthūm** (q.v.) and **Zaynab** (q.v.), wife of **'Alī b. Abī Ṭālib** (q.v.), and mother of **al-Ḥasan b. 'Alī** (q.v.) and **al-Ḥusayn b. 'Alī** (q.v.). Of all the daughters of the Prophet Muḥammad, she has indisputedly been the most respected and revered by Muslims down the ages. Her name has become enveloped with much legend but the following historical points are worthy of note: she was immensely fond of her father and looked after his wounds after the Battle of Uḥud; she married 'Alī after the **Hijra** (q.v.) and accompanied Muḥammad at the surrender of **Mecca** (q.v.). She was present at his death bed. Fāṭima ranks as one of the five 'People (or Companions) of the Cloak' (*Ahl al-Kisā'* or *Aṣḥāb al-Kisā'*), a name which derived from the famous occasion when Muḥammad took 'Alī, Fāṭima, al-Ḥasan and al-Ḥusayn under his cloak and described them as members of his family, an event of immense significance for **Shī'ism** (q.v.). (*See* **Uḥud, Battle of**)

Fāṭimids Major dynasty in mediaeval Islamic history which flourished in North Africa (from 297/909) and later in Egypt (from 358/969–567/1171). It derived its name from **Fāṭima** (q.v.), the daughter of **Muḥammad**, and its caliphs claimed descent from Fāṭima and **'Alī b. Abī Ṭālib** (q.v.). The Fāṭimids made their principal capital in **Cairo** (q.v.). The dynasty, whose theology was Ismā'īlī, was responsible for much fine art and architecture. In Egypt the Fāṭimids reached the peak of their power under **al-Mustanṣir** (q.v.) before declining towards a final overthrow by the **Ayyūbids** (q.v.). (*See* **al-Ḥākim Bi-Amr Allāh**; **Ibn Killis**; **Ismā'īlīs**; **Ṣalāḥ al-Dīn**.)

al-Fāṭir (Ar.) The title of the 35th **sūra** of the **Qur'ān**; it means 'The Creator' and the reference is, of course, to God Himself.

The *sūra* belongs to the Meccan period and has 45 verses. Its title is drawn from the 1st verse which opens by praising God, Creator of the Heavens and the earth and the One who has made the angels His envoys or emissaries. This reference here to the angels has also led some commentators to give the title 'The Angels' to this *sūra*. It calls on men to remember God's generosity of provision to them. Hell fire awaits the disbeliever but God's true believers will enter the gardens of Eden. The partners whom the unbelievers associate with God, and invoke, are incapable of creation. God sustains the Heavens and earth in existence. (*See* **'Adn**.)

Fatwā (Ar.) [pl. *fatāwā*] A technical term used in Islamic law to indicate a formal legal judgement or view. (*See* **Muftī**.)

Fayḍ (Ar.) In its technical philosophical sense, as used by the Islamic philosophers, *fayḍ* meant 'emanation'. The contrast often posed was between a world created *ex nihilo* at a moment in time by God, and a world which *emanated* eternally from that Deity. The latter position was frequently condemned as heretical by the **'ulamā'** (q.v.). (*See* **Falsafa; al-Fārābī; Ibn Sīnā; Neoplatonism, Islamic**)

Feast *See* **'Īd; Mawlid.**

Fez Anglicized form of Arabic *Fās*, an important town in Morocco. Founded by the Idrīsids towards the end of the 2nd/8th century, it was conquered by the **Almoravids** (q.v.) in the 5th/11th century, and afterwards by the **Almohads** (q.v.). It was the Almoravid period which was the great one for the development of Islamic art and architecture: this is to be seen most notably in the enlargement and decoration of the al-Qarawiyyīn Mosque which is a superb monument to the skills of Hispano-Moorish art in the Almoravid period. (*See* **Art and Architecture, Islamic**)

al-Fīl (Ar.) The title of the 105th **Sūra** of the **Qur'ān**. It means 'The Elephant'. The *sūra* belongs to the Meccan period and has 5 verses. The title is taken from the 1st verse which asks whether the actions of God with the men of the elephant have not been noticed. The reference here is to the attack on **Mecca** (q.v.) by **Abraha** (q.v.) which, as the rest of the *sūra* shows, was unsuccessful.

Fiqh (Ar.) In its technical sense the word means 'Islamic jurisprudence'. Originally the word meant 'understanding' or 'knowledge'. **Sunnī** (q.v.) jurisprudence is founded upon, or divided into, the four major Schools of law of the **Ḥanafīs** (q.v.), **Ḥanbalīs** (q.v.), **Mālikīs** (q.v.), and **Shāfi'īs** (q.v.). The **Khārijites** (q.v.) and the Shī'ites have their own separate systems of jurisprudence. (*See* **Faqīh**; **Farḍ**; **Madhhab**; **Sharī'a**; **Shī'ism**; **Subsidiary Principles of Law**; **Uṣūl al-Fiqh**.)

Fir'awn (Ar.) Pharaoh. He is a figure frequently encountered in the **Qur'ān**, especially in his dealings with **Mūsā** (q.v.) and **Hārūn** (q.v.). Notable encounters include that in which Mūsā performs various miracles before Pharaoh (*see* vv.106–117 of **Sūrat al-A'rāf** (q.v.)), and the conversion to Mūsā's God, and subsequent crucifixion, of Pharaoh's magicians (*see* ibid., vv.121–126). Among other episodes, the Qur'ān refers to the drowning of Pharaoh's people (*see* v.50 in **Sūrat al-Baqara** (q.v.)) and the commissioning by Pharaoh of Hāmān to build him a high castle or tower so that he can reach Mūsā's God (*see* v.38 of **Sūrat al-Qaṣaṣ**). (*See also* **Sūrat Ghāfir**.)

Firdaws (Pers.) *See* **al-Janna**.

Fitna (Ar.) [pl. *fitan*] Temptation, trial, enchantment, civil war, strife. It is a term often used in Islamic history with the specific historical sense of Civil War, particularly with reference to the era of conflict between **'Alī b. Abī Ṭālib** (q.v.) and **Mu'āwiya b. Abī Sufyān** (q.v.). The word *fitna* also appears frequently in the **Qur'ān**, for example in v.28 of **Sūrat al-Anfāl** (q.v.) where man's wealth and children are described as a temptation (*fitna*).

Five Pillars of Islam *See* **Arkān**.

Followers *See* **Tābi'ūn**.

Forgiveness *See* **Tawba**.

Fornication *See* **Zinā'**.

Foundation, Religious *See* **Waqf**.

Foundations of Islamic Jurisprudence *See* **Uṣūl al-Fiqh**. *See also* **Subsidiary Principles of Law**.

Free Will *See* **Ghaylān b. Muslim; Qadar; Qadariyya**.

Friday *See* **Yawm al-Jum'a**.

Fundamentalism, Islamic These words have been variously interpreted and endlessly debated. However, in essence, they seem to indicate a desire to return to an 'ideal' Islam, perhaps that of the age of the **Rāshidūn** (q.v.). Many Islamic fundamentalists believe that the Islam of the modern era, and the so-called 'Islamic' states, as they perceive them, have been corrupted. They desire a return to 'true' Islam, shorn of any modern compromises with secularism. This has sometimes engendered a profound hostility towards the West which is often perceived as secular and even atheistic. The spirit of Islamic fundamentalism has imbued many Islamic groups ranging from the **Wahhābīs** (q.v.) to **Ḥizb Allāh** (q.v.) and the Shī'ite **Amal** (q.v.). (*See* **Salafiyya; Shī'ism**.)

al-Furqān (Ar.) The title of the 25th **sūra** of the **Qur'ān**; *al-Furqān* is a name applied to the Qur'ān and means literally 'The Distinguisher between Good and Evil' or 'The Proof'. The *sūra* belongs to the Meccan period and has 77 verses. The title of the *sūra* is drawn from v.30. A major theme of this chapter is the foolishness of the polytheists and unbelievers. The *sūra* also stresses the humanity of God's messengers (v.20), and the coming punishment for idolaters, polytheists and disbelievers. By contrast, Paradise will be the reward of the Godfearing. (*See* **al-Janna**.)

Fuṣṣilat (Ar.) The title of the 41st **sūra** of the **Qur'ān**; it means 'They have been Made Clear' and the title is drawn from v.3 in which reference is made to the Qur'ān whose verses have been made clear. (The *sūra* is sometimes also called *Hā' Mīm* [*al-Sajda*] after the two **Mysterious Letters of the Qur'ān** (q.v.) which constitute the first verse of this *sūra*. It should not be confused with *Sūra* 32 which also bears the title **al-Sajda** (q.v.)). *Sūrat Fuṣṣilat* belongs to the Meccan period and has 54 verses. It stresses the themes of the oneness of God and reminds man what happened to **'Ād** (q.v.) and **Thamūd** (q.v.). God's enemies will perish in Hell. (*See* **al-Nār**.)

al-Fusṭāṭ First Muslim city in Egypt, established by **'Amr b. al-'Āṣ** (q.v.) who also built here the first mosque in Egypt. Al-Fusṭāṭ preserved its prosperity even into the period of the **Fāṭimids** (q.v.) and their foundation of **Cairo** (q.v.). Al-Fusṭāṭ was rebuilt after a major fire in the 6th/12th century but began to decline under the **Mamlūks** (q.v.).

Gabriel *See* **Jibrīl**.

Gambling The **Qur'ān** forbids gambling and games in which chance is involved. *See* v.219 of **Sūrat al-Baqara** (q.v.) and v.90 of **Sūrat al-Mā'ida** (q.v.).

Genghis Khan *See* **Bābur**; **Mongols**.

Genie *See* **Jinn**.

Ghadīr al-Khumm (Ar.) The name of an oasis between **Mecca** (q.v.) and **Medina** (q.v.). The phrase means 'The Pool (or

Creek) of al-Khumm'. Here the Prophet **Muḥammad**, after the famous Pilgrimage of Farewell, raised the hands of **'Alī b. Abī Ṭālib** (q.v.) and declared that whoever held himself, Muḥammad, as his master, should view 'Alī in a similar fashion. Shī'ites believe that by these words and actions Muḥammad designated 'Alī as his direct successor. (*See* **Ḥajj al-Wadā'**; **Shī'ism**.)

Ghāfir (Ar.) The title of the 40th **sūra** of the **Qur'ān**; it means 'Forgiver', i.e. God. The *sūra* belongs to the Meccan period and has 85 verses. Its title is drawn from v.3 which refers to God as Forgiver of sin and Accepter of repentance. The *sūra* is one of seven which begin with the **Mysterious Letters of the Qur'ān** (q.v.) *hā' mīm*. The *sūra* stresses God's unity and power and provides considerable detail about the life of the prophet **Mūsā** (q.v.) and his dealings with Pharaoh. A significant verse (v.67) traces man's life from dust to old age. (*See* **Fir'awn**; **al-Ḥisāb**.)

al-Ghāshiyya (Ar.) The title of the 88th **sūra** of the **Qur'ān**; the word has been translated as 'The Enveloper', 'The Enveloping' and 'The Calamity' and clearly indicates the Day of Resurrection. The *sūra* belongs to the Meccan period and has 26 verses. Its title comes from v.1. The *sūra* notes that on that Day of Resurrection those destined for Hell fire will have tired and work-weary faces, by contrast with the happy faces of the inhabitants of Paradise. (*See* **Ba'th**; **al-Janna**; **al-Nār**; **Yawm al-Qiyāma**.)

Ghayba (Ar.) Occultation, absence, concealment, invisibility. The best-known occultation or absence is that of the Twelfth Shī'ite Imām **Muḥammad al-Qā'im** (q.v.). Twelver Shī'ites identify a lesser and a greater period of *ghayba* for this figure: the first lasted for about 67 years from 260/874; the second has lasted from 329/941 and will only end with the reappearance of this Imām. (*See* **Imām**; **Ithnā 'Asharīs**.)

Ghaylān b. Muslim (died first half of the 2nd/8th century) Leading early proponent of free will who lived in **Damascus**

(q.v.) and was a contemporary of the Christian John of Damascus. Ghaylān was executed by the Umayyad caliph **Hishām** (q.v.) because of his views on free will. (*See* **Qadariyya**; **Umayyads**.)

al-Ghazālī, Abū Ḥāmid Muḥammad (450/1058–505/1111) One of Islam's greatest theologians, a major **ṣūfī** (q.v.) and an outstanding scholar of Islamic philosophy, though by no means an original philosopher. He was also very well versed in the doctrines of the **Ismā'īlīs** (q.v.) which he refuted. Al-Ghazālī taught at the Niẓāmiyya College in **Baghdād** (q.v.) until a psychosomatic illness impeded his academic career in 488/1095. He made the pilgrimage to **Mecca** (q.v.) and later retired to his birthplace Ṭūs (in Khurāsān) to live as a ṣūfī. It was at this time that he wrote his great *Revival of the Religious Sciences* (*Iḥyā' 'Ulūm al-Dīn*). He briefly returned to academe before going back once more to Ṭūs. Al-Ghazālī's career thus neatly combines the spiritual and ascetic, and the academic. He came to hold the belief that he would be the Renewer of Islam for the new Islamic century. Towards the end of his life he wrote a notable autobiography which is a mixture of Augustinian *Confessions* and Newmanesque *Apologia pro Vita Sua*. It constitutes one of the most moving and honest, if possibly somewhat artifically structured, Islamic spiritual testaments. Its significant title was *The Deliverer from Error* (*al-Munqidh min al-Ḍalāl*). Abū Ḥāmid al-Ghazālī should be distinguished from his ṣūfī brother Aḥmad. A very readable account of the life and work of Abū Ḥāmid al-Ghazālī will be found in Watt's *Muslim Intellectual* (see back of this *Dictionary* for full bibliographical details). (*See* **Falsafa**; **Taṣawwuf**.)

Ghaznavids Major mediaeval Islamic dynasty which flourished between 366/977–582/1186, ruling an area which stretched from Khurāsān in the West, through Afghanistan to the North of India in the East. The Ghaznavid empire reached a peak during the reign of Maḥmūd (*reg*. 388/998–421/1030) but thereafter gradually disintegrated. The Afghānī **Ghūrids** (q.v.) finally overthrew the Ghaznavids in 582/1186. The Ghaznavids played an important part in the development of Islamic art and architecture: the minarets in the ruins at Ghazna are of particular interest, especially in their use of brick. (*See* **Art and Architecture, Islamic**)

Ghūrids Minor Islamic dynasty in mediaeval Islam which flourished between *c.* 390/1000–612/1215 and overthrew the last of the **Ghaznavids** (q.v.). They ruled in Afghanistan and areas formerly held by the Ghaznavid dynasty. The Ghūrids in turn were overthrown by the Khwārazm-Shāhs.

Ghusl (Ar.) Major ritual washing of the whole body to achieve a state of purity, before visiting a mosque and after such occasions as childbirth, menstruation, sexual intercourse, contact with a dead body, or before events such as formal admission to the Islamic faith. (*See* **Ḥammām**; **Mīḍa'a**; **Wuḍū'**.)

God *See* **Allāh**.

Gog and Magog In Arabic these two figures are called Ya'jūj and Ma'jūj. They appear in the **Qur'ān** in **Sūrat al-Kahf** (q.v.) as epitomes or representatives, either of the forces of chaos or, alternatively, of tribes of warring barbarians.

Gondēshāpūr or **Jundaysābūr** Major centre of Greek learning, philosophy and medicine, situated in Khūzistān, established by the Sāsānian ruler Shāpūr I (*reg.* AD 241–271), but in ruins by the 6th/12th century. Gondēshāpūr was a major vehicle in early Islamic times for the transmission into Islamic thought and philosophy of Greek elements and also a provider for the **'Abbāsids** (q.v.) of well-trained physicians. (*See* **Bīmāristān**; **Ḥarrān**.)

Granada Important city in mediaeval Islamic Spain, known in Arabic as Gharnāṭa. It was also the name given to the Province within which the city stood. After being ruled by the **Almoravids** (q.v.) and the **Almohads** (q.v.), Granada later became the seat of the Naṣrids in 535/1238. Granada remained a final major bastion of Islam in Spain until it was captured by the Christians in 897/1492. Its crowning architectural glory is, of course, the **Alhambra** (q.v.). (*See* **al-Andalus**.)

Group Solidarity *See* **'Aṣabiyya**.

Guardian Angels *See* **Kirām al-Kātibīn**.

al-Ḥabash *See* **Ethiopia**.

Hābīl *See* **Qābīl and Hābīl**.

Habous *See* **Waqf**.

Ḥaḍāna (Ar.) A technical term in **fiqh** (q.v.) meaning the right to 'custodyship' of children. An intricate, large and varying body of law has developed among the four law schools on this subject. It is of particular significance in the event of the separation or divorce of the parents. (*See* **Madhhab**; **Ṭalāq**.)

Ḥadd (Ar.) [pl. *ḥudūd*] Literally, 'edge', 'boundary', 'limit'. As a technical term in Islamic law it indicates God's 'limits' and denotes the punishments for certain crimes which are mentioned in the **Qur'ān**. There are five of these and they are listed here with the formal punishment in brackets: (1) Fornication or adultery (**zinā'** (q.v.)), (stoning or 100 lashes); (2) False accusation of unchastity (*qadhf*), (80 lashes); (3) Wine drinking, (80 lashes); (4) Theft, (amputation of hand(s) and/or feet); and (5) Highway robbery, (execution if homicide occurs). Some commentators and jurists have added, not quite accurately, apostasy to this list. (*See* **Ilḥād**; **Irtidād**; **Khamr**; **Nabīth**; **Sariqa**.)

al-Ḥadīd (Ar.) The title of the 57th **sūra** of the **Qur'ān**; it means 'The Iron'. The *sūra* belongs to the very late Medinan period and has 29 verses. It is so-called after the reference to the iron which God has sent down for the use of man, in v.25. The *sūra* begins by praising God the omniscient Creator and stresses later that the life of this world is as transient as the green plants which follow a fall of rain.

Ḥadīth (Ar.) [pl *aḥādīth*] This Arabic word has a large number of meanings including 'speech', 'report' and 'narrative'. It also has the very important specialist sense of *tradition*, i.e. a record of the sayings and doings of the Prophet **Muḥammad** and his companions, and as such is regarded by Muslims as a source of Islamic law, dogma and ritual second only in importance to the **Qur'ān** itself. The subject matter and range of the *ḥadīth* literature are vast and can only be outlined here. A *ḥadīth* is traditionally supported by an **isnād** (q.v.) or chain of authorities. It contains a main text (*matn*) and may conclude with a moral. *Ḥadīths* and their *isnāds* have been subjected to a wide range of types of categorization. A basic one is to classify the *ḥadīth* under one of several major categories of trustworthiness: **ṣaḥīḥ** (q.v.), **ḥasan** (q.v.), **ḍa'īf** (q.v.) and **saqīm** (q.v.). The two most famous and revered compilations of *ḥadīth* are those by **al-Bukhārī** (q.v.) and **Muslim b. al-Ḥajjāj** (q.v.). Four other compilations are particularly respected, forming a classic six *in toto*: their authors are **Abū Dā'ūd** (q.v.), **Ibn Māja** (q.v.), **al-Nasā'ī** (q.v.) and **al-Tirmidhī** (q.v.). (*See also* **Abū Hurayra**; **Mawḍū'**; **Mutawātir**; **al-Nawawī**; **Ṣaḥāba**; **Sunna**; **Tadlīs**.)

Ḥadīth Qudsī (Ar.) A sacred, or holy, tradition. This is the name given to a tradition which records God's own utterances as opposed to those of the Prophet **Muḥammad**. The latter type of tradition is called in Arabic by the term *ḥadīth nabawī*, meaning 'Prophetic tradition'.

Ḥaḍra (Ar.) Literally, 'presence'. The word has acquired a technical meaning in **taṣawwuf** (q.v.) and come to indicate the **dhikr** (q.v.) recited communally, often on a Friday. This word *ḥaḍra* has replaced the older term **samā'** (q.v.).

Ḥafṣa bint 'Umar b. al-Khaṭṭāb (died 45/665 but other dates are given) A wife of the Prophet **Muḥammad** and daughter of the 2nd caliph, **'Umar b. al-Khaṭṭāb** (q.v.). She is particularly important in the traditional history of the collection of the **Qur'ān** in the caliphate of **'Uthmān b. 'Affān** (q.v.) since she was the guardian of some of the earliest sheets of Qur'ānic text. These sheets were utilized by 'Uthmān's committee and then returned to Ḥafṣa. (*See* **Zayd b. Thābit**.)

Ḥafṣids The Banū Ḥafṣ, to give them their Arabic name, were a mediaeval Islamic dynasty which flourished between 625/1228 and 982/1574 in **Tūnis** (q.v.). The dynasty gained its name from a companion of the Almohad Ibn Tūmart, called Abū Ḥafṣ 'Umar b. Yaḥyā al-Hintātī. Early Ḥafṣid rule brought a period of peace and tranquillity to Ḥafṣid Ifrīqiya. The ruler al-Mustanṣir (*reg.* 647/1249–675/1277) concluded a treaty with the Crusaders who had been led by St. Louis; the latter died in Carthage in 669/1270. On al-Mustanṣir's death the period of tranquillity came to an end. The early Ḥafṣids were Almohad in orientation but the Mālikī **madhhab** (q.v.) was allowed to flourish. (*See* **Almohads**; **Crusades**; **Mālikīs**.)

al-Ḥajar al-Aswad (Ar.) 'The Black Stone', set in the **Ka'ba** (q.v.); those pilgrims near enough to it will attempt to kiss the Black Stone during their circumambulation (**ṭawāf** (q.v.)) of the *Ka'ba* during the Islamic pilgrimage. Tradition associates the stone with **Ādam** (q.v.) and **Ibrāhīm** (q.v.). (*See* **Ḥajj**; **Qarāmiṭa**.)

Ḥajj (Ar.) [pl. *ḥajjāt*] Pilgrimage. This is one of the five **arkān** (q.v.) or Pillars of Islam. All Muslims, provided a number of conditions including good health and financial ability are present, have a duty to make a pilgrimage to **Mecca** (q.v.) at least once in their lifetimes. This major pilgrimage must be made in the Month of Pilgrimage (**Dhū 'l-Ḥijja** (q.v.)), the last month of the

Muslim lunar calendar, between the 8th day of the month and the 12th or 13th. (A minor pilgrimage to Mecca, which does not count towards fulfilment of the religious duty and is called in Arabic an *'umra*, may be made at any time and requires less ceremonial.) Before arrival in Mecca the pilgrim dons white garments and is then in a state of **iḥrām** (q.v.) or ritual consecration during which he or she will abstain from sexual intercourse, perfume, the wearing of sewn garments and the cutting of hair and nails. A number of ritual ceremonies are undertaken in Mecca including a sevenfold circumabulation (**ṭawāf** (q.v.)) of the **Ka'ba** (q.v.) and a sevenfold 'running' between **al-Ṣafā** (q.v.) and **al-Marwa** (q.v.). On the 9th day of the month of Dhū 'l-Ḥijja occurs the standing (**wuqūf** (q.v.)) in the Plain of **'Arafa** (q.v.) outside Mecca. This is an essential part of the pilgrimage and if it is omitted, the pilgrimage is considered invalid. Prayers are said at 'Arafa and pilgrims listen to a sermon. On the 10th of Dhū 'l-Ḥijja pilgrims sacrifice an animal at **Minā** (q.v.), imitating the projected sacrifice by **Ibrāhīm** (q.v.) of **Ismā'īl** (q.v.), and this day constitutes one of the great feast days of the Muslim calendar, **'Īd al-Aḍḥā** (q.v.). Not all the ceremonies of the pilgrimage have been described here in this necessarily brief entry but the above will indicate the profoundly moving nature of the whole experience of the *Ḥajj*. After the pilgrimage proper, pilgrims frequently include a visit to the tomb of the Prophet **Muḥammad** at **Medina** (q.v.). The **Qur'ān** provides a considerable amount of detail about the pilgrimage, especially in vv.196–200 of **Sūrat al-Baqara** (q.v.) and vv.26–30 of **Sūrat al-Ḥajj** (q.v.). Those who undertake the pilgrimage are entitled to bear the honorific title *ḥājj*, expressed more colloquially as *ḥājjī* or *ḥāggī*. Most introductory books on Islam provide an account of the pilgrimage and its ceremonies. For a full account, which also covers the social aspects, see the article by Wensinck, Jomier and Lewis in vol. 3 of the new 2nd edn. of *The Encyclopaedia of Islam* (s.v. *Ḥadjdj*) (see the back of this *Dictionary* for full bibliographical details). (*See also* **al-Jamra**; **Maḥmil**; **Mīqāt**; **Muṭawwif**; **Muzdalifa**; **Sa'y**.)

al-Ḥajj (Ar.) The title of the 22nd **sūra** of the **Qur'ān**; it means 'The Pilgrimage'. The *sūra* belongs to the Medinan period and has 78 verses. The *sūra* is so-called because vv.26–30 provide instruction about the pilgrimage. The *sūra* begins with warnings about the Day of Judgement, describes the progress of man from a speck of dust to old age, and promises Hell for the disbelievers but the joys of Paradise for the believers. **Muḥammad** had come as a clear warner (*nadhīr mubīn*). (*See* **Ḥajj**; **al-Janna**; **al-Nār**.)

Ḥajj al-Wadā' (Ar.) 'The Pilgrimage of Farwell', undertaken and led by the Prophet **Muḥammad** himself to **Mecca** (q.v.) in 10/632, which became a model for future pilgrimages. (*See* **Ghadīr al-Khumm**.)

al-Ḥākim Bi-Amr Allāh (375/985–411/1021) The 6th caliph of the dynasty of the **Fāṭimids** (q.v.) in Egypt, who succeeded his father at the age of eleven in 386/996. Al-Ḥākim's was a strange and, some believe, fanatical reign. He gained a reputation for madness which a few scholars have claimed was undeserved. Among his many edicts were laws enacted against the Jews and Christians and a ban on the popular Egyptian food *mulūkhiyya*. On one infamous occasion he also ordered his troops to burn **al-Fusṭāṭ** (q.v.). Towards the end of his life he came, or was led, to believe that he was divine. He disappeared in the Cairene Muqaṭṭam Hills in 411/1021 where he was probably murdered. The Mosque of al-Ḥākim in **Cairo** (q.v.) has been much restored. (*See* **Dhimmī**; **Druze**.)

Ḥalab *See* **Aleppo**.

Ḥalāl (Ar.) That which is permitted or lawful. (*See* **al-Aḥkām al-Khamsa**; **Ḥarām**.)

Ḥalīma bint Abī Dhu'ayb Foster mother and wet nurse of the Prophet **Muḥammad**, for his first two years of life. She belonged to the Banū Sa'd b. Bakr, a branch of the Ḥawāzin tribe.

al-Ḥallāj, al-Ḥusayn b. Manṣūr (244/857-8–309/922) Famous, indeed notorious, mystic whose utterances, actual and alleged, provoked much controversy both in his own lifetime and later. The best known of these was the phrase 'I am the [Divine] Truth' (*Anā 'l-Ḥaqq*). There were probably political as well as religious motivations behind his cruel execution in **Baghdād** (q.v.). (*See* **al-Bisṭāmī**; **Taṣawwuf**.)

Ḥalqa (Ar.) [pl. *ḥalaqāt*] Circle, link, ring. The term has a number of technical meanings in **taṣawwuf** (q.v.): it can mean, for example, a group of students studying with a ṣūfī shaykh, or the circle of ṣūfīs formed to perform a **dhikr** (q.v.). (*See* **Shaykh**; **Ṣūfī**.)

al-Hamadhānī, 'Ayn al-Quḍāt (492/1098–525/1131) Famous **ṣūfī** (q.v.) who was born in Hamadhān. He immersed himself in the religious sciences from an early age and also became a *ṣūfī* in his youth. His teachings and ecstatic utterances (*shaṭḥiyāt*) aroused the wrath of the orthodox and, like **al-Ḥallāj** (q.v.) before him, he was brutally executed in 525/1131 for heresy. Perhaps his best known written work is his *Shakwā al-Gharīb* which may be translated as *The Complaint of the Stranger*. (*See* **Taṣawwuf**.)

Ḥamdānids Mediaeval Islamic dynasty which ruled in **Aleppo** (q.v.) and elsewhere, in the 4th/10th century and achieved a peak of fame with the Aleppan ruler Sayf al-Dawla (*reg*. 333/944–356/967). The Ḥamdānids proper ruled Aleppo from 333/944 until 392/1002. Sayf al-Dawla's court became famous for the poets, scholars and writers who congregated at it. These included the great philosopher **al-Fārābī** (q.v.) and the equally distinguished Arab poet al-Mutanabbī (303/915–354/965).

al-Ḥamdu li 'llāh (Ar.) A very commonly used Muslim invocation meaning 'Praise be to God' or 'Thank God'.

al-Ḥāmidī, Ibrāhīm b. al-Ḥusayn (died 557/1162) High ranking Yemeni Ismā'īlī propagandist whose principal work was

The Book of the Youth's Treasure (*Kitāb Kanz al-Walad*). Al-Ḥāmidī uses the traditional Ismā'īlī negative terminology of God and his thought is much influenced by Neoplatonism. (*See* **Dā'ī; Ismā'īlīs; Neoplatonism, Islamic**)

Ḥammām (Ar.) [pl. *ḥammāmāt*] Bath, steam bath, swimming pool. Such buildings have existed in Islam in the sense of bath house since the time of the **Umayyads** (q.v.) and even before. From the point of view of **ghusl** (q.v.), the major ablution, the *ḥammām* had a religious as well as a recreational function. Notable examples of *ḥammāmāt* existed in **Damascus** (q.v.) and **Istanbul** (q.v.). (*See* **Art and Architecture, Islamic**)

Ḥamza b. 'Abd al-Muṭṭalib (died 3/625) Famous uncle of the Prophet **Muḥammad** on his father's side. At first Ḥamza opposed the new Islamic faith but later became one of its most valiant adherents. He fought bravely at the Battle of Badr in 2/624 but later died fighting at the Battle of Uḥud in 3/625. Much legend later accumulated round his name and valiant deeds. (*See* **Badr, Battle of; Hind; Uḥud, Battle of**)

Ḥanafīs Adherents of one of the four main law schools (*madhāhib*) of **Sunnī** (q.v.) Islam, named after the great jurist **Abū Ḥanīfa** (q.v.). The Ḥanafī law school developed from the ancient legal systems of **al-Kūfa** (q.v.) and **al Baṣra** (q.v.) in Iraq. The development of a formal School of law was more the work of Abū Ḥanīfa's disciples, Abū Yūsuf and al-Shaybānī, than Abū Ḥanīfa himself. The Ḥanafī **madhhab** (q.v.) gained its greatest sphere of influence in the Middle East and the Indian sub-continent. (*See* **Fiqh**; **Ḥanbalīs**; **Ḥiyal**; **Istiḥsān**; **Mālikīs**; **Shāfi'īs**; **Sharī'a**.)

Ḥanbalīs Adherents of one of the four main law schools (*madhāhib*) of **Sunnī** (q.v.) Islam, named after the distinguished jurist and theologian **Aḥmad b. Ḥanbal** (q.v.). The School of law has gained a reputation for being the most rigorous of the four law schools and it was one of the foundations upon which the **Wahhābīs** (q.v.) built their movement. Ḥanbalism is the official **madhhab** (q.v.) of Saudi Arabia. (*See* **Fiqh**; **Ḥanafīs**; **Ibn Taymiyya**; **Mālikīs**; **Shāfi'īs**; **Sharī'a**.)

Ḥanīf (Ar.) [pl. *ḥunafā'*] Monotheist. The word occurs several times in its singular and plural forms in the **Qur'ān**. Here it basically indicates those who were neither Christians nor Jews but *were* monotheists. **Ibrāhīm** (q.v.) constitutes the basic paradigm of such usage (*see* v.67 of **Sūrat Āl 'Imrān** (q.v.)). The Qur'ānic usage of the word must be distinguished from that of pre-Islamic poetry where *ḥanīf* could mean a pagan or idol worshipper.

al-Ḥaqq (Ar.) The truth/Divine Truth. This is a word of immense significance in the intellectual and linguistic development of Islam. *Ḥaqq* can be both a noun and an adjective, meaning 'truth' and 'rightness' and also 'true', 'right' and 'correct'. However, it also has a more technical sense as an attribute and name of God. As such it is not to be borne by any human being. The great mystic **al-Ḥallāj** (q.v.) proclaimed 'I am the [Divine] Truth' (*Anā 'l-Ḥaqq*) with fatal results. In the **Qur'ān** (q.v.) the word *ḥaqq* is used in a variety of contexts.

al-Ḥāqqa (Ar.) The title of the 69th **sūra** of the **Qur'ān**; it may variously be translated as 'That Which is Inevitable', 'The Calamity' or 'The Resurrection', but whichever one chooses the reference is clearly to the Last Day. The *sūra* belongs to the Meccan period and contains 52 verses. Its title is drawn from the first three verses. The punishments which overtook **'Ād** (q.v.) and **Thamūd** (q.v.) are also mentioned at the beginning. The *sūra* continues with a description of the Day of Judgement and its judgement with books: the man who is given the book itemizing his deeds on earth in his right hand will taste the joys of Paradise, but he who receives his book in the left hand will be consigned to Hell which the Qur'ān here calls **al-Jaḥīm** (q.v.). (*See* **Ba'th**; **al-Ḥisāb**; **al-Janna**; **Yawm al-Qiyāma**.)

Ḥaram (Ar.) [pl. *aḥrām*] Sanctuary. The Arabic word indicates an area of a particularly sacred nature. Examples include **Mecca** (q.v.) and **Medina** (q.v.), both of which are forbidden to non-Muslims. (*See* **al-Ḥaram al-Sharīf**; **al-Ḥaramān**; **al-Masjid al-Ḥarām**.)

Ḥarām (Ar.) That which is forbidden and unlawful, also sinful. (*See* **al-Aḥkām al-Khamsa**; **Ḥalāl**.)

al-Ḥaram al-Sharīf (Ar.) The Noble Sanctuary. This is the third holiest sanctuary in Islam after **Mecca** (q.v.) and **Medina** (q.v.). Situated in the Temple area of **Jerusalem** (q.v.), the **Ḥaram** contains, *inter alia*, **al-Aqṣā** (q.v.) Mosque, and the **Qubbat al-Ṣakhra** (q.v.). (*See* **al-Ḥaramān**.)

al-Ḥaramān or **al-Ḥaramayn** (Ar.) The Two Sacred Sanctuaries, i.e. **Mecca** (q.v.) and **Medina** (q.v.); **Jerusalem** (q.v.) bears the title in Islam of 'the Third Sacred Sanctuary' (*Thālith al-Ḥaramayn*). (*See* **Ḥaram**; **al-Haram al-Sharīf**.)

Ḥarrān The Roman Carrhae. This was a city in Northern Syria which played a considerable role in the development of mediaeval philosophy in the Middle East. It was the home of the **Sabaeans** (q.v.) whose theology was much influenced by Neoplatonism; among a variety of distinguished scholars produced by the Sabaeans was the great 3rd/9th century Thābit b. Qurra. Ḥarrān also became home for the Alexandrian philosophers from the middle of the 3rd/9th century. (*See* **Alexandria**; **Falsafa**; **Neoplatonism, Islamic**)

Hārūn al-Rashīd (149/766–193/809) The 5th, and perhaps most famous caliph of the **'Abbāsids** (q.v.) around whom much legend has accumulated as a result of such works as *The Thousand and One Nights*. The reality was more prosaic. Hārūn spent most of his rule from 170/786–193/809 fighting, away from **Baghdād** (q.v.) the capital of the Arab empire. Before his death

Hārūn announced plans for the division of his empire between his sons, one of whom was the famous **al-Ma'mūn** (q.v.), and thus he laid the foundations of the civil war which followed.

Hārūn b. ʻImrān The Aaron of the **Qur'ān**. Here Hārūn is portrayed as an associate and brother of **Mūsā** (q.v.) who stands beside him before Pharaoh. At one point Mūsā scolds Hārūn because of the calf worship which has taken place in Mūsā's absence. The death of Hārūn attracted the attention of later Muslim commentators who wove much legend around the event. (*See* **Firʻawn; Sūrat al-Aʻrāf; Sūrat Ṭāhā.**)

Hārūt and Mārūt Two angels mentioned in v.102 of **Sūrat al-Baqara** (q.v.) who either taught men sorcery or how to avoid sorcery. Commentators further explain that they came to earth, having accepted God's challenge to behave better than sinful man. However, they committed murder and fornication and, choosing to make reparation on earth, they were imprisoned and tormented in a Babylonian well.

Ḥasan (Ar.) Fair or Good. The word is used as a technical term in **ḥadīth** (q.v.) criticism to indicate the relative strength and reliability of a tradition. A *ḥasan* tradition was not regarded as quite as strong as one which was **ṣaḥīḥ** (q.v.), but it was better than those which were **ḍaʻīf** (q.v.) or **saqīm** (q.v.). Various types of *ḥasan* tradition exist.

Ḥasan al-ʻAskarī (230/844–260/874) Eleventh Shīʻite Imām. Born in **Medina** (q.v.) he lived a restricted life in the army camp (*ʻaskar*) and city of **Sāmarrā** (q.v.) being imprisoned at one point by the caliph al-Muʻtamid. The death of Ḥasan provoked considerable debate over his successor, and the Shīʻites believe that he was poisoned on the orders of al-Muʻtamid. He married a slave girl called Narjis (or Ṣaqīl) and it is she who is considered to have been the mother of the twelfth Imām, **Muḥammad al-Qā'im** (q.v.). (*See* **Ithnā ʻAsharīs.**)

al-Ḥasan al-Baṣrī (21/642–110/728) One of the **tābi'ūn** (q.v.) noted for his piety and sermons. The latter were infused with a strong streak of asceticism and detachment from worldly things. In this respect he may be considered as a prototype of the early ascetical **ṣūfī** (q.v.). After campaigning in Eastern Iran in his youth, he settled in **al-Baṣra** (q.v.) where he lived until he died. His prose style, as displayed in his sermons, found many early admirers. Many of the ṣūfī orders include him in their **silsilas** (q.v.). (*See* **Ṭarīqa**; **Wāṣil b. 'Aṭā'**.)

al-Ḥasan b. 'Alī (3/624-5–*c.* 49/669-70) Son of **'Alī b. Abī Ṭālib** (q.v.) and **Fāṭima** (q.v.), grandson and favourite, with his brother **al-Ḥusayn b. 'Alī** (q.v.), of the Prophet **Muḥammad**, and Second Shī'ite Imām. Al-Ḥasan abdicated the caliphate in favour of **Mu'āwiya b. Abī Sufyān** (q.v.). (*See* **Shī'ism.**)

Ḥasan -i Ṣabbāḥ (died 518/1124) Leader of the **Assassins** (q.v.) of **Alamūt** (q.v.), scholar, administrator and ascetic, and propagandist *par excellence* of the Nizārī Ismā'īlī mission (*da'wa*). Born in Qum, he spent a few years in Egypt before seizing Alamūt in 483/1090 which he made the centre of his mission. He lived an ascetical life there, executing both his less rigorous sons. (*See* **Ismā'īlīs**; **Nizārīs**.)

Hāshim (1) Great-grandfather of the Prophet **Muḥammad** whose name was borne by the Prophet's own clan. Hāshim was the son of **'Abd Manāf** (q.v.) and also the father of **'Abd al-Muṭṭalib b. Hāshim**. Hāshim was responsible for provisioning pilgrims and is also credited with having dug a number of wells. (*See* **Hāshim** (2); **Quraysh**.)

Hāshim (2) Meccan clan to which the Prophet **Muḥammad** belonged; it was part of the tribe of **Quraysh** (q.v.).

Hāshimiyya A term used generally to designate the **'Abbāsids** (q.v.) and their supporters, but also more specifically to denote a

Shīʻite revolutionary group from **al-Kūfa** (q.v.) which emerged at the end of the rule of the **Umayyads** (q.v.). (It was named after its Imām, Abū Hāshim ʻAbd Allāh b. Muḥammad al-Ḥanafiyya.) The Hāshimiyya became ardent propagandists for the ʻAbbāsids in Khurāsān, and played an important role in the overthrow of the Umayyads. (*See* **Shīʻism**.)

al-Ḥashr (Ar.) The title of the 59th **sūra** of the **Qur'ān**; it means 'The Gathering' but also 'The Exile'. The *sūra* belongs to the Medinan period and has 24 verses. Its title is drawn from a phrase in v.2 which has been variously interpreted. Much of the *sūra* concerns Jewish-Muslim relations and, in particular, the breaking by the Jewish tribe of al-Naḍīr of a treaty of neutrality which it had made with **Muḥammad**. V.21 uses a most striking image in which God tells his people that if the Qur'ān had been sent down on a mountain, they would have seen that very mountain submissive and cleft open in fear of God.

Ḥaṭṭīn, Battle of This was one of the great battles of mediaeval Islamic history. It was fought in an area North West of Lake Tiberias, between the Christian troops and those of **Ṣalāḥ al-Dīn** (q.v.) in 583/1187. The Christian forces, who were decisively beaten, included such notables as Raymond of Tripoli and Reginald of Kerak. The latter was personally killed by Ṣalāḥ al-Dīn. Ḥaṭṭīn was a decisive battle in the course of the **Crusades** (q.v.), opening the way for the Muslim capture of **Jerusalem** (q.v.) itself, as well as Acre, and provoking the Third Crusade. (*See* **Ayyūbids**.)

Ḥawḍ (Ar.) [pl. *aḥwāḍ*] Basin, pool, pond, cistern. In Islamic architecture the cistern has an ancient pedigree since mosques from the earliest times required water for the performance of the ritual ablutions. The word *ḥawḍ* also has a notable eschatological significance, indicating the pool in Paradise where **Muḥammad** on the Day of Resurrection will meet members of the Islamic community. The **ḥadīth** (q.v.) literature provides a considerable amount of information about the *ḥawḍ* in this sense. For example, the *ḥawḍ* is a place of purification from sin on Judgement Day, before entry to Paradise, after the Prophet Muḥammad's **shafā'a** (q.v.) with God for sinners. (*See* **al-Janna**; **Masjid**; **Yawm al-Qiyāma**.)

al-Hāwiya (Ar.) The Abyss or the Chasm. Considered to be bottomless, this is one of the seven ranks or layers of Hell. Tradition later consigned the hypocrites to this layer of Hell but the word only appears once in the **Qur'ān**, in v.9 of **Sūrat al-Qāri'a** (q.v.). Here Hell, called Hāwiya, is promised to the sinner whose good deeds weigh lightly in the scales at the Judgement. (*See* **al-Ḥisāb**; **al-Nār**.)

Ḥawwā' (Ar.) The name given by Muslim authors to Eve, the wife of **Ādam** (q.v.). The name is un-Qur'ānic: in that text Eve is referred to as 'spouse' or 'partner' (*zawj*). She joined with Ādam in his disobedience and was accordingly cast out with him. Later, after an initial separation, Eve encountered Ādam again at **'Arafa** (q.v.). Her name, like that of her husband, has become embroidered with much legend. Eve's tomb was traditionally located in what is now the Red Sea Arabian port of Jidda (Judda), known in the West as Jeddah. The name has been held by some to derive from the Arabic *jadda* or *jidda* meaning 'grandmother', in reference to Eve, but this has been denied by others.

Heaven *See* **al-Janna**.

Hell *See* **al-Hāwiya**; **al-Ḥuṭama**; **Jahannam**; **al-Jaḥīm**; **Laẓā**; **al-Nār**; **Sa'īr**; **Saqar**.

Hereafter *See* **al-Ākhira**; **al-Ma'ād**.

Heresy *See* **Bid'a**; **Ilḥād**.

Heretic *See* **Ilḥād**; **Zindīq**.

Hezbollah *See* **Ḥizb Allāh.**

Hidden Imām *See* **Muḥammad al-Qā'im.**

Ḥijāb (Ar.) [pl. *ḥujub*] Veil. Worn by many Muslim women out of modesty, the veil is also a striking symbol of pride in being a Muslim which many younger Muslims, as well as the older generation, are pleased to wear, contrary to popular belief. It can in some cases also signal an adherence to Islamic fundamentalism. The **Qur'ān** enjoins women to dress modestly and the extent of veiling, and the size of the veil, varies from Muslim country to country in accordance with local custom. It may be a plain piece of cloth or highly coloured and decorated, again depending both on local custom and the wish of the wearer. (*See* **Burqu'**; **Chādor**; **Fundamentalism, Islamic**; **Purdah**.)

al-Ḥijr (Ar.) The title of the 15th **sūra** of the **Qur'ān**; al-Ḥijr is a place name. Some commentators associate it with the tribe of **Thamūd** (q.v.) but others with the people of **Ṣāliḥ** (q.v.). The *sūra* refers to 'the people of al-Ḥijr' (*aṣḥāb al-Ḥijr*) in v.80. The *sūra* belongs mainly to the Meccan period and contains 99 verses. It describes among other things the disobedience of **Iblīs** (q.v.) after the creation of **Ādam** (q.v.). In v.34 Iblīs is described as 'stoned' or 'cursed' (*rajīm*).

al-Hijra (Ar.) The Migration: specifically, in Islamic religious history, the migration or emigration of the Prophet **Muḥammad** from **Mecca** (q.v.) to **Medina** (q.v.) in AD 622, which became Year 1 of the Muslim lunar calendar. This was one of the great seminal events of Islamic history and paved the way for the conquest of Mecca by Muḥammad and the final settlement of Islam in Arabia from whence it would emerge to become a major world religion. (*See* **Calendar**.)

Hijra or **Hujra** (Ar.) [pl. *hijar* or *hujar*] Wahhābī Ikhwān agricultural village in Arabia, designed to establish and promote bedouin settlement. The Ikhwān became characterized by their religious fervour and eventually rebelled against the founder of the *hijar*, 'Abd al-'Azīz b. 'Abd al-Raḥman Āl Su'ūd (Ibn Su'ūd). Their rebellion was put down in 1348/1930. (*See* **Ikhwān**; **Wahhābīs**.)

Hilāl (Ar.) [pl. *ahilla*] Crescent, new or half moon. This is an Islamic symbol frequently found on domes and minarets. Religiously the new moon was of considerable significance because its sighting signalled, for example, the start and finish of **Ramaḍān** (q.v.). (*See* **Manāra**; **Qubba**; **Red Crescent**.)

Hilāl, Banū Arab tribe, originally from Najd, some of whose members later migrated to Egypt. **Ibn Khaldūn** (q.v.) describes their brigand-like activities in North Africa, which began in the middle of the 5th/11th century. Much legend has grown up around this unruly tribe notably propagated in the famous Sagas of the Banū Hilāl. They achieved notoriety with their sacking of **Qayrawān** (q.v.) in 449/1057.

Himyarites *See* **Ma'rib Dam**.

Hind Wife of **Abū Sufyān** (q.v.). At her instigation, one of her slaves speared and killed **Ḥamza b. 'Abd al-Muṭṭalib** (q.v.) at the Battle of Uḥud. (*See* **Uḥud, Battle of**)

Ḥirā', Mount Situated North East of **Mecca** (q.v.), this mountain is irrevocably associated with the first revelation of the **Qur'ān** via the angel **Jibrīl** (q.v.) to **Muḥammad**. The Prophet had an annual custom of spending time in one of the caves of Mount Ḥirā': there Muḥammad received the first revelation of the Qur'ān, i.e. the verses of **Sūrat al-'Alaq** (q.v.), in AD 610. This mountain also bears the title of 'The Mountain of Light' (*Jabal al-Nūr*). (*See* **Laylat al-Qadr**; **Taḥannuth**.)

al-Ḥisāb (Ar.) Literally, 'Reckoning'. The Day of Judgement is called in Arabic 'The Day of Reckoning' (*Yawm al-Ḥisāb*), among other names (*see* v.27 of **Sūrat Ghāfir**). The **Qur'ān** gives a considerable amount of detail about the Day of Judgement: in particular, two styles of judgement, with scales and with books, are mentioned. *See*, for example, vv.8–9 of **Sūrat al-A'rāf** (q.v.) and vv.7—12 of **Sūrat al-Inshiqāq** (q.v.). (*See also* **al-Sā'a**; **Yawm al-Qiyāma**.)

Ḥisba *See* **Muḥtasib**.

Hishām (72/691–125-6/743) Notable 10th caliph of the dynasty of the **Umayyads** (q.v.) and perhaps their last really strong and able ruler before the 'Abbāsid Revolution. He assumed the caliphate in 105/724. His reign saw a variety of military campaigns including a continuation of low-scale warfare with Byzantium. During his rule the Arabs reached the end of their northwards advance into Europe, being stopped by Charles Martel at the Battle of Poitiers in 114/732. (*See* **'Abbāsids**; **Khalīfa**; **Poitiers, Battle of**.)

Ḥiyal (Ar.) [sing. *ḥīla*] Devices, tricks, ruses, subterfuges. In the law the word acquired the technical sense of 'a legal stratagem' which often frustrated the intention and spirit, if not the actual letter, of the law. The use of such *ḥiyal* in the mediaeval practice of law became particularly associated with the **Ḥanafīs** (q.v.). Some Shāfi'ī scholars also allowed *ḥiyal* but both the **Mālikīs** (q.v.) and the **Ḥanbalīs** (q.v.) condemned the practice. (*See* **Shāfi'īs**; **Sharī'a**.)

Ḥizb (Ar.) [pl. *aḥzāb*] A word which has acquired a number of technical meanings in **taṣawwuf** (q.v.). The most important of these is its use to designate a prayer of particular efficacy. Perhaps the most famous *ḥizb* of all is the 'Prayer (or Litany) of the Sea' (*Ḥizb al-Baḥr*) by al-Shādhilī, often sung during a **ṣūfī** (q.v.) **ḥaḍra** (q.v.). The prayer was much favoured by sea travellers and is recorded, for example, by that great Islamic traveller, **Ibn Baṭṭūṭa** (q.v.), at the beginning of his *Riḥla*. The word *ḥizb* was also used in another sense to mean a 60th part of the **Qur'ān** (q.v.). (*See* **Riḥla**; **Shādhiliyya**; **Tawassul**; **Wird**.)

Ḥizb Allāh (Ar.) The Party of God. This is the name borne by a major fundamentalist Shī'ite grouping, founded after the 1979 Iranian Revolution. The name finds its origins in the **Qur'ān**: both **Sūrat al-Mā'ida** (q.v.) (v.56) and **Sūrat al-Mujādila** (q.v.) (v.22) associate the believers with 'the party of God'. (*See* **Amal**; **Fundamentalism, Islamic**)

Hojatoleslam *See* **Ḥujjat 'l-Islām.**

Holy War *See* **Jihād.**

Hour, The *See* **al-Sā'a**.

Houris Anglicized version of the Arabic *ḥuriyya* or *ḥawrā'* [pl. *ḥūr*]. The houris are the virginal female companions of the blessed in Paradise. They appear several times in the **Qur'ān**. For example, in v.20 of **Sūrat al-Ṭūr** (q.v.) the blessed are told that they will be wed to houris as one of the many delights of Paradise. Later tradition considerably embellished the basic Qur'ānic data. (*See* **al-Janna**.)

Hubal Major idol of pre-Islamic **Mecca** (q.v.) which had a cultic place and role within the **Ka'ba** (q.v.).

Hūd The title of the 11th **sūra** of the **Qur'ān**; Hūd is the proper name of a prophet sent to the people of **'Ād** (q.v.). The *sūra* belongs to the Meccan period and has 123 verses. The story of the prophet Hūd, from which the title of the *sūra* derives, occupies vv.50–60. It tells how Hūd goes to the people of 'Ād to warn them. They reject him and accuse Hūd of not bringing them a clear proof. Disaster, in consequence, overtakes the tribe of 'Ād. The story of Hūd and 'Ād in this *sūra* is followed by the similar ones of **Ṣāliḥ** (q.v.) and **Thamūd** (q.v.), and **Shu'ayb** (q.v.) and Midian (**Madyan** (q.v.)). (*See* **Ibrāhīm** (1)).

al-Ḥudaybiyya, Treaty of Major treaty (called after a village outside **Mecca** (q.v.)), concluded between **Muḥammad** (q.v.) and the Meccans in 6/628. Under its terms Muḥammad agreed, with his followers, to give up the pilgrimage which they had intended to make at that moment, in return for being allowed to perform a minor pilgrimage (*'umra*) the following year. Other terms included a mutual 'no-raiding' pact, and a pledge by Muḥammad to return to Mecca any junior member of the tribe of **Quraysh** (q.v.) who went over to him lacking the sanction of his or her guardian. The treaty, intended to remain in force for ten years, in fact only lasted until circumstances precipitated Muḥammad's conquest of Mecca in 8/630. (*See* **Ḥajj**; **Sūrat al-Fatḥ**.)

Ḥujjat 'l-Islām (Ar./Pers.) Rank of would-be **mujtahid** (q.v.), below that of **Āyatullāh** (q.v.) in Iran. The phrase means literally 'The Proof of Islam'.

al-Ḥujurāt (Ar.) The title of the 49th **sūra** of the **Qur'ān**; it means 'The Rooms' or 'The Chambers'. The *sūra* belongs to the Medinan period and has 18 verses. The title comes from a reference in v.4 to the Prophet **Muḥammad**'s rooms (in his house) and a belligerent visit by some of the tribe of **Tamīm** (q.v.) to the adjacent mosque of the Prophet. The *sūra* warns against contempt for others and backbiting. It was revealed not long before Muḥammad's death.

al-Hujwīrī (died *c.* 467–8/1075) A famous **ṣūfī** (q.v.) from Ghazna in Afghanistan who, in his written portrayal of the ṣūfī path, presented a learned, varied, wide but, sometimes, also incoherent picture. He taught a variety of ascetical practices including celibacy. His most famous work, and the only one which is extant, is his *Disclosure of the Concealed* (*Kashf al-Maḥjūb*). Like **al-Ghazālī** (q.v.) he insisted in his ṣūfism that every ṣūfī had to obey the **sharī'a** (q.v.).

Humāyūn (913/1508–963/1556) Eldest son of **Bābur** (q.v.) and one of the great Mughal rulers. He ruled from 937/1530 until 963/1556 with a fifteen year interregnum in the latter part of his life. Much of his reign was spent in warfare, either against his own family or other foes. Intensely superstitious, he was also a cultured and religiously tolerant man. He died as a result of falling downstairs from the roof of his library.

al-Humaza (Ar.) The title of the 104th **sūra** of the **Qur'ān**; it means 'The Slanderer'. The *sūra* belongs to the Meccan period and contains 9 verses. Its title is drawn from the 1st verse which commences a severe warning to every money-grabbing and miserly slanderer: he will be thrown into the fire of **al-Ḥuṭama** (q.v.).

Ḥunayn, Battle of Important battle which took place in the valley oasis of Ḥunayn (lying on a route from **Mecca** (q.v.) to **al-Ṭā'if** (q.v.)) between the tribes of Hawāzin plus **Thaqīf** (q.v.), and **Muḥammad**, in 8/630. Muḥammad's vanguard was led by **Khālid b. al-Walīd** (q.v.) while his opponents were commanded by Mālik b. 'Awf. The Muslim army won decisively with small losses, thereby consolidating Muḥammad's position in Arabia. The Battle of Ḥunayn is mentioned by name in vv.25–26 of **Sūrat al-Tawba** (q.v.) in the **Qur'ān**.

Ḥunayn b. Isḥāq (192-3/808-9–260/873 Doyen of the Arab translation movement. He studied at **Gondēshāpūr** (q.v.) among other places and was one of the most important channels of Greek learning to the Arabs, acquiring an extremely good knowledge of the Greek language. He translated into both Arabic and Syriac. It is due to the early spadework of Ḥunayn and his school that much Greek learning early infused Islamic philosophy. (*See* **Falsafa**.)

Ḥusayn, Ṭāhā (1306-7/1889–1393/1973) Egyptian literary critic, novelist, belletrist and scholar, and probably one of the most prominent literary figures of the 20th century in the Arab world. Blind from the age of two, yet the later possessor of doctorates from both Cairo University and the Sorbonne, Ṭāhā Ḥusayn succeeded in outraging Islamic opinion in 1926 with a book entitled *On Pre-Islamic Poetry*. In this work he examined the poetry allegedly written in the pre-Islamic period and came to the conclusion that most of it was later forgery. However, outraged Islamic theologians of the day held that his view constituted in some way an attack on the language of the **Qur'ān** itself and its much-vaunted superiority over pre-Islamic antecedents. Ḥusayn's book was withdrawn, revised and published anew in 1927 under a modified title.

al-Ḥusayn b. 'Alī (4/626–61/680) Born in **Medina** (q.v.), the Third Shī'ite Imām, known among the Shī'ites as 'the Prince of the Martyrs', was one of the grandsons of the Prophet **Muḥammad** and the son of the 4th caliph **'Alī b. Abī Ṭālib** (q.v.) and **Fāṭima** (q.v.). After the death of **Mu'āwiya b. Abī Sufyān** (q.v.) in 60/680, al-Ḥusayn took up arms against the **Umayyads** (q.v.) and headed for **al-Kūfa** (q.v.). He was brutally massacred with his few companions at the Battle of Karbalā' in 61/680, an event which has been invested by the Shī'ites down the ages with immense significance. Al-Ḥusayn is greatly revered by both the **Sunnī** (q.v.) branch of Islam and the **Shī'ites** (q.v.) alike. The Mosque of Sayyidnā 'l-Ḥusayn in **Cairo** (q.v.), where his head is enshrined, is a major popular focal point for Muslim pilgrimage and petition. This mosque is also an arena for the performance of *zikr* or **ḥaḍra** (q.v.) by the **Burhāniyya** (q.v.), especially in **Ramaḍān** (q.v.). A notice hanging on one of the walls of the al-Ḥusayn Mosque reads: 'The Prophet of God, blessing and peace be upon him, said: "Al-Ḥusayn supports me and I support al-Ḥusayn" (*Al-Ḥusayn minnī wa anā min al-Ḥusayn*).' (*See* **'Āshūrā'**; **Dhikr**; **Karbalā', Battle of**; **al-Muḥarram**; **Ta'ziya**.)

al-Ḥuṭama (Ar.) Literally, 'that which shatters, wrecks or smashes'. *Al-Ḥuṭama* is one of the seven ranks of Hell to which tradition later assigned the Jews. The word occurs only twice in the **Qur'ān**, both times in **Sūrat al-Humaza** (q.v.). Here, in v.6, it is precisely defined as 'the kindled fire of God'. (*See* **al-Nār**.)

Hypocrisy *See* **Munāfiqūn, Sūrat al-Munāfiqūn**.

Hypocrites *See* **Munāfiqūn**.

'Ibāda (Ar.) [pl. *'ibādāt*] Worship, devotional action, observance required by the Islamic faith, e.g. **ṣalāt** (q.v.). In **fiqh** (q.v.) the *'ibādāt* contrast technically with the *mu'āmalāt*, the former being basically the *rituals* enjoined by Islamic law, and the latter the *social obligations* enjoined by that same law, embracing such aspects of it as inheritance and contracts. There is a saying, cited by Fyzee (*see* back of the *Dictionary* for full bibliographical details), that marriage (**nikāḥ** (q.v.)) has aspects of both *'ibāda* and *mu'āmala*.

Ibāḍīs Members of a branch of the **Khārijites** (q.v.), named after their alleged founder 'Abd Allāh b. Ibāḍ, a 1st/7th century Khārijite leader. Ibāḍīs represent a moderate wing of the Khārijites. The law of the former has much in common with that of the **Mālikīs** (q.v.) while Ibāḍī theology was clearly influenced by the doctrines of the **Mu'tazila** (q.v.). There are Ibāḍīs today in Oman, East Africa and North Africa.

al-Ibāḍiyya *See* **Ibāḍīs**.

Iblīs (Ar.) The Devil. The Arabic word may derive from the Greek word *diábolos*. Made out of fire, he was cast down by God for refusing, alone of all the angels, to bow down and acknowledge God's new creation **Ādam** (q.v.) who was made out of clay. The story of Iblīs may be constructed from the considerable detail about him which is given in the **Qur'ān**, especially in **Sūrat al-Baqara**, **Sūrat al-A'rāf**, **Sūrat al-Ḥijr**, **Sūrat al-Isrā'**, **Sūrat Ṭāhā**, and **Sūrat Ṣād** (qq.v.). In the Garden of Paradise Iblīs tempted Ādam and Eve and precipitated their downfall. He is also called 'The Satan' (*al-Shayṭān*). There is some debate among the commentators as to whether Iblīs should be regarded as an angel or, in agreement with v.50 of **Sūrat al-Kahf**, as one of the **jinn** (q.v.). (*See* **Ḥawwā'**; **al-Janna**; **al-Nār**; **al-Rajīm**.)

Ibn 'Abbās (AD 619–*c.* 67-8/686-8) Name often borne by 'Abd Allāh b. al-'Abbās, a much revered Muslim exegete.

Ibn 'Abd al-Wahhāb, Muḥammad (1115/1703–1206/1792) Founder and inspiration of the **Wahhābīs** (q.v.) and adherent of Ḥanbalism. After much travel and study, he gained the support of the chieftain of the village of Dir'iyya (Dar'iyya) in Arabia, named Muḥammad b. Su'ūd. The latter began to extend his power and thus the power of the Wahhābīs in Arabia. Muḥammad b. Su'ūd's successor, called 'Abd al-'Azīz, kept Muḥammad b. 'Abd al-Wahhāb as his spiritual mentor and thus ensured the consolidation and spread of the latter's views, ably expressed in his best known work *The Book of the Assertion of God's Unity* (*Kitāb al-Tawḥīd*). Ibn 'Abd al-Wahhāb was much influenced by **Ibn Taymiyya** (q.v.). (*See* **Ḥanbalīs**; **Hijra**; **Ikhwān**.)

Ibn al-'Arabī (560/1165–638/1240) One of the great **ṣūfī** (q.v.) masters of all time, deservedly referred to as 'The Greatest Shaykh' (*al-Shaykh al-Akbar*). Born in Murcia, he later lived in Seville, North Africa and **Damascus** (q.v.), as well as travelling widely in the Near and Middle East. The two most important extant works of his, from a huge known corpus, are *The Meccan Revelations* (*al-Futūḥāt al-Makkiyya*) and *The Bezels of Wisdom* (*Fuṣūṣ al-Ḥikam*). The **ṣūfī** doctrine irrevocably associated with him, even if he does not himself use the term, is that of 'the Oneness (or Unity) of Being' (*Waḥdat al-Wujūd*). Muslim opinion has always been split about Ibn al-'Arabī: for some he is a great heretic; for others, a great saint. (*See* **Shaykh**.)

Ibn 'Arabī *See* **Ibn al-'Arabī**.

Ibn Bājja (*c.* 500/1106–533/1138) Islamic philosopher who became known by the name of Avempace in mediaeval Europe. We only have a few details of his life; it is alleged that he was poisoned in **Fez** (q.v.) in 533/1138. He was one of the principal members of the Hispano-Arab philosophy school and his thought was influenced by both Aristotle and Plotinus. It is well-known that Ibn Bājja influenced in turn the great **Ibn Rushd** (q.v.). (*See* **Aristotelianism, Islamic; Ibn Gabirol**; **Neoplatonism, Islamic)**

Ibn Baṭṭūṭa (703/1304–770 or 779/1368–9 or 1377) The Marco Polo of the Islamic world and author of the most famous *Travelogue* (*Riḥla*) in Arabic literature. Leaving Tangiers in 725/1325, he roamed over much of the known world including Arabia, **Delhi** (q.v.), Ceylon, and allegedly, China. Borrowing often from an earlier 6th/12th century traveller, Ibn Jubayr, the *Riḥla* of Ibn Baṭṭūṭa provides some very important detailed descriptions of **Mecca** (q.v.) and **Medina** (q.v.). Ibn Baṭṭūṭa belonged to the Mālikī School of law and he served as a **qāḍī** (q.v.) in both Delhi and the Maldive Islands. (*See* **Ḥizb**; **Mālikīs**; **Maḥfūẓ, Najīb**; **Riḥla**.)

Ibn Gabirol (*c.* 411/1021-2–*c.*450/1058?) Jewish Spanish philosopher whom the Latins knew as Avicebron; he was a major exponent of Neoplatonism from the Hispano-Arab philosophy school and wrote in both Hebrew and Arabic. (*See* **Ibn Bājja**; **Neoplatonism, Islamic)**

Ibn Ḥanbal *See* **Aḥmad b. Ḥanbal**.

Ibn Ḥazm (384/994–456/1064) Mediaeval Spanish theologian, philosopher, jurisprudent, moralist, politician, poet, and writer on comparative religion. Ibn Ḥazm was one of the foremost proponents of the *Ẓāhirī* or 'Literalist' School of law but it is perhaps his books on other religions and ethics which have given him the reputation which he has of being one of mediaeval Spain's foremost thinkers. (*See* **Ẓāhirīs**.)

Ibn Hishām *See* **Ibn Isḥāq**.

Ibn Isḥāq (*c*. 85/704–*c*. 150/767) Born in **Medina** (q.v.), his principal claim to fame rests in his collecting substantial materials for his life of the Prophet **Muḥammad**. These were edited into their most popular form by Ibn Hishām (died 218/833 or 213/828) who spent his life in Egypt. The resulting *Book of the Life of the Prophet of God* (*Kitāb Sīrat Rasūl Allāh*) is regarded as one of the most important of all sources for the life of the Prophet. (*See* **Sīra**.)

Ibn Khaldūn (732/1332–808/1406) One of the best known of all Arabo-Islamic figures in the West, revered by Arnold J. Toynbee, for example, in that historian's famous and multi-volumed *Study of History* where he described him as 'An Arabic genius'. Toynbee's assessment was right. Ibn Khaldūn was Islam's greatest late-mediaeval proto-sociologist and historian though it is through the spectacles of Arab history and achievement, rather than Western intellectual polemic and 'colonization' that he must rightly be judged. Born in **Tūnis** (q.v.), he ended his days in **Cairo** (q.v.). Public and political highlights of a long and varied career included his several appointments as Mālikī **qāḍī** (q.v.) in Cairo and later meeting with the famous **Tīmūr-i Lang** (q.v.). The literary highlight of his career was undoubtedly his *Muqaddima* or *Introduction* to history and historiography. Ibn Khaldūn is well-known for his cyclical theory of history: put simplistically and crudely, a nomad tribe struggles to achieve urban power, becomes corrupt and luxurious after a few generations having achieved that power, and is in turn overthrown by a rising and less effete tribe. Ibn Khaldūn's writings and career defy neat analysis and are particularly unsusceptible to proper encapsulation in brief articles such as this. His thought is multi-faceted and precludes snap judgements though many have been the perpetrators of such. For a standard introduction to the subject in English, the reader is referred to al-Azmeh's *Ibn Khaldūn* (see back of this *Dictionary* for full bibliographical details). (*See also* **'Aṣabiyya**.)

Ibn Killis, Ya'qūb (318/930–380/991) Famous **wazīr** (q.v.) of the 5th Fāṭimid caliph al-'Azīz (*reg.* 365/975–386/996). He was of Baghdādī Jewish origin but later became a Muslim. Egypt flourished during his administration. (*See* **Baghdād**; **Fāṭimids**.)

Ibn Māja (209/824-5–273/887) His full name was Abū 'Abd Allāh Muḥammad b. Yazīd al-Raba'ī al-Qazwīnī ibn Māja; he ranks as one of the six principal compilers of Islamic tradition (**ḥadīth** (q.v.)) in **Sunnī** (q.v.) Islam. His traditions were collected in his book called *The Book of Traditions* (*Kitāb al-Sunan*). Other works, now lost, are attributed to the pen of Ibn Māja. His life was a notable mirror of the Prophet **Muḥammad**'s injunction to travel in search of knowledge. (*See* **Riḥla**.)

Ibn Mālik *See* **Mālik b. Anas**.

Ibn Mas'ūd (died *c.* 33/653) Notable companion of the Prophet **Muḥammad** and very early convert to Islam. He was among the migrants to **Ethiopia** (q.v.) but later joined the Prophet in **Medina** (q.v.) and witnessed the Battles of Badr and Uḥud. Towards the end of his life he took up residence in **al-Kūfa** (q.v.) but later fell out with the caliph **'Uthmān b. 'Affān** (q.v.). Ibn Mas'ūd is of particular interest in Qur'ānic studies since the text which he had seems to have differed from the 'Uthmānic version in a number of respects. (*See* **Badr, Battle of**; **Qur'ān**; **Ṣaḥāba**; **Uḥud, Battle of**)

Ibn Rushd, Abū 'l-Walīd Muḥammad b. Aḥmad (520/1126–595/1198) Known in the West as Averroes, he was perhaps Spain's greatest Hispano-Arab philosopher; certainly he was Spain's most notable commentator on Aristotle. Falsely accused of espousing a 'double-truth' position (where what was considered true in philosophy was regarded as false in theology, and vice versa), Ibn Rushd gave his name to the Averroist movement in Europe. Among the posts which he held were those of **qāḍī** (q.v.) in Seville and **Cordova** (q.v.) and principal doctor to the Almohad ruler. At one point in his career orders were given for his books to be burned. (*See* **Almohads**; **Aristotelianism, Islamic**)

Ibn Sīnā, Abū 'Alī al-Ḥusayn (369/979–428/1037) Known in the West as Avicenna, Ibn Sīnā was undoubtedly Islam's greatest Neoplatonic philosopher, even if he did lack the originality of his predecessor **al-Fārābī** (q.v.). His career is astonishing: Ibn Sīnā was a polymath who wrote major works on medicine as well as metaphysics and other aspects of philosophy. He was a minister and friend of princes. Perhaps his greatest work was *The Book of the Cure* (*Kitāb al-Shifā'*). Yet the philosopher had a mystical side too which should not be underestimated. Born near **Bukhārā** (q.v.) he lived in a variety of places all over Persia, dying finally in Hamadān. (*See* **Neoplatonism, Islamic**)

Ibn Taymiyya (661/1263–728/1328) Distinguished Ḥanbalī jurist and theologian. He was born in **Ḥarrān** (q.v.) and later established himself in **Damascus** (q.v.) where he studied, taught and died. He is important for maintaining that the gate of **ijtihād** (q.v.) remained open and his thought had a profound impact on the **Wahhābīs** (q.v.). (*See* **Ḥanbalīs**; **Taqlīd**.)

Ibn Ṭufayl, Abū Bakr (died 581/1185-6) Important figure in the Hispano-Arab school of mediaeval philosophy whom the West knew as Abubacer. **Ibn Rushd** (q.v.) was one of his protégés. His epistle, named after its hero, entitled *Ḥayy b. Yaqẓān* provided via its English translation, a model for Defoe's *Robinson Crusoe*.

Ibn Ṭūlūn, Aḥmad (220/835–270/884) Founder of an important dynasty in Egypt, the Ṭūlūnids. Egypt became prosperous under his rule. Nominally, Aḥmad arrived in Egypt as a deputy of the **'Abbāsids'** (q.v.) governor in that country but it was not long before he had carved out his own power base and, indeed, extended it to other regions like Syria. The Ṭūlūnids were eventually overthrown by the 'Abbāsid caliph's general in 292/905. From the perspective of Islamic architecture, Aḥmad b. Ṭūlūn is famous for his building of the great mosque in **Cairo** (q.v.) which bears his name, and which possessed a unique spiral minaret, allegedly modelled on that of the great mosque of **Sāmarrā** (q.v.).

Ibrāhīm (1) (Ar.) Abraham, a great Islamic prophet, patriarch and ardent proponent of monotheism who figures prominently in the **Qur'ān**. In **Sūrat Āl 'Imrān** (q.v.) Ibrāhīm is described as being neither a Jew nor a Christian but a **ḥanīf** (q.v.) and a **muslim** (q.v.). The Qur'ān retails several major incidents from his life: Allāh brings four birds to life for him (v.260 of **Sūrat al-Baqara** (q.v.)); angels forecast the birth of his son **Isḥāq** (q.v.) (vv.69–73 of **Sūrat Hūd** (q.v.)); he is compassionate towards his father **Āzar** (q.v.) and prays for him, despite the latter's idolatry; he is cast into a fire by a ruler whom the commentators call **Nimrod** (q.v.) and saved by God, according to some commentators by the intercession of the angel **Jibrīl** (q.v.) (vv.68—69 of **Sūrat al-Anbiyā'** (q.v.)); and he is commanded by God to sacrifice his son (identified as **Ismā'īl** (q.v.) rather than **Isḥāq** (q.v.)), but Ismā'īl is saved at the last moment by God (vv.102–107 of **Sūrat al-Ṣāffāt**.). (*See also* **Sūrat al-Naḥl**.)

Ibrāhīm (2) (Ar.) Abraham: the title of the 14th **sūra** of the **Qur'ān**; the reference is to the great prophet and patriarch Ibrāhīm (see above entry). The *sūra* belongs mainly to the Meccan period and has 52 verses. It bears the name Ibrāhīm because vv.35 ff make considerable reference to him. **Isḥāq** (q.v.) and **Ismā'īl** (q.v.) are also mentioned. The *sūra* begins with three of the **Mysterious Letters of the Qur'ān** (q.v.) and refers to the signs conveyed by **Mūsā** (q.v.) as well as warning what happened to the people of **Nūḥ** (q.v.), **'Ād** (q.v.) and **Thamūd** (q.v.). The tyrant will enter **Jahannam** (q.v.) and be given pus to drink which will be very difficult to swallow.

Ibrāhīm (3) (Ar.) Abraham, the son of the Prophet **Muḥammad** and **Māriya the Copt** (q.v.). He died in infancy. (*See* **'Abd Allāh b. Muḥammad; al-Qāsim.**)

'Īd (Ar.) [pl. *a'yād*] Feast, holiday, festival. Islam has fewer great feast days in the formal sense than a number of other major religions. The two most important feasts are **'Īd al-Fiṭr** (q.v.) and **'Īd al-Aḍḥā** (q.v.). (*See* **Ḥajj; Mawlid; Mawlid al-Nabī; Ramaḍān; Ṣawm.**)

'Īd al-Aḍḥā (Ar.) The Feast of Sacrifice, one of the greatest feasts in the Muslim calendar. It is celebrated on the 10th day of the month of **Dhū 'l-Ḥijja** (q.v.). (*See* **Ḥajj; 'Īd; 'Īd al-Fiṭr; Mawlid.**)

'Īd al-Fiṭr (Ar.) The Feast of Breaking the Fast of **Ramaḍān** (q.v.), one of the greatest feasts in the Muslim Calendar. (*See* **'Īd; 'Īd al-Aḍḥā; Mawlid; Ṣawm.**)

'Īd al-Qurbān *See* **'Īd al-Aḍḥā; Qurbān.**

'Idda (Ar.) Legal 'waiting period' before a divorced or widowed woman may remarry. The rules in **fiqh** (q.v.) governing *'idda* are complex but basically derive from the **Qur'ān**, especially **Sūrat al Baqara** (q.v.) and **Sūrat al-Ṭalāq** (q.v.). (*See* **Ṭalāq.**)

Idolatry *See* **Shirk.**

Idrīs A figure whose name occurs twice in the **Qur'ān**. In **Sūrat Maryam** (q.v.) he is called a prophet and bears the epithet 'true' (*ṣiddīq*); while in **Sūrat al-Anbiyā'** (q.v.) he is described as patient and righteous. A considerable amount of legend has grown up round his name. Most often Idrīs is identified with Enoch. (*See* **Abū Bakr**; **al-Ṣiddīq**; **Sūrat Yūsuf**.)

Ifāḍa *See* **Muzdalifa**.

Ifṭār (Ar.) The first meal eaten at the end of a day's fasting in **Ramaḍān** (q.v.).

Iḥrām (Ar.) State of ritual consecration and purification during the **Ḥajj** (q.v.), symbolized by the wearing of two, usually white, garments by male pilgrims (one of which may later be used as their shroud), and the observance of certain taboos. The Arabic word *iḥrām* is also used to designate the garments themselves as well as the state of consecration. (*See* **Mīqāt**.)

I'jāz (Ar.) Inimitability, especially of the **Qur'ān**. The sacred text challenges those who oppose it to produce its like.

Ijmā' (Ar.) In jurisprudence the term may be translated as 'consensus'. This can be of two types: consensus of a local group of jurisprudents in a particular generation; and the consensus, far harder to ascertain, of the whole Muslim community. For the father of Islamic jurisprudence, **al-Shāfi'ī** (q.v.), *ijmā'* of the latter type ranked as one of the four main sources (*uṣūl*) of law. (*See* **Uṣūl al-Fiqh**.)

Ijtihād (Ar.) In jurisprudence this term means 'the exercise of independent judgement' unfettered by case law or past precedent. Its opposite is **taqlīd** (q.v.) which means literally 'imitation'. Contrary to popular opinion, the 'gate of *ijtihād*' was never closed. In modern times the figure of **'Abduh** (q.v.) was associated with the concept of neo-*ijtihād*. Among the **Ithnā 'Asharīs** (q.v.) the exercise of any *ijtihād* is the province of the **mujtahid** (q.v.) in the absence of the **Imām** (q.v.). The word *ijtihād* derives from the same Arabic root as **jihād** (q.v.). (*See* **Ibn Taymiyya**.)

al-Ikhlāṣ (Ar.) The title of the 112th **sūra** of the **Qur'ān**; it means literally 'loyalty' or 'sincerity' and has been variously translated here as 'Pure (or Sincere) Religion' and 'Purity of Faith'. The *sūra* belongs to the Meccan period and, like the other *sūras* towards the end of the Qur'ān, it is extremely short having only 4 verses. The title of the *sūra* reflects the general orientation of these verses. The first two stress the Oneness and eternal nature of God while the second two stress that He has neither father nor son nor equal. The *sūra* is sometimes called *The Sūra of Unity* and is said to encapsulate the essence of the whole Qur'ān.

Ikhtilāf (Ar.) Difference. Technically speaking, this word indicates the differences between and within the four Schools of law (*madhāhib*) on points of **fiqh** (q.v.). A well-known **ḥadīth** (q.v.) from the Prophet **Muḥammad** states that such difference of opinion in his community is a sign of the mercy (*raḥma*) of God. (*See* **Ḥanafīs**;**Ḥanbalīs**; **Madhhab**; **Mālikīs**; **Shāfi'īs**.)

Ikhwān (Ar.) Brethren. A title borne by a variety of groups from mediaeval to modern times. Among the most interesting, from an Islamic point of view, are: (1) The Brethren of Purity (**Ikhwān al-Ṣafā'** (q.v.)); (2) the Ikhwān of the **Wahhābīs** (q.v.). This strongly religious and militant group was founded by Ibn Su'ūd early in the 20th century but they later revolted against him. (*See* **Hijra**); (3) the Muslim Brotherhood or Brethren (**al-Ikhwān al-Muslimūn** (q.v.)) or, to give them their full Arabic title, *Jam'iyyat al-Ikhwān al-Muslimīn*, which was founded by **al-Bannā'** (q.v.) in Egypt in 1928.

al-Ikhwān al-Muslimūn (Ar.) The Muslim Brotherhood. This organization was founded by Ḥasan **al-Bannā'** (q.v.) in 1346–7/1928 with a view to advocating a return to true Islam via the **Qur'ān** (q.v.) and the **ḥadīth** (q.v.). The Brotherhood was vehemently opposed to Western imperialism, especially in Islamic countries, and it aimed at the establishment of an ideal single Muslim state. The Brotherhood was banned by the Egyptian government in 1373–4/1954 but has since functioned underground in Egypt and other Middle Eastern states. (*See* **Quṭb, Sayyid**.)

Ikhwān al-Ṣafā' (Ar.) Brethren of Purity. These were a group of Arab philosophers, theologians and intellectuals who flourished most probably in **al-Baṣra** (q.v.) in the 4th/10th or 5th/11th centuries. Their exact names and dates are a matter of some dispute. However, they produced a famous corpus of fifty-two *Epistles* (*Rasā'il*) which were encyclopaedic in range, covering subjects as diverse as music, astronomy, embryology and philosophy. The *Epistles* are highly syncretic and draw on the Christian and Judaic traditions for material, as well as the Islamic. Though not actually **Ismā'īlīs** (q.v.) the Ikhwān were profoundly influenced by the doctrines of that sect. Philosophically and theologically the Ikhwān al-Ṣafā' are of particular interest: from the former point of view their syncretism is again readily apparent, their philosophy being a mixture of Neoplatonism and Aristotelianism. Theologically, their view of God is by turns the Unknowable One of Plotinus on the one hand, and the Creator God of the **Qur'ān**, who operates directly within and on man's history, on the other. No attempt is made by the Ikhwān to reconcile these two opposing views. The standard book in English on the Ikhwān al-Ṣafā', and, indeed, the only full-length English treatment thus far, is Netton's *Muslim Neoplatonists* (see back of this *Dictionary* for full bibliographical details). (*See also* **Aristotelianism, Islamic; Neoplatonism, Islamic**)

Iktisāb *See* **Kasb.**

Ilḥād (Ar.) Heresy. The Arabic word is also translated sometimes as 'apostasy'. *Ilḥād* means literally 'a deviation (from the correct path)'. (*See* **Bid'a**; **Irtidād**; **Ridda**.)

Illiterate (of Muḥammad) *See* **Ummī**.

'Ilm (Ar.) [pl. *'ulūm*] Knowledge, learning, science. A tradition from the Prophet **Muḥammad** enjoins that knowledge should be sought even as far as China. Travel in search of knowledge became a popular and well-recognized scholarly activity in the Islamic Middle Ages. A distinction has been made by some scholars between scientific or book knowledge (*'ilm*) and intuitive or gnostic-type knowledge (*ma'rifa*), but other scholars have denied that there was any real distinction at first between the two Arabic words. Rosenthal has calculated that the Arabic root from which *'ilm* derives, in all its forms, occurs approximately 750 times in the **Qur'ān** (see back of this *Dictionary* for full bibliographical details of his book *Knowledge Triumphant*). (*See also* **Riḥla**.)

Ilyās One of the prophets of the **Qur'ān**, often identified with Elijah (Elias). See especially vv.123–125 of **Sūrat al-Ṣāffāt** (q.v.).

Ilyās, Mawlānā Muḥammad (1302-3/1885–1363/1944) Founder of the **Faith Movement** (q.v.) in India. He became profoundly interested in **taṣawwuf** (q.v.) early in life and was a member of the **Čishtiyya** (q.v.) order. After two pilgrimages to **Mecca** (q.v.) he concluded that he had a vocation to preach to those Indian masses who had little or no proper knowledge of their Islamic faith. He suffered from poor health throughout his life but this did not prevent him from much travel and teaching.

Images There is a myth that the representation of the human form in Islam is forbidden by the **Qur'ān**; this is not the case. It was the **ḥadīth** (q.v.) literature which instituted such a prohibition, advising that the artist would receive severe punishment on Judgement Day. What the *Qur'ān* specifically forbids is the worship of *idols* (*anṣāb*); otherwise it shows **Sulaymān** (q.v.) causing the **jinn** (q.v.) to build him statues (*tamāthīl*). Although the *ḥadīth* prohibition held sway, particularly in the Islamic Middle Ages, it was often ignored at the caliphal courts during this and later times. Sometimes, however, the artist would portray **Muḥammad** with his face blanked out, as happened in some illustrated volumes of the life of the Prophet Muḥammad. This dislike of representing the human form is seen most clearly today in the mosque where the decoration is usually calligraphic or mosaic or **arabesque** (q.v.). Similarly, one would not find the representation of the human form in a copy of the Qur'ān: here the decoration is mainly calligraphic, often of the most beautiful kind. (*See* **Masjid**.)

Imām (Ar.) [pl. *a'imma*] An Arabic word with a variety of connotations, each of which needs to be carefully distinguished: (1) Deriving as it does from an Arabic word meaning 'to head', 'to lead in prayer', *imām* has the primary meaning of prayer leader. Islam has no priests and thus the *imām* attached to a mosque is not ordained. However, any male Muslim may lead the prayer in the absence of a mosque *imām*; (2) The twelve early leaders of the **Ithnā 'Asharīs** (q.v.) or Twelver Shī'ites are referred to as the Twelve *Imāms*; (3) The **Ismā'īlīs** (q.v.) acknowledge Seven early *Imāms* and the concept of *imām* plays a key role in the complex doctrines of Ismā'īlism. (*See also* **Āghā Khān**); (4) In early Islamic history the title *Imām* was associated with the **khalīfa** (q.v.); (5) It has been used simply as a title of respect, for example, by and for the Āyatullāh **Khumaynī** (q.v.) who, in fact, preferred the title *Imām* to that of Āyatullāh. (*See* **Ijtihād**; **Muḥammad al-Qā'im**; **Mujtahid**; **Shaykh**.)

al-Imām al-Muntaẓar *See* **Muḥammad al-Qā'im.**

Imāmites *See* **Ithnā 'Asharīs**.

Īmān (Ar.) Theologically and Qur'ānically this Arabic word has come to mean 'faith', 'belief', 'right belief' (i.e. in Islam). (*See* **'Aqīda**; **Qur'ān**.)

Immanence *See* **Allāh**; **Tanzīh**; **Tashbīh**.

Indemnity *See* **Diya**.

Infallibility *See* **'Iṣma**.

Infidel *See* **Kāfir**.

Infidelity *See* **Kufr**.

al-Infiṭār (Ar.) The title of the 82nd **sūra** of the **Qur'ān**; it means 'The Cleaving' or 'The Splitting'. The *sūra* belongs to the Meccan period and has 19 verses. Its title is drawn from the 1st verse which refers dramatically to '[the] heaven' (*al-samā'*) being cleft, one of the signs of the beginning of the Day of Resurrection. The *sūra* goes on to remind man of the Recording Angels (called here 'Keepers' or 'Guardians', *al-Ḥāfiẓīn*) and that man's deeds will determine his ultimate fate: the pious will go to heaven while the debauched will burn in Hell (**al-Jaḥīm** (q.v.)). (*See* **Ba'th**; **Ishārāt al-Sā'a**; **al-Janna**; **Kirām al-Kātibīn**; **al-Sā'a**; **Yawm al-Qiyāma**.)

Inheritance An immensely complex subject in Islamic law but one of the areas where the **Sharī'a** (q.v.) has some impact on modern codes of legislation. The *Sharī'a* itself contains considerable diversity between the four major **Sunnī** (q.v.) Schools of law. The starting point, however, for any discussion of inheritance in Islam is the **Qur'ān** and the data which it provides for the legal doctrine of Qur'ānic heirs or sharers. The Qur'ānic legislation considerably ameliorated the old pre-Islamic customs of inheritance and gave women the right of inheritance for the first time. It should be noted that the principles of the Shī'ite law of inheritance differ considerably from those of Sunnī law. (*See* **Ikhtilāf**; **Shī'ism**; **Sūrat al-Nisā'**.)

Inimitability of the Qur'ān *See* **I'jāz**.

al-Injīl (Ar.) The Gospel. This is mentioned several times in the **Qur'ān**. Islam believes that at one time there was a proto-Gospel which accorded with all the data of the Qur'ān. However, according to the doctrine of **taḥrīf** (q.v.), that Gospel has been or become corrupted; hence the present disparity between the Gospels as Christians have them today and the message of the Qur'ān.

Inquisition *See* **Miḥna**.

al-Insān (Ar.) The title of the 76th **sūra** of the **Qur'ān**; the Arabic word means 'Man'. The *sūra* belongs to the Medinan period and has 31 verses. Its title is drawn from the reference to man in the 1st verse. The *sūra* begins by dividing mankind into the grateful and their opposite, reiterating the reward for each. The rewards of the good are outlined in considerable detail: among the delights of Paradise is the Fount of **Salsabīl** (q.v.). The end of this *sūra* provides encouragement for **Muḥammad** in his mission. (*See* **al-Janna**; **Kāfūr**.)

In Shā'a Allāh (Ar.) If God Wills. This is a very common Muslim expression, the equivalent of the Latin *Deo Volente*. Vv.23–24 of **Sūrat al Kahf** (q.v.) counsel that one should not say that one will do something tomorrow but rather 'If God wills'.

al-Inshiqāq (Ar.) The title of the 84th **sūra** of the **Qur'ān**; it means 'The Splitting Apart'. The *sūra* belongs to the Meccan period and has 25 verses. Its title is taken from the 1st verse which refers to '[the] heaven' being split apart. This may be compared with the opening verse of **Sūrat al-Infiṭār** (q.v.). The *sūra* goes on to mention the judgement with books on the Last Day: the sinner will receive his book behind his back and be consigned to Hell (**Sa'īr** (q.v.)). (*See* **al-Ḥisāb**.)

Intention *See* **Niyya**.

Intercession *See* **Shafā'a**; **Tawassul**.

Interpretation (of the Qur'ān) *See* **Tafsīr**; **Ta'wīl**.

Interpreters of the Qur'ān *See* **Mufassir**.

al-'Iqāb, Battle of *See* **Las Navas de Tolosa, Battle of**.

Iqbāl, Muḥammad (1290-3/1873-6–1357/1938) Born in Sialkot, Iqbāl studied in **Lahore** (q.v.), Cambridge and Munich before taking up residence in Lahore again. He was one of India's most famous polymaths, achieving fame as a poet, lawyer, politician, and philosopher. As an Ash'arite theologian he practised a speculative exegesis of the **Qur'ān**. He championed the right of **ijtihād** (q.v.) and believed that **ijmā'** (q.v.) could result from a parliamentary system. His most famous book was his *Reconstruction of Religious Thought in Islam*, an attempt at synthesizing Eastern and Western thought. (*See* **al-Ash'arī**; **Tafsīr**.)

Iram of the Pillars In **Sūrat al-Fajr** (q.v.) of the **Qur'ān** reference is made in v.7 to 'Iram of the Pillars' (*Iram dhāt al-'Imād*). Although most probably the name of a town, commentators have differed widely over its precise identification. Suggestions include the town of **'Ād** (q.v.), **Damascus** (q.v.) and the early site of **Alexandria** (q.v.).

Irtidād (Ar.) Apostasy, also called **ridda** (q.v.) in Arabic. An apostate is called a *murtadd*. The death penalty for apostasy is not prescribed in the **Qur'ān** itself but is articulated in both the **ḥadīth** (q.v.) literature and **fiqh** (q.v.). (*See* **Bid'a**; **Ḥadd**; **Ilḥād**.)

'Īsā (Ar.) Jesus. He is a major prophet for Muslims who has a prominent place in the **Qur'ān**. Islam regards Jesus as purely human and not as the Son of God. Muslims thus have no concept of salvation history associated with Jesus. The latter's annunciation by **Jibrīl** (q.v.) and subsequent birth is described in some detail in **Sūrat Maryam** (q.v.). Jesus performs the miracle of the table in **Sūrat al-Mā'ida** (q.v.); and he is not crucified but rather taken up to God in **Sūrat al-Nisā'** (q.v.). Jesus is frequently called 'Son of Mary' in the Qur'ān and he is portrayed as speaking in the cradle in **Sūrat Maryam**. Eschatological **ḥadīth** (q.v.) texts portray Jesus coming near the end of time to destroy **al-Dajjāl** (q.v.). (*See* **Aḥmadiyya** (1).)

Isaac *See* **Isḥāq**.

Iṣfahān One of the great historic cities of Iran, famous for its mosques, especially the Great Mosque of Iṣfahān, also called the Friday Mosque. The history of the mosque mirrors much of the history of the city itself, and the impact of such dynasties as the **Būyids** (q.v.), **Saljūqs** (q.v.) and Ilkhānids. The city of Iṣfahān also contains many of the glories of the art and architecture of a later dynasty, the **Ṣafavids** (q.v.). (*See* **Masjid**; **Shīrāz**.)

al-'Ishā', Ṣalāt (Ar.) The Night Prayer. (*See* **Ṣalāt**.)

Isḥāq (Ar.) Isaac, the son of **Ibrāhīm** (q.v.) and younger brother of **Ismā'īl** (q.v.). Muslim commentators often identify Isḥāq as the reward given to Ibrāhīm after the latter's obedience with Ismā'īl. Isḥāq's birth is foretold by angels in **Sūrat Hūd** (q.v.).

Ishārāt al-Sā'a (Ar.) The Signs of the Hour (i.e. of the Last Day). There are a large number of signs given both in the **Qur'ān** and the **ḥadīth** (q.v.) literature. The former talks of a darkening sun, boiling seas and moving mountains; the latter chronicles a general breakdown in morals followed by the arrival of such figures as **al-Dajjāl** (q.v.), **'Īsā** (q.v.) and the **Mahdī** (q.v.). **Gog and Magog** (q.v.) will also appear as cannibals to terrify the earth. (*See* **Muḥammad al-Qā'im**; **al-Sā'a**.)

Ishmael *See* **Ismā'īl** (1).

al-Iskandar *See* **Dhū 'l-Qarnayn**.

al-Iskandariyya *See* **Alexandria**.

Islām (Ar.) A word meaning literally 'submission' (to the will of God). Islam is the name of one of the world's great monotheistic religions: it was founded by the Prophet **Muḥammad** in the 7th century AD as a result of the revelation of the **Qur'ān** which he received via the angel **Jibrīl** (q.v.) from God. This *Dictionary* is an attempt to survey and articulate at a *popular* level some of the principal facets of the Islamic religion. (*See* **Muslim**.)

Islamic Banking A banking system which incorporates adherence to the prohibition on **ribā** (q.v.) enshrined in the **Qur'ān**. It is an important principle of Islamic economics that there should be equality of risk. From a banking point of view this means that the risks and rewards should be shared between borrower, bank and depositor. Muslim banks should not finance goods or schemes which are themselves forbidden by Islam. Other important differences between Western and Islamic banking systems are that the latter guarantees no return and does not regard money as having any time value. (*See* **Dār al-Māl al-Islāmī**; **Muḍāraba**.)

Islamic Conference Organisation [ICO] Organization established by the Islamic countries whose representatives met at Jeddah between 14th–18th Muḥarram 1392/29th February–4th March 1972 to approve and promulgate its Charter. Article 2 of the Conference Charter states that its first objective is 'to promote Islamic solidarity among member states'. One of the most important committees of the ICO is the al-Quds Committee, established to deal with the question of **Jerusalem** (q.v.). (*See* **al-Muḥarram**.)

Islamic Council of Europe An organization based in London which was set up in 1974. It pursues a large range of activities including publishing and the holding of conferences, and generally attempts to help all Muslims in a pastoral and educational capacity. In 1979 the Islamic Council of Europe produced a draft 'Islamic Charter of Human Rights'.

'Iṣma (Ar.) Infallibility. This is a quality attributed by the **Shī'ites** (q.v.) to their Imāms. *'Iṣma* also embraces the idea of sinlessness, and a number of Shī'ite traditions relate to the sinlessness of the twelve Imāms as well as that of figures like **Muḥammad** and **Fāṭima** (q.v.). (*See* **Imām**.)

Ismā'īl (1) (Ar.) The prophet Ishmael, son of **Ibrāhīm** (q.v.) and Hājar (Hagar). He is identified by most commentators with the son who is nearly sacrificed by Ibrāhīm out of obedience to God. On being cast out by Ibrāhīm (after the birth of **Isḥāq** (q.v.)), Ismā'īl, together with Hājar, found themselves on the site of present-day **Mecca** (q.v.). Hājar frantically ran backwards and forwards between two small hills called **al-Ṣafā** (q.v.) and **al-Marwa** (q.v.) trying to find water to quench her son's thirst. This event is commemorated by the sevenfold **sa'y** (q.v.) between the two points during the **Ḥajj** (q.v.) today. Water was eventually discovered and the Well of **Zamzam** (q.v.) appeared beneath Ismā'īl. (Pilgrims drink the waters of Zamzam during the Pilgrimage.) According to one tradition, the spring appeared as a direct result of Ismā'īl poking the sand; but another tradition attributes the appearance of the spring of Zamzam to the direct intervention of the angel **Jibrīl** (q.v.). Islamic tradition also reveres Ismā'īl, together with his father Ibrāhīm, as a co-builder of the **Ka'ba** (q.v.). (*See* **Ibrāhīm** (1); **Ibrāhīm** (2).)

Ismā'īl (2) (Ar.) (died 145/762) Eldest son of **Ja'far al-Ṣādiq** (q.v.) and brother of **Mūsā al-Kāẓim** (q.v.). (*See* **Ismā'īlīs**.)

Ismā'īlīs (Ismā'īliyya) Adherents of branch of Shī'ite Islam so-called after Ismā'īl, the eldest son of **Ja'far al-Ṣādiq** (q.v.). Members of this branch are also called Seveners (since they acknowledge seven principal Imāms after the death of the

Prophet **Muḥammad**), and *Bāṭiniyya* (because of their emphasis in exegesis on **bāṭin** (q.v.) interpretation). The theology of the Ismā'īlīs was profoundly influenced by Neoplatonism and characterized by a cyclical theory of history centred on the number seven, a number which assumes an enormous significance in Ismā'īlī belief and cosmology. As has been indicated, Ismā'īlī exegesis of the **Qur'ān** holds that the sacred text is capable of both a *bāṭin* and a **ẓāhir** (q.v.) interpretation. Today, Ismā'īlīs of varying kinds are to be found all over the world but, in particular, in the Indian sub-continent and East Africa, as well as the UK and USA. Total numbers are very difficult to ascertain but probably number several million. (*See* **Āghā Khān**; **Assassins**; **Bohorās**; **al-Ḥāmidī**; **Imām**; **Ismā'īl** (2); **Ithnā 'Asharīs**; **Khojas**; **al-Kirmānī**; **Musta'lians**; **Neoplatonism, Islamic**; **Nāṭiq**; **Nizārīs**; **Qarāmiṭa**; **Shī'ites**; **al-Sijistānī**; **Ta'wīl**.)

Isnād (Ar.) Chain of authorities at the beginning of a **ḥadīth** (q.v.). Mediaeval Islam developed a highly complex science of *isnād* criticism. (*See* **'An**; **Matn**; **Mutawātir**.)

Isrā' (Ar.) Night journey. The most famous night journey in Islam was that made by the Prophet **Muḥammad** through the air, mounted on **al-Burāq** (q.v.), from **Mecca** (q.v.) to **Jerusalem** (q.v.); thence he made the Ascension (**Mi'rāj** (q.v.)) through the Seven Heavens, borne by **Jibrīl** (q.v.) and entered God's presence. The Night Journey and the *Mi'rāj* are together celebrated in the Islamic world on the 27th day of the Islamic month of Rajab. (*See* **al-Aqṣā, al-Masjid**).

al-Isrā' (Ar.) The title of the 17th **sūra** of the **Qur'ān**; it means literally 'The Night Journey'. The *sūra* belongs to the Meccan period and contains 111 verses. The title of the *sūra* is derived from verse 1 which refers to the Night Journey (*see* above entry) of the Prophet **Muḥammad** to *al-Masjid al-Aqṣā*. (The *sūra* is also called **Sūrat Banī Isrā'īl** meaning 'The *Sūra* of the Sons of

Israel', because of the references to them towards the end of the *sūra* and also at its beginning.) One widely recorded tradition associates the practice of praying *five* times a day with the Night Journey, and so, this *Sūra*, Muḥammad having been initially commanded by God to pray fifty times a day but finally managing, on the advice of **Mūsā** (q.v.), to have the number reduced to five. (*See* **al-Aqṣā, al-Masjid**; **Iblīs**; **Sūrat al-Najm**; **Ṣalāt**.)

Isrāfīl One of the great Islamic angels. He is often called 'The Lord of the Trumpet' because it is his task to sound that instrument on the Day of Resurrection. In Islamic art he is often portrayed poised, ready to blow the trumpet on the Last Day at God's express command. Isrāfīl is not mentioned by name in the **Qur'ān** but there is much tradition about him. For example, the spirits of some of the dead who wait for the Resurrection inhabit the holes in the mighty trumpet of Isrāfīl. What is mentioned in the Qur'ān is the actual sounding of the trumpet at the end of time. (*See* **Angel**; **Archangel**; **Art and Architecture, Islamic**; **Ba'th**; **Yawm al-Qiyāma**.)

Istanbul Former capital of the Ottoman empire and still a major city in modern Turkey. Constantinople was captured by the **Ottomans** (q.v.) from the Byzantines in 857/1453, renamed Istanbul, and replaced **Bursa** (q.v.) and the later Edirne (Adrianople) as the Ottoman capital. The capture inaugurated a great golden age of Turkish Islamic art and architecture under such architects as **Sinān** (q.v.). Today Istanbul is still a treasure house of Islamic architecture with monuments ranging from the Topkapi Palace, and the converted Hagia Sophia of Justinian (into a mosque), to the magnificent Süleymāniye Mosque and the Blue Mosque with its six tall minarets. (*See* **Art and Architecture, Islamic**; **Mehmet II 'The Conqueror'**; **Süleymān 'The Magnificent'**.)

Istawā (Ar.) Literally, this Arabic verb means 'to be straight', 'to stand erect', 'to sit down', 'to mount', and even 'to be properly cooked'. However, its sense and translation, where it appears in the **Qur'ān** in such Arabic phrases as *Istawā 'alā 'l-'arsh* (*see* v.54 of **Sūrat al-A'rāf** (q.v.)) has given rise to considerable problems from mediaeval times onwards, because of the debate about anthropomorphism and the attributes of God. Some theologians believed that to translate the above-cited Qur'ānic phrase as 'He *sat* on the throne' was to endow God with human attributes and was therefore inadmissable as a translation. (*See* **Aḥmad b. Ḥanbal**; **'Arsh**; **al-Ash'arī**; **Bilā Kayf**; **Ṣifāt Allāh**; **Tashbīh**; **Ta'ṭīl**.)

Istiḥsān (Ar.) Legal discretion, preference. This was a source of law additional to the usual quartet of **Qur'ān**, **Sunna** (q.v.), **Ijmā'** (q.v.) and **Qiyās** (q.v.), particularly liked by the **Ḥanafīs** (q.v.). The term *istiḥsān* came to be opposed to *qiyās* though it was considered as a 'hidden *qiyās*' by the Ḥanafīs. However, the principle of *istiḥsān* was never accepted by the great scholar jurist **al-Shāfi'ī** (q.v.). (*See* **Istiṣḥāb**; **Istiṣlāḥ**.)

Istiṣḥāb (Ar.) Literally, 'seeking a companion or link'. In Islamic law this word has a special technical sense of 'maintenance of the *status quo*'. In other words, the law presumes a past situation or state to continue until the opposite is shown. Subjects dealt with under *istiṣḥāb* include the status of missing persons, their rights of inheritance and those of others etc. This subordinate principle of law is particularly liked by the **Shāfi'īs** (q.v.). (*See* **Istiḥsān**; **Istiṣlāḥ**.)

Istiṣlāḥ (Ar.) Taking into account the public good. This was a supplementary principle of Islamic law particularly liked by the **Mālikīs** (q.v.). The principle is narrower in scope than **istiḥsān** (q.v.). Since *istiṣlāḥ* in theory and effect seeks to discover the *maṣlaḥa* (which may be translated here as 'public welfare') it is not surprising that the practice of *istiṣlāḥ* has not been confined to the Mālikīs. (*See* **Istiṣḥāb**.)

Ithnā 'Asharīs (Ithnā 'Ashariyya) Twelvers. Their name derives from the Arabic word for 'twelve'. These make up the majority branch of **Shī'ites** (q.v.) and they are called 'Twelvers' because they acknowledge twelve principal Imāms after the death of the Prophet **Muḥammad**. The Twelfth Shī'ite Imām, **Muḥammad al-Qā'im** (q.v.), disappeared and his return is awaited by Twelver Shī'ites. The latter differ from **Sunnīs** (q.v.) over a variety of issues, notably the question of who should have succeeded Muḥammad – **'Alī b. Abī Ṭālib** (q.v.) in Shī'ite belief – but also on a number of legal points including marriage and inheritance. (Twelvers permit the concept of **mut'a** (q.v.) or temporary marriage.) Today the country with the largest number of Twelver Shī'ites is Iran (most of the population) but Southern Iraq also has substantial numbers constituting in total perhaps as many as 50% of the total Iraqi population. (*See* **Amal**; **Āyatullāh**; **Ghadir al-Khumm**; **Ghayba**; **al-Ḥasan b. 'Alī**; **Ḥizb Allāh**; **Ḥujjat 'l-Islām**; **al-Ḥusayn b. 'Alī**; **Imām**; **al-Muḥurram**; **Mujtahid**; **Ṣiffīn, Battle of**; **Ta'ziya**.)

Īwān (Ar.) or **Līwān** (Ar.) Arched hall. Originally this word indicated a recessed reception room, having a raised floor, abutting a courtyard. In Islamic architecture the term is more frequently used to designate the vaulted areas round the central yard of a mosque or **madrasa** (q.v.). This vault was usually open only on one side and possessed an arch on that side which was called the *īwān* arch, a feature having much in common with the Gothic window or arch in Western architecture. (*See* **Art and Architecture, Islamic**; **Masjid**.)

'Izrā'īl (Ar.) Azrael. He is the principal Islamic angel of death with a reputation in tradition for toughness and ruthlessness. He is mentioned in the **Qur'ān** but as 'The Angel of Death' (*Malak al-Mawt*) rather than by name (*see* v.11 of **Sūrat al-Sajda** (q.v.)). We depend on the tradition literature for our information about him. He is of gigantic size and has a roll with the names of all mankind inscribed upon it. He does not know, however, when each person will die. An individual's death is signalled by a leaf falling from the tree beneath God's throne on which the fated person's name appears. It is then 'Izrā'īl's task to separate that person's soul from his or her body. 'Izrā'īl has been called Azrael in Western literature. (*See* **Angel**; **Archangel**.)

Jabr (Ar.) Compulsion, predestination, fate, determinism, determination. This was a word of considerable theological significance in the debates of mediaeval Islam. (*See* **Jahm b. Ṣafwān**; **Qadar**.)

Jacob *See* **Ya'qūb**.

Ja'far al-Ṣādiq (80/669-700 or 83/702-3 or 86/705–died 148/765) The Sixth Shī'ite Imām, and the last to be commonly recognized and revered by *both* **Ismā'īlīs** (q.v.) and **Ithnā 'Asharīs** (q.v.). He was born, lived and taught in **Medina** (q.v.) and was buried there when he died. He was a notable scholar of **ḥadīth** (q.v.) and in his own life gained a massive reputation for his knowledge and holiness. His life and death marked a major split in the Shī'ite community. It is reported that he was offered the caliphate by the **'Abbāsids** (q.v.) at the time of the 'Abbāsid Revolution which overthrew the **Umayyads** (q.v.), but he refused it. (*See* **Imām**; **Ismā'īl** (2); **Mūsā al-Kāẓim**.)

Jahān, Shāh *See* **Shāh Jahān**.

Jahāngīr (977/1569–1037/1627) Mughal emperor who ruled in India from 1013/1605 until his death. He was a son of **Akbar** (q.v.). Jahāngīr was the object of a number of rebellions and revolts and during his rule relations considerably worsened between the Sikhs and Indian Muslims as a result of Jahāngīr's execution of a major Sikh guru for supporting the emperor's rebellious son. Jahāngīr's wife, the Shī'ite Nūr Jahān, wielded much power behind the throne. Jahāngīr himself was a mixture of alcoholic and opium addict on the one hand, and scholarly patron of letters on the other. From the point of view of Islamic arts, he is of particular interest for the development of the Mughal garden. (*See* **Shāh Jahān**.)

Jahannam (Ar.) Gehenna. This is one of the seven ranks of Hell. The word has connotations in Arabic of 'depth' and is very commonly used in the **Qur'ān** to designate Hell, appearing 77 times. Tradition consigned unrepentant wicked Muslims to this layer of Hell to suffer for a while until their eventual transfer to Paradise. When no longer needed Jahannam will be obliterated. (*See* **Hell**; **al-Janna**; **al-Nār**.)

Jāhiliyya (Ar.) State of ignorance. The Arabic word is used to designate the pre-Islamic period.

al-Jaḥīm (Ar.) One of the seven ranks of Hell. The word appears 25 times in the **Qur'ān** and is the region of Hell to which tradition consigns idolaters. (*See* **Hell**; **al-Nār**; **Ṣirāṭ al-Jaḥīm**; **Sūrat al-Ḥāqqa**; **Sụrat al-Infiṭār**.)

al-Jāḥiẓ, Abū 'Uthmān 'Amr b. Baḥr (*c.* 160/776–255/868-9) One of the most distinguished and prolific mediaeval Arabic writers and, in particular, a major exponent of the **adab** (q.v.) genre. From an Islamic religious point of view, al-Jāḥiẓ is of special interest because of his Mu'tazilī writings and interests. He was called *al-Jāḥiẓ*, meaning 'the Goggle-eyed', because of an eye defect. (*See* **Mu'tazila**.)

Jahm b. Ṣafwān (executed 128/745-6) Early theologian who exercised much influence on the development of the **Mu'tazila** (q.v.). He denied the eternity of Hell and Paradise and believed that the attributes of God mentioned in the **Qur'ān** were to be subjected to allegorical interpretation. The early Jahmiyya sect, which championed **jabr** (q.v.) and belief in a created Qur'ān, was called after him. (*See* **al-Janna**; **al-Nār**; **Ṣifāt Allāh**; **Ta'ṭīl**; **Ta'wīl**.)

Jalāl al-Dīn Rūmī *See* **Rūmī, Jalāl al-Dīn**.

Jamā'at-i Islāmī (Ur.) 20th century Muslim revivalist and fundamentalist movement and party which had a particular impact in Pakistan, founded by Mawdūdī in 1360/1941. The aim of the Jamā'at in Pakistan was to implement a religious Islamic revival and to change Pakistan into what Mawdūdī termed in his book *Islamic Law and Constitution* 'a theo-democracy'.

Jāmi' *See* **Masjid**.

al-Jamra (Ar.) [pl. *jimār*] Literally, 'the pebble'. Three stopping places in the Valley of **Minā** (q.v.), each called a *jamra*, are visited by returning pilgrims from **'Arafa** (q.v.) during the Pilgrimage, the **Ḥajj** (q.v.). Each *jamra*, which has a different name from its fellows, contains a stone column with a surrounding trough to receive all the stones thrown by the pilgrims. The stones are thrown in emulation of **Ibrāhīm** (q.v.), **Ismā'īl** (q.v.) and Hājar who were each tempted by **Iblīs** (q.v.) to disobey God's command to sacrifice Ismā'īl. Each drove Iblīs off with stones. Variants of this tradition show just one of the above three protagonists doing all the stone throwing. The ritual lapidation at Minā is a compulsory part of the pilgrimage.

al-Janna (Ar.) Literally, 'The Garden'. This is the most common name by which Paradise is referred to in the **Qur'ān**. Though Paradise, like Hell, is described in the Qur'ān in very physical terms, some have preferred to interpret these descriptions allegorically or metaphorically. A well-known **ḥadīth** (q.v.) espoused by Rashīd **Riḍā** (q.v.) in modern times holds that Paradise may best be characterized as a state which has not been seen by the human eye nor heard by the human ear. Other words, apart from *al-Janna*, used in the Qur'ān for Paradise, include *'Adn* (Eden) and the Persian term *Firdaws*. Basing themselves upon the Qur'ān, later traditions identified seven Heavenly gardens, which contrasts neatly with the seven Qur'ānic divisions of **Hell** (q.v.). The Qur'ān specifically promises Paradise to those who do good, avoid evil, exhibit true repentance and believe in the Qur'ān. (*See* **Ḥawḍ**; **Kāfūr**; **al-Kawthar**; **al-Nār**; **Salsabīl**; **Sidrat al-Muntahā**; **Tasnīm**.)

Jarḥ wa Ta'dīl (Ar.) 'Rubbishing and declaring reliable': technical term used in **ḥadīth** (q.v.) criticism with regard to the transmission of traditions.

al-Jāthiyya (Ar.) The title of the 45th **sūra** of the **Qur'ān**; it means literally 'The Kneeling'. The *sūra* belongs to the Meccan period and has 37 verses. Its title is drawn from v.28 which refers to every nation kneeling. The *sūra* begins with two of the **Mysterious Letters of the Qur'ān** (q.v.) and reiterates a number of the ways in which God has provided for man. Then, by contrast, the pains of **Jahannam** (q.v.) are threatened for those who reject God's signs and blessings. Reference is made to God who has sovereignty over the Heavens and the earth and who will assemble all mankind on the Day of Resurrection. The *sūra* ends with a hymn of praise to God. (*See* **Yawm al-Qiyāma**.)

Jawhar (Ar.) [pl. *jawāhir*] Technical term in Islamic philosophy meaning 'substance'. It derives from Aristotelian metaphysical terminology and is an Arabic translation of the Greek word *ousía*. However, as distinct from Aristotle, several of the great Islamic philosophers like **al-Kindī** (q.v.) and **Ibn Sīnā** (q.v.) believed that God should not be described by the term 'substance'. In this respect both shared the view of the Neoplatonist philosopher and founder of Neoplatonism, Plotinus (AD 204-5–AD 270). (*See* **'Araḍ**; **Aristotelianism, Islamic**; **Falsafa**; **Neoplatonism, Islamic**)

Jeddah *See under* **Ḥawwā'**,

Jerusalem In Arabic this major city is called *al-Quds*, a word which means 'The Holy'. Jerusalem is revered as the third holiest city in Islam, after **Mecca** (q.v.) and **Medina** (q.v.) since it is the site from which the Prophet **Muḥammad** made his famous **Mi'rāj** (q.v.) through the Seven Heavens. The city was conquered for Islam by the army of **'Umar b. al-Khaṭṭāb** (q.v.) in 17/638. Later it was captured by the Crusading armies in 492/1099 but retaken by the Muslim general **Ṣalāḥ al-Dīn** (q.v.) in 583/1187. From early in the 10th/16th century Jerusalem was ruled by the **Ottomans** (q.v.) but it became the capital of the British Mandate of Palestine after the First World War. Jerusalem is currently part of the State of Israel (established in 1367/1948). The status of Jerusalem is one of the most sensitive issues in the Muslim world today. (*See* **al-Aqṣā, al-Masjid**; **Crusades**; **al-Ḥaram al-Sharīf**; **al-Ḥaramān**; **Isrā'**; **Qubbat al-Ṣakhra**.)

Jesus *See* **'Īsā**.

Jibrīl (Ar.) The angel Gabriel. He is one of the greatest of all the Islamic angels since he was the channel through which the Holy **Qur'ān** was revealed from God to the Prophet **Muḥammad**. He is mentioned by name three times in the Qur'ān (*see* vv.97, 98 of **Sūrat al-Baqara** (q.v.) and v.4 of **Sūrat al-Taḥrīm**) and elsewhere referred to by names like 'The Spirit'. Much tradition has accumulated in Islam round the figure of Gabriel: for example, he showed **Nūḥ** (q.v.) how to build the ark and lured Pharaoh's army into the Red Sea. He pleaded with God for, and tried to rescue, **Ibrāhīm** (q.v.) when the latter was on the point of being burned to death by **Namrūd** (q.v.), (*see* vv.68–70 of **Sūrat al-Anbiyā'** and vv.97–98 of **Sūrat al-Ṣāffāt**). (*See also* **Angel**; **Archangel**; **Fir'awn**; **Ḥirā', Mount**.)

Jihād (Ar.) Holy war. The word derives from an Arabic root meaning basically 'to strive'. Jihād is sometimes considered by some groups to be a sixth pillar of Islam, for example by the **Khārijites** (q.v.) and the **Ibāḍīs** (q.v.). Of course, all Muslims are obliged to wage a spiritual jihād in the sense of striving against sin and sinful inclinations within themselves: this is the other major sense of jihād. It is interesting, albeit ultimately superficial, to compare the concept of jihād with that which underpinned the **Crusades** (q.v.). (*See* **Arkān**.)

al-Jīlānī, 'Abd al-Qādir (470/1077-8–561/1166) Notable Ḥanbalī preacher and ascetic after whom the famous **ṭarīqa** (q.v.) of the **Qādiriyya** (q.v.) was later named. He spent large parts of his life in **Baghdād** (q.v.) where he is buried. His tomb, because of his great reputation for sanctity, has been much visited over the centuries. (*See* **Ḥanbalīs**.)

Jināḥ, Muḥammad 'Alī (*c.* 1293/1876–1367/1948) His name is more commonly spelled Jinnah. He was the founder of Pakistan where he is called 'Greatest Leader' (*Qā'id A'ẓam*). He trained as a lawyer in England and practised in Bombay. Later he became a member of the Imperial Legislative Council but resigned after nine years. He won presidency of the **Muslim League** (q.v.) which championed the cause of a Muslim state separate from India. Jināḥ became the first Governor General of an independent Pakistan (in 1366/1947), and President of that country's Constituent Assembly.

Jinn (Ar.) [sing. *jinnī*] Intelligent, often invisible, beings made from flame (by contrast with the angels, made from light, and mankind, made from clay). The jinn also have the ability to assume various kinds of perceptible forms. They are mentioned in the **Qur'ān** and, like man, some will be saved and go to Paradise since there are good as well as bad jinn, and jinn who help men as well as those who hinder and harm as they meddle in the lives of men. The mission of the Prophet **Muḥammad** was both to mankind and to the jinn. **Iblīs** (q.v.) is described in the Qur'ān as both one of the jinn and an angel. A huge amount of folklore and tradition has grown up about the jinn in the Near and Middle East. (*See* **Angel**; **al-Janna**; **Sūrat al-Jinn**; **al-Ṭā'if**.)

al-Jinn (Ar.) The title of the 72nd **sūra** of the **Qur'ān**; it means 'The Jinn'. The *sūra* belongs to the Meccan period and has 28 verses. Its title is drawn from the references to the jinn in the first eight verses, which describe the jinn listening to the Qur'ān and accepting its message. Stress is placed on the principal mission of **Muḥammad**: whoever disobeys either the Prophet or God will burn in the fire of **Jahannam** (q.v.) forever.

Jinnah *See* **Jināḥ**.

Jizya (Ar.) Poll tax imposed in mediaeval times on non-Muslims who were **Ahl al-Kitāb** (q.v.) in areas ruled by Muslims. However, the subject of taxation in early Islam is an immensely complicated one and it is worth noting that the terms *jizya* and land tax (**kharāj** (q.v.)) were sometimes used in a variety of non-specific senses, indicating simply a general tax. **Sūrat al-Tawba** (q.v.) in v.29 sanctions the payment of *jizya* by the *Ahl al-Kitāb*.

Job *See* **Ayyūb**.

John *See* **Yaḥyā**.

Jonah *See* **Yūnus**.

Joseph *See* **Yūsuf**; **Sūrat Yūsuf**.

Judge *See* **Qāḍī**.

Judgement *See* **al-Ḥisāb**; **Yawm al-Qiyāma**.

al-Jum'a (Ar.) The title of the 62nd **sūra** of the **Qur'ān**; it means 'Friday'. The *sūra* belongs to the Medinan period and has 11 verses. The title of the *sūra* is drawn from v.9 which counsels the believers, when they hear the call to prayer on Friday (*Yawm al-Jum'a*) to hurry to 'the remembrance of God' and to cease trading. (*See* **Adhān**.)

Jundaysābūr *See* **Gondēs͟hāpūr**.

Jurisprudence *See* **Fiqh**.

al-Juwaynī, ʻAbd al-Malik (419/1028–478/1085) Persian theologian of Ashʻarite persuasion who instructed among others **al-Ghazālī** (q.v.). Because al-Juwaynī taught in both **Mecca** (q.v.) and **Medina** (q.v.) over the space of four years he gained the title 'Imām of the Two Sanctuaries' (*Imām al-Ḥaramayn*). He is to be distinguished from the 7th/13th century Persian historian 'Alā' al-Dīn 'Aṭā-Malik al-Juwaynī. (*See* **al-Ashʻarī**; **al-Ḥaramān**.)

Juwayriyya A wife of the Prophet **Muḥammad**.

Kaʻba (Ar.) Literally, 'cube'. The **Kaʻba**, which is in **Mecca** (q.v.) is a cube-shaped building within the precincts of the Great Mosque of Mecca. It is covered by the **kiswa** (q.v.). **Ibrāhīm** (q.v.) and **Ismāʻīl** (q.v.) are revered as re-builders of the **Kaʻba** originally established by **Ādam** (q.v.). After the conquest of Mecca by the Prophet **Muḥammad**, the idols which had been placed in the *Kaʻba* during the period of the **Jāhiliyya** (q.v.) were removed. Muslims all over the world direct their prayers five times a day towards the *Kaʻba* in Mecca, and it also constitutes a primary focal point during the **Ḥajj** (q.v.). However, it is most important to note here that Muslims do not *worship* the *Kaʻba*, nor the **Ḥajar al-Aswad** (q.v.) set within one of its corners. The *Kaʻba* is an ancient sanctuary whose presence is designed to raise man's heart and worship to *God*. (*See* **Hubal**; **Qarāmiṭa**; **Qibla**; **Ṣalāt**; **Ṭawāf**.)

Kāfir (Ar.) [pl. *kāfirūn*] Infidel, unbeliever, atheist.

al-Kāfirūn (Ar.) The title of the 109th **sūra** of the **Qur'ān**; it means 'The Infidels'. The *sūra* belongs to the Meccan period and has 6 verses. Its title derives from the 1st verse which reads 'Say, oh infidels'. The *sūra* encapsulates the belief that religions should be freely chosen and held, and stresses the unswerving allegiance of the Prophet **Muḥammad** to the worship of the One true God. (*See* **Compulsion**).

Kāfūr (Ar.) Camphor. A cup of *Kāfūr*, sometimes identified by tradition as a river in Paradise, will be drunk by the pious (*see* v.5 of **Sūrat al-Insān** (q.v.) in the **Qur'ān**). However, the Qur'ān itself, in v.6 of this *sūra*, describes *Kāfūr* as a fountain or spring (*'ayn*[an]). (*See* **al-Janna**; **al-Kawthar** (2); **Salsabīl**; **Tasnīm**.)

al-Kahf (Ar.) The title of the 18th **sūra** of the **Qur'ān**; it means 'The Cave'. The *sūra* belongs mainly to the Meccan period but contains some Medinan verses. In all there are 110 verses. The title of the *sūra* is drawn from a major piece of Qur'ānic narrative which occupies vv.9–26 and gives the story of 'the Companions of the Cave' (**Aṣḥāb al-Kahf** (q.v.)). According to this, a number of young men seek refuge in a cave, fleeing religious persecution. They fall asleep and awake after a considerable period of time has elapsed. The story has parallels in the Christian tradition with the Seven Sleepers of Ephesus. Another major piece of narrative, this time with a particularly mystical orientation, occupies vv.60–82. This is the story of the testing of **Mūsā** (q.v.) by one of God's Servants who is endowed with great knowledge. The Servant is not named in the Qur'ān but is usually identified with **al-Khaḍir** (q.v.) (al-Khiḍr). Other major figures mentioned in this *sūra*, which is one of the most vivid in the entire Qur'ān, include **Ādam** (q.v.), **Iblīs** (q.v.), **Dhū 'l-Qarnayn** (q.v.), and **Gog and Magog** (q.v.). It is also in this *sūra* that Muslims are instructed to use the phrase **In shā'a Allāh** (q.v.).

Kairouan *See* **Qayrawān**.

Kalām (Ar.) Literally, 'speech'. However, the word also had the more technical sense in mediaeval Islam of '(scholastic) theology', especially within the phrase *'Ilm al-Kalām* which may be rendered in English as 'The Science of (Scholastic) Theology'. Included under the general heading of *kalām* may be placed many of the great debates of Islamic theology, provoked by the **Mu'tazila** (q.v.) and others, which dealt with such subjects as **tashbīh** (q.v.), **Ṣifāt Allāh** (q.v.) and **jabr** (q.v.).

Karbalā'(Ar.) Central Iraqi city with a domed tomb-shrine containing the body of **al-Ḥusayn b. 'Alī** (q.v.). This is one of the holiest of all the shrines of the **Ithnā 'Asharīs** (q.v.). (*See* **Cairo**; **Karbalā', Battle of**; **al-Najaf**.)

Karbalā', Battle of Very famous early battle fought in an area South West of **Baghdād** (q.v.) between the tiny army of supporters of **al-Ḥusayn b. 'Alī** (q.v.) and the overwhelming forces of the **Umayyads** (q.v.) commanded by 'Umar b. Sa'd, in 61/680. Al-Ḥusayn and his few companions were defeated and massacred. The circumstances of the night before the battle, and the battle itself, have become invested with much legend. The battle took place on the tenth day of the Muslim month of **al-Muḥarram** (q.v.) and this day each year is held to be particularly sacred, especially by **Shī'ites** (q.v.). (*See* **'Āshūrā'**; **Ta'ziya**.)

Kasb (Ar.) or **Iktisāb** (Ar.) Mediaeval theological doctrine of 'acquisition', often associated with, but probably not invented by, **al-Ash'arī** (q.v.). According to this doctrine God creates any action but man 'acquires' it. This was a valiant attempt by mediaeval Islamic theologians to solve an age-old problem: how did one reconcile, on the one hand, God's total omnipotence and omniscience with, on the other, man's free will and responsibility for his own actions? (*See* **Ḍirār b. 'Amr**; **Mu'tazila**; **Qadar**; **Qadariyya**; **Taqdīr**.)

al-Kawthar (1) (Ar.) The title of the 108th **sūra** of the **Qur'ān**; it means literally 'The Abundant'. The *sūra* belongs to the Meccan period and has 3 verses. Its title is drawn from the 1st verse in which God states that He has given man *al-Kawthar*. The remaining two verses urge man to pray to God and offer sacrifice. The man who hates the Prophet **Muḥammad** will remain without offspring. (*See* **al-Kawthar** (2).)

al-Kawthar (2) (Ar.) Literally, 'The Abundant'. This is the name of a river in Paradise, identified by many commentators with *al-Kawthar* in **Sūrat al-Kawthar** (see above). The **Qur'ān** does not actually specify that *al-Kawthar* is a *river*. (*See* **al-Janna**; **Kāfūr**; **Salsabīl**; **Tasnīm**.)

Kāẓimayn (Ar.) Literally, 'the two Kāẓims'. Kāẓimayn is a site in **Baghdād** (q.v.) containing a splendid shrine over the tombs of **Mūsā al-Kāẓim** (q.v.) and **Muḥammad al-Taqī** (q.v.). The shrine, which goes back to the **Būyids** (q.v.), was built in its present form by the **Ṣafavids** (q.v.) and redecorated by the **Qajars** (q.v.) among others. The suburb is known as Kāẓimiyya.

Kerbala *See* **Karbalā'**.

Khadīja bint Khuwaylid (*c.* AD 554–AD 619) First wife of the Prophet **Muḥammad** and also revered as the first Muslim after him. She was a member of the tribe of **Quraysh** (q.v.) via **'Abd al-'Uzzā** (q.v.) and **Asad** (q.v.). A widow with considerable wealth, for whom Muḥammad had originally worked, she married the Prophet when she was aged 40 and he aged 25. While she remained alive, the Prophet did not take any other wives. Khadīja bore the Prophet six children: two boys, **'Abd Allāh** (q.v.) and **al-Qāsim** (q.v.), both of whom died very young, and four girls, **Fāṭima** (q.v.), **Ruqayya** (q.v.), **Umm Kulthūm** (q.v.) and **Zaynab** (q.v.). Khadīja was buried in **Mecca** (q.v.). (*See* **Waraqa b. Nawfal**.)

al-Khaḍir or **al-Khiḍr** (Ar.) Mystical Islamic figure whose name derives from an Arabic root meaning 'green'. A huge amount of information is available on this figure in the **Tafsīr** (q.v.), **Ḥadīth** (q.v.) and historical literature of Islam. What might be described as the key primal text concerning al-Khaḍir occurs in **Sūrat al-Kahf** (q.v.). Here he appears, unnamed, as the mystic sage or **pīr** (q.v.) *par excellence*, familiar with God's ways and competent to test others, like **Mūsā** (q.v.), about those ways. The moral of this text here in the **Qur'ān** is clearly that

God's ways are not man's ways, and the actions of the former, imbued with prescient and universal knowledge, only *seem* bizarre. Al-Khaḍir appears to have a foot in both the human and celestial spheres and he ranks as a saint in popular and **ṣūfī** (q.v.) circles alike. (*See* **Walī**.)

Khālid b. al-Walīd (died 21/641) Belonged to the clan of **Makhzūm** (q.v.) in the tribe of **Quraysh** (q.v.). Having fought against the Prophet **Muḥammad** at the Battle of Uḥud, he later converted to Islam and became one of its noted generals receiving the title 'Sword of God' (*Sayf Allāh*) from Muḥammad himself. Khālid fought at the Battles of 'Aqrabā', Ajnādayn, and Yarmūk among others. (*See* **Ajnādayn, Battle of**; **'Aqrabā', Battle of**; **Uḥud, Battle of**; **Yarmūk, Battle of**)

Khalīfa (Ar.) [pl. *khulafā'*] Caliph, Head of the Islamic Community. The Arabic word in early Islamic history meant literally 'successor' or 'deputy' (i.e. of the Prophet **Muḥammad**). This technically elective office (in **Sunnī** (q.v.) Islam) combined *in theory* a spiritual and secular function, though *in practice*, under such dynasties as the **Umayyads** (q.v.), it was the latter function which was generally prominent at the expense of the former. Sunnī theorists such as **al-Māwardī** (q.v.) later developed a complex theory of the caliphate. A variety of dynastic leaders throughout Islamic history have claimed the title of caliph: it was used, for example, of **'Abd al-Ḥamīd II** (q.v.). In the early decades of the 14th/20th century unsuccessful attempts were made to revive the caliphate (*khilāfa*). From the point of view of usage in the **Qur'ān** it is of interest that both **Ādam** (q.v.) in **Sūrat al-Baqara** (q.v.) and **Dāwūd** (q.v.) in **Sūrat Ṣād** (q.v.) are given the title *khalīfa*. This word also has the more specialized **ṣūfī** (q.v.) sense indicating the leader in a ṣūfī procession, often on horseback. (*See* **Amīr al-Mu'minīn**; **Taṣawwuf**.)

al-Khalīl (Ar.) 'The Friend'. Ibrāhīm bears the title 'The Friend of God' (*Khalīl Allāh*). (*See* **Ibrāhīm** (1).)

Khalwa (Ar.) Literally, 'isolation', 'seclusion'. It has the technical sense in ṣūfism of a place or state of retreat, or a hermitage. (*See* **Taṣawwuf**.)

Khamr (Ar.) [pl. *khumūr*] Wine. The drinking of wine and spirits is prohibited by Islam. See v.219 of **Sūrat al-Baqara** (q.v.) and vv.90–91 of **Sūrat al-Mā'ida** (q.v.) in the **Qur'ān**. (*See* **Ḥadd**; **Khayyām**; **Nabīdh**.)

Khān, Sayyid Aḥmad (1232/1817–1316/1898) Modernist Indian educational reformer and Muslim religious and political thinker. He was the founder of the Muhammadan Anglo-Oriental College at **Aligarh** (q.v.). His theological ideas are encapsulated in his two books *The Exegesis of the Qur'ān* (*Tafsīr al-Qur'ān*) and *Freedom in the Sources of Exegesis* (*al-Taḥrīr fī Uṣūl al-Tafsīr*). Sir Sayyid Aḥmad Khān saw no contradiction between nature and scripture and he championed the historicity of the **Qur'ān** and the possibility of interpreting it in a rational way. With regard to such age-old problems as that of the attributes of God, he held that these were to be understood as being the same as God's Self. He detected a complete sociology within the confines of the Qur'ān. His view of the **ḥadīth** (q.v.) literature, however, was somewhat less respectful and he viewed the historicity of it with much suspicion. He refused to accept the **ijmā'** (q.v.) of the **'ulamā'** (q.v.) as a legal source. Not surprisingly, some of Sir Sayyid Aḥmad Khān's theological ideas were the object of vociferous opposition. (*See* **Mu'tazila**; **Ṣifāt Allāh**.)

Khānagāh (Pers.) [pl. *khānagāhā*]/**Khānqāh** (Ar.) [pl. *khawāniq*] **Ṣūfī** (q.v.) dwelling for board and instruction, often containing a mausoleum. During the era of the **Mamlūks** (q.v.), particularly in Egypt, there was a considerable proliferation of such buildings. It appears that the *khānagāh* was not necessarily tied to any particular **ṭarīqa** (q.v.). (*See* **Ribāṭ**; **Tekkē**; **Zāwiya**.)

al-Khandaq, Siege and Battle of The Arabic word means 'the Ditch' or 'the Trench'. After the Battles of Badr and Uḥud, al-Khandaq was the third major confrontation between **Muḥammad** in **Medina** (q.v.) and his enemies from **Mecca** (q.v.). To protect Medina from the encroaching Meccans in 5/627, Muḥammad, on the advice of **Salmān al-Fārisī** (q.v.), had a trench dug to the North of the oasis. The siege lasted about two weeks and, despite several assaults, the trench successfully guarded the oasis of Medina and the besiegers retired. The siege is of particular significance in that it consolidated Muḥammad's position and paved the way for the conquest of Mecca a few years later. (*See* **Sūrat al-Aḥzāb**.)

Kharāj (Ar.) Literally, 'yield' or 'produce'. In Islamic history the word came to bear the specific meaning of 'land tax'. However, see the remarks under **Jizya**. Like the latter it was imposed on non-Muslims but, unlike the *jizya*, it had no basis in the **Qur'ān**.

Khārijites Members of early Islamic sect, the origins of which are confused and obscure but which may be reconstructed as follows. The name of the group's members, in Arabic *Khawārij*, means 'those who seceded' (i.e. from supporting **'Alī b. Abī Ṭālib** (q.v.)); it derives from the Arabic verb 'to go out', 'to secede' (*kharaja*). The first notable secession was that of a group of 'Alī's soldiers at the Battle of Ṣiffīn who objected to any form of arbitration at the battle and protested that the judgement should be left to God alone, before leaving the main army. They were joined on a later occasion by other erstwhile supporters of 'Alī from **al-Kūfa** (q.v.) and it is this later incident which gave the Khārijites their name. Khārijism, whose beliefs were by no means uniform, divided into a number of sub-sects, some increasingly fanatical and exclusivist, teaching, for example, that grave sinners would go to Hell and that they thereby placed themselves outside the community; that non-Khārijites were **kāfirs** (q.v.) and could thus be killed; and that any upright believer, even a black slave, could become **Imām** (q.v.), whether or not he was descended from the **Quraysh** (q.v.). The modern descendants of the Khārijites today are the **Ibāḍīs** (q.v.). (*See* **Ṣiffīn, Battle of**)

Khātam al-Nabiyyīn (Ar.) The Seal of the Prophets. This title, borne by the Prophet **Muḥammad** derives from v.40 of **Sūrat al-Aḥzāb** (q.v.) in the **Qur'ān**.

Khatm al-Anbiyā' *See* **Khātam al-Nabiyyīn**.

Khawārij *See* **Khārijites**.

Khaybar, Battle of Khaybar was a wealthy Jewish oasis in the Northern Ḥijāz, attacked and successfully captured by **Muḥammad** in 7/628. Muḥammad believed that the people of Khaybar were fomenting discontent with Islam and its adherents. Some of the Jews of Khaybar had been exiled from **Medina** (q.v.). (*See* **al-Naḍīr**.)

Khayyām, 'Umar (Omar Khayyam) (*c.* 439/1048–died *c.* 519/1125-527/1132) Astronomer, mathematician, poet, and possible **ṣūfī** (q.v.), of Nishapur (Nayshābūr) in Iran. It was as a poet that he achieved his greatest fame, particularly in the West: a much translated series of quatrains (*rubā'iyyāt*) is attributed to him. There is a very real sense in which the 'great' Khayyām is a Western 'invention'. Some interpret the language of the *Rubā'iyyāt*, with their wine-filled and sceptical imagery, as the effusions of an irreligious hedonist. Others, however, see the references to wine as part of the symbolism of the ṣūfī. An attractive but unlikely legend portrays 'Umar Khayyām as a school-fellow of **Ḥasan-i Ṣabbāḥ** (q.v.) and the great **wazīr** (q.v.) Niẓām al-Mulk in Nishapur. (The latter was later assassinated by an assassin from **Alamūt** (q.v.)!).

al-Khazraj Major Arab tribe in **Medina** (q.v.), possibly originating in the Yemen, at the time of the **Hijra** (q.v.) of **Muḥammad**. (*See* **al-Aws**.)

al-Khiḍr *See* **al-Khaḍir**.

Khilāfa *See under* **Khalīfa**.

Khitān (Ar.) Circumcision. This is a widespread custom in Islam but it is not mentioned in the **Qur'ān**. Circumcision was probably practised in pre-Islamic Arabia and tradition teaches that the great prophet **Ibrāhīm** (q.v.) was circumcised when he reached his 80th year. The age today at which boys are circumcised varies from country to country. In Egypt, for example, the circumcision of boys can take place within a few hours or days of birth, but it may be delayed even several years if the mother wishes the circumcision of her son to be performed during a **mawlid** (q.v.) like that of **al-Badawī** (q.v.). Female circumcision is also practised in some areas of the Islamic world, particularly those influenced by African custom. The barbarity of female circumcision, more properly called *khafḍ* in Arabic, owes nothing to Islam.

Khojas The majority of Khojas in India and Pakistan are **Nizārīs** (q.v.) and the majority of these also acknowledge the leadership of the **Āghā Khān** (q.v.). Spiritually they are heirs of those who supported the claims of Nizār as Fāṭimid caliph in Egypt on the death of **al-Mustanṣir** (q.v.) in 487/1094. The word *khoja* derives from the Persian *khwāja* meaning 'lord' or 'master'. It originally indicated an Indian Islamic caste which had converted from Hinduism to Ismā'īlism in the 9th/15th century. There are large numbers of Khojas to be found in East Africa, Bombay and Gujarat. Apart from the Nizārī Khojas, there are also a few Sunnī and Ithnā 'Asharī Khojas: neither of the latter acknowledge the Āghā Khān as spiritual leader. (*See* **Bohorās**; **Fāṭimids**; **Ismā'īlīs**; **Ithnā 'Asharīs**; **Sunnī**.)

Khomeini, Ayatollah *See* **Khumaynī, Āyatullāh Rūḥullāh**.

Khuld (Ar.) Eternity, endless time, Paradise is sometimes called in Arabic *Dār al-Khuld*, meaning 'The House of Eternity'.

Khumaynī, Āyatullāh Rūḥullāh (*c.* 1320/1902–1409/1989) Spiritual head of Iran after the Revolution of 1398–9/1978–9, and leading proponent of the doctrine of 'Government by the jurist' (*Vilāyat-i faqīh* (Pers.)/*Wilāyat al-faqīh* (Ar.)). After years of exile in such places as Turkey, Iraq and France he returned to his native Iran in triumph after the overthrow of the Shāh and became the most powerful and significant figure of the Revolution. He stands as a landmark in modern Iranian history and was bitterly mourned by people of all classes when he died. (*See* **Āyatullāh**; **Imām**; **Ithnā 'Asharīs**; **Mujtahid**.)

Khuṭba (Ar.) [pl. *khuṭab*] Sermon, address; in particular the sermon delivered during the Friday prayer in the mosque. During the *khuṭba* blessings are invoked on the ruler and thus, in mediaeval times, in the absence of modern methods of communication like radio, TV and telephone, the *khuṭba* could serve to announce a change of **khalīfa** (q.v.) or even dynasty to the assembled congregation. (*See* **Ṣalāt**; **Yawm al-Jum'a**.)

Khuzā'a Arab tribe in the region of **Mecca** (q.v.). It was the retaliatory killing of some members of this tribe in 8/629 which precipitated the series of events leading up to the conquest of Mecca by **Muḥammad** in 8/630.

al-Kindī (died after 252/866) The 'Father of Islamic Philosophy' who paved the way for his successors like **al-Fārābī** (q.v.) and **Ibn Sīnā** (q.v.). During his lifetime his library was temporarily confiscated and he was beaten. This may have been the result of political intrigue or the Mu'tazilite strand in his thought and his association with Mu'tazilite rulers. There are, however, other strands in his thought, notably Qur'ānic and Aristotelian but also some Neoplatonic as well. Al-Kindī's major contribution to Islamic philosophy was to provide – and often, invent – a metaphysical terminology upon which his successors would build. He believed that philosophy and theology were compatible and he remained, at heart, a Qur'ānic Muslim, despite the accusations levelled at him in his own age. One of his most notable works, in what is an extensive corpus, is his *Epistle on First Philosophy* (*Fī 'l-Falsafa al-Ūlā*). (*See* **Aristotelianism, Islamic**; **Mu'tazilla**; **Neoplatonism, Islamic**)

Kirām al-Kātibīn (Ar.) Literally, 'the Noble Writers' or 'the Noble Scribes'. Attached to every person are a pair of Angels whose function it is to record that person's good and evil acts. These angels are referred to in vv.10–12 of **Sūrat al-Infiṭār** (q.v.) and vv.17–18 of **Sūrat Qāf** (q.v.) in the **Qur'ān**. They are regularly greeted during the prayer when the worshipper moves his head to the right and the left saying 'Peace be upon you' (*al-Salāmu 'alaykum*) on each occasion. (*See* **Angel**; **Ṣalāt**.)

al-Kirmānī, Ḥamīd al-Dīn Aḥmad b. 'Abd Allāh (died *c.* 412/1021) Major Fāṭimid Ismā'īlī missionary (*dā'ī*) and theologian who worked in the Iraq area for much of his life, as well as Iran. Because of this he was called *Ḥujjat al-'Irāqayn* meaning 'Proof of the Two Iraqs', i.e. Iraq and Iran). Al-Kirmānī's major theological work was his *The Repose of the Intellect* (*Rāḥat al-'Aql*). Like **al-Fārābī** (q.v.) al-Kirmānī held to a hierarchical Neoplatonic doctrine of ten intellects, each of which had its astral associations. (*See* **Fāṭimids**; **al-Ḥāmidī**; **Ismā'īlīs**; **Neoplatonism, Islamic**; **al-Sijistānī**.)

Kiswa (Ar.) Brocaded black cover of silk and cotton which adorns the **Ka'ba** (q.v.); it is changed once a year for a new one.

Knowledge *See* **'Ilm**.

Konya Known as Iconium in ancient times, Konya in Asia Minor became the capital of the **Saljūqs** (q.v.) of Rūm and later, a major city of the **Ottomans** (q.v.). The city boasts much fine Islamic architecture and also contains the tomb of **Rūmī** (q.v.). (*See* **Bursa**; **Istanbul**.)

Koran *See* **Qur'ān**.

al-Kūfa Major city of the Islamic Middle Ages in Iraq, ranking in importance with **al-Baṣra** (q.v.). The origins of the word 'Kūfa' are obscure. The city was founded in 17/638 and functioned as a military citadel, frequently being involved in the politics of the day. Like al-Baṣra, al-Kūfa was important for the development of Islamic and Arab culture as well. Theologically it is of interest in the way that it served as a host for Shī'ite belief and thought. One of the most important early episodes in the history of al-Kūfa was the pro-Shī'ite revolt of al-Mukhtār in 66-7/685-6. From the point of view of Islamic art it may be noted that al-Kūfa gave its name to Kūfic script, a monumental style used in both mosque decoration and the writing of early copies of the **Qur'ān**. It is regarded as the oldest style of writing in Arabic in the post-**Muḥammad** age. Modern Kūfa is a thriving agricultural city, full of date groves, through which the main branch of the River Euphrates runs. It is very near the sacred city of **al-Najaf** (q.v.). Kūfa still contains the Mosque of **'Alī b. Abī Ṭālib** (q.v.) where the latter was assassinated, and this is the focus of pious visits. (*See* **Ḥanafīs**; **Shī'ism**.)

Kūfic Script *See* **al-Kūfa**.

Kufr (Ar.) Infidelity, unbelief, atheism.

Kuttāb (Ar.) [pl. *katātīb*] Qur'ānic elementary school. (*See* **Qur'ān**; **Sabīl**.)

Lāhawr *See* **Lahore**.

Lahore (Lāhawr) Major city of the Pakistani Punjab. It has been ruled throughout its history by a variety of dynasties including the **Ghaznavids** (q.v.), the **Ghūrids** (q.v.), the Delhi Sultanate and the **Mughals** (q.v.). It was during the rule of the latter that many of its greatest Islamic and other monuments were erected. (*See* **Delhi**.)

Lā ilāha illā 'llāh (Ar.) The first part of the **shahāda** (q.v.): it means 'There is no god but God'.

Land Tax *See* **Kharāj**.

Las Navas de Tolosa, Battle of Battle fought near the present Spanish town of Santa Elena between the **Almohads** (q.v.) and Christian forces from Castile, Leon, Aragon and Navarre in 609/1212. The Christian army was commanded by Alfonso VIII of Castile while the Muslims were led by the 4th Almohad caliph Muḥammad al-Nāṣir. The result was a devastating defeat for the Almohads which signalled the beginning of the end as far as their real power in Spain was concerned. The battle is called *al-'Iqāb* by the Arabic sources. (*See* **al-Andalus**.)

Last Day, The *See* **Yawm al-Qiyāma**.

Last Judgement, The *See* **al-Ḥisāb**.

al-Lāt (Ar.) Literally, 'The Goddess'. Major pre-Islamic Arabian female deity, particularly revered by the tribe of **Thaqīf** (q.v.). (*See* **Manāt**; **al-'Uzzā**.)

Law *See* **Sharī'a**.

al-Lawḥ al-Maḥfūẓ (Ar.) The Preserved Tablet. This is a tablet in Heaven on which is to be found the original text of the **Qur'ān**. The Qur'ān itself specifically refers to the Tablet in the 22nd and last verse of **Sūrat al-Burūj** (q.v.). (*See* **al-Janna**.)

al-Layl (Ar.) The title of the 92nd **sūra** of the **Qur'ān**; it means 'The Night'. The *sūra* belongs to the Meccan period and has 21 verses. Its title is drawn from the reference to the night in the 1st verse. The *sūra* begins with three distinct formal oaths: By the night, by the day and by God himself, the Creator. It goes on to promise a happy end to the generous and pious man but the opposite to the miser. Riches will not help the latter when he dies. The *sūra* is particularly significant in its stressing the doctrine that it is good deeds *as well as* good faith which will bring a person to Paradise. (*See* **al-Janna**; **Sūrat al-'Aṣr**.)

Laylat al-Mi'rāj (Ar.) The Night of the Ascension (of the Prophet **Muḥammad**). A popular festival celebrates this event on the 27th of the Muslim month of Rajab. It is known in some Asian countries and communities as Shab-i Miraj. (*See* **Mi'rāj**.)

Laylat al-Qadr (Ar.) The Night of Power (or Decree) which is believed to be the night between the 26th and 27th of **Ramaḍān** (q.v.), or the 27th night. The Night has a very special significance in the Muslim calendar because it is the anniversary of that night when the **Qur'ān** was first revealed to the Prophet **Muḥammad**. In **Sūrat al-Qadr** (q.v.), this Night is described as 'better than 1000 months'. Tradition holds that requests made to God during *Laylat al-Qadr* will be granted.

Laẓā (Ar.) Literally, 'flame', 'blazing fire'. Laẓā is one of the seven ranks of Hell to which tradition later consigned the Christians. The word only occurs once in the **Qur'ān** in **Sūrat al-Ma'ārij** (q.v.). Here, in v.15, Laẓā is described as a great furnace which will burn off the sinner's scalp and swallow up the miser and those who turned their backs on the truth. (*See* **Hell**; **al-Nār**.)

Lepanto, Battle of Lepanto is situated on the Gulf of Corinth and called in Turkish Aynabakhti. It gave its name to the great sea-battle fought nearby between a Christian European alliance led by Don Juan of Austria, and an Ottoman Turkish fleet commanded by 'Alī Pasha, in 979/1571. Don Juan's success in the battle, in which he sank 200 ships, was immortalized in a famous poem entitled *Lepanto* by G. K. Chesterton (see below). The battle was of greater significance in raising morale in Europe (as the first major defeat of the **Ottomans** (q.v.) since the 9th/

15th century) than in terms of lasting concrete gains: Venice, whose island of Cyprus had been invaded in the previous year by the army of the Ottoman Sultan Selīm II, thus precipitating the European response, surrendered the island to the Ottomans in 980/1573. Although Chesterton's poem about the battle is a highly romanticized, exotic and 'orientalist' production, and contains lines that are erroneous or misleading about Islam, its *opening* lines are worth quoting for the sense which they convey of the sheer Ottoman power of the age. (The reference is clearly to the Ottoman Sultan Selīm II (*reg.* 974/1566–982/1574)):

> White founts falling in the courts of the sun,
> And the Soldan [Sultan] of Byzantium is smiling as they run;
> There is laughter like the fountains in that face of all men feared,
> It stirs the forest darkness, the darkness of his beard,
> It curls the blood-red crescent, the crescent of his lips,
> For the inmost sea of all the earth is shaken with his ships.

Perhaps the best-known of all those who fought at the Battle of Lepanto was the great Spanish writer Cervantes who was wounded in the left hand and chest. (*See* **Sulṭān**.)

Lifespan *See* **Ajal**.

Light *See* **Sūrat al-Nūr**.

Light Verse *See* **Sūrat al Nūr**.

Litany *See* **Dhikr**; **Ḥizb**; **Wird**.

Līwān *See* **Īwān**.

Lot *See* **Lūṭ**.

Lote Tree, Lotus Tree *See* **Sidrat al-Muntahā**.

Luqmān (1) Wise man known to the Arabs in the **Jāhiliyya** (q.v.) whose wisdom is vaunted in early Arabic poetry. In the

Qur'ān an entire **sūra** is named after him (see below). Here he is celebrated as a figure who believes in one God, and the provider of good advice to his son. Luqmān is not mentioned in any other part of the Qur'ān. He appears as a sage in many works of Arabic literature and much legend has accumulated round him. He has often been identified with - or likened to - Aesop.

Luqmān (2) Luqmān: the title of the 31st **sūra** of the **Qur'ān**; Luqmān is a proper name sometimes likened to, or even identified with, the Greek Aesop. The *sūra* belongs to the Meccan period and contains 34 verses. Its title is drawn from vv.12 ff which portray Luqmān being granted wisdom (*al-ḥikma*) by God and then counselling his son to remain a monotheist and giving other good advice. In v.17, for example, he exhorts his son to observe the prayer ritual and to command the good and forbid evil. Apart from the references to Luqmān, there are some other interesting elements in the *sūra* as well. It begins with three of the **Mysterious Letters of the Qur'ān** (q.v.) and goes on to announce that the verses which follow are from the Wise Book. God's power is apparent in the creation of the pillarless Heavens and His provision of life-giving water to the earth. His words are infinite and could not be encompassed or exhausted even if all the trees on earth became pens dipped in seven seas (of ink). (*See* **al-Amr bi 'l-Ma'rūf**; **Luqmān** (1).)

Lūṭ (Ar.) Lot. One of the messengers, whose story is recorded in several *sūras* of the **Qur'ān**, who is sent by God to warn his people; their crimes include sodomy. His people's city is destroyed but Lūṭ and nearly all his family are saved: only Lūṭ's wife, who lingers, is destroyed.

al-Ma'ād (Ar.) The Hereafter, a synonym of **al-Ākhira** (q.v.). The word *al-Ma'ād* also encompasses all the things which will happen on the Day of resurrection. (*See* **Yawm al-Qiyāma**.)

al-Ma'ārij (Ar.) The title of the 70th **sūra** of the **Qur'ān**; it means 'The Ascents' or 'The Stairs'. The *sūra* belongs to the

Meccan period and has 44 verses. Its title reflects v.3 where God is described as 'The Lord of the Ascents' (*Thī 'l-Ma'ārij*). The majesty of God is vividly and beautifully emphasized at the beginning of the *sūra* with a reference to the angels ascending to God in a day whose measure is deemed to be 'fifty thousand years'. The terrors of the Day of Judgement are described. The wicked will go to Hell while the trustworthy and pious will be honoured in Paradise. (*See* **al-Ḥisāb**; **al-Janna**; **Laẓā**; **al-Nār**; **Yawm al-Qiyāma**.)

al-Ma'arrī, Abū 'l-'Alā' (363/973–449/1057) A Syrian who was one of the greatest poets and writers of mediaeval Arabic literature. He did not allow his blindness to inhibit a prolific and brilliant output. Al-Ma'arrī's religious scepticism aroused suspicions. One of his most interesting pieces of writing is his *Epistle of Pardon* (*Risālat al-Ghufrān*) in which he portrays a Danteesque visit to Heaven with many of the great heathen poets of the past forgiven and at peace in Paradise. (*See* **al-Janna**; **al-Nār**.)

Madhāhib (Ar.) Schools of law; plural of the Arabic word **madhhab** (q.v.).

Madhhab (Ar.) [pl. *madhāhib*] This Arabic word has a range of meanings including 'ideology', 'doctrine', 'creed', and 'movement'. In **fiqh** (q.v.) it indicates one of the four major Schools of law. The reader is referred to the following headings in this *Dictionary*: **Ḥanafīs**; **Ḥanbalīs**; **Mālikīs**; and **Shāfi'īs**. In addition to these **Sunnī** (q.v.) Schools it must also be noted here that there are a number of Shī'ite Schools of law. (*See* **Shī'ism**.)

al-Madīna *See* **Medina**.

Madrasa (Ar.) [pl. *madāris*] School, college, place of education, often linked to, or associated with, a mosque. The *madrasa* was a primary focus for the study of the Islamic sciences. (*See* **al-Azhar**; **Īwān**; **Masjid**; **al-Zaytūna**.)

Madyan Early and mediaeval Madyan Shu'ayb was the name of a North Western Arabian *town*: as such it was mentioned by the Islamic geographers. Archaeologists in modern times claim to have identified the ruins of the mediaeval town. However, the **Qur'ān** seems to refer to Madyan mainly as a *people*; most notably they are a people who receive divine punishment because they reject the message of the prophet who has been sent to them, **Shu'ayb** (q.v.). (*See* **Sūrat al-A'rāf**; **Sūrat Hūd**.)

Maghāzī (Ar.) [sing. *maghzāt*] Raids, military campaigns, expeditions, especially those undertaken by the Prophet **Muḥammad**. (*See* **al-Wāqidī**.)

al-Maghrib (Ar.) The Maghreb; literally, 'the place of sunset', 'the West'. Loosely, the word designates in Arabic the whole of North West Africa. Specifically, it designates Morocco.

al-Maghrib, Ṣalāt (Ar.) The Evening or Sunset Prayer. (*See* **Ṣalāt**.)

al-Mahdī (Ar.) Literally, 'the One who is Rightly Guided'. The Mahdī is a figure of profound eschatological significance in Islam and a title often claimed by diverse leaders throughout Islamic history. His just rule will herald the approach of the end of time. Both Sunnīs and Shī'ites adhere to a belief in the Mahdī, though **Shī'ism** (q.v.) has developed the doctrine perhaps rather more deeply, tying up with it the concept of **ghayba** (q.v.) and the Twelfth Shī'ite Imām. (*See* **Ishārāt al-Sā'a**; **Muḥammad al-Qā'im**; **Sunnī**.)

al-Mahdī al-Muntaẓar *See* **Muḥammad al-Qā'im.**

Mahfouz, Naguib *See* **Maḥfūẓ, Najīb.**

Maḥfūẓ, Najīb (Naguib Mahfouz) (1329/1911–) The Arab world's most famous novelist and writer. Egyptian by birth,

Maḥfūẓ won the Nobel Prize for Literature in 1408-9/1988. The themes in Maḥfūẓ's novels are manifold and universal but all are informed by a profound rejection of fanaticism in all its guises. Two of his novels are of particular interest for the student of Islam: (a) His satirical allegory *Awlād Ḥāratinā* (a title which has been rendered in English as *Children of Gebelawi*) published in 1959, incurred the wrath of the religious authorities in Egypt; it portrays in thinly veiled form many of the great figures and prophets sacred to one or more of the three monotheistic religions of Islam, Christianity and Judaism, as well as the death of Gebelawi (=God Himself) at the end of the novel. Although serialized in the Egyptian daily newspaper, *al-Ahrām*, in 1378-9/1959, the work was - and remains - banned in Egypt, and has never been published in book form there. It was, however, published in full book form in Lebanon in 1386-7/1967, slightly expurgated. (b) Maḥfūẓ's other novel which is of particular Islamic interest is his *Voyage of Ibn Faṭṭūma* (*Riḥlat Ibn Faṭṭūma*), published in 1403-4/1983. Maḥfūẓ's *Riḥla* draws consciously and deliberately on the well-known **Riḥla** (q.v.) of the great mediaeval Arab traveller **Ibn Baṭṭūṭa** (q.v.) and combines this with a kind of Arab Bunyan's *Pilgrim's Progress*.

Maḥmil or **Maḥmal** (Ar.) [pl. *maḥāmil*] Litter carried on a camel or palanquin. Specifically, it has a technical sense where it refers to one of the mediaeval customs of the **Ḥajj** (q.v.) in which Islamic princes and rulers would send a very ornate litter to **Mecca** (q.v.). The *maḥmil* sent to the *Ḥajj* had a profoundly political significance, representing as it did the power, authority and prestige of the ruler who sent it. Among areas which sent a *maḥmil* were Egypt, Syria and the Ottoman empire. (*See* **Ottomans**).

Mahr (Ar.) [*muhūr*] Dowry, bridal gift, bride-price, bride-wealth. Islamic law enjoins that the bridegroom give his bride a gift when the marriage contract is instituted. In the period of the **Jāhiliyya** (q.v.) the *mahr* was given to the bride's father or male guardian. However, the **Qur'ān** decreed that it should be the wife who received the *mahr* and that it was hers to keep, even in the event of a future divorce. If the marriage is dissolved before it has been consummated, the prospective bride is still entitled to half of the dowry. The amount of *mahr* varies considerably: the **Sharī'ia** (q.v.) does not stipulate a maximum amount and so it has happened sometimes that greedy families have felt free to ask for a *mahr* much larger than the other family can bear. But however high or low the amount, the *mahr* is legally an integral and *necessary* aspect of the marriage contract. (*See* **Mut'a**; **Nikāḥ**.)

al-Mā'ida (Ar.) The title of the 5th **sūra** of the **Qur'ān**; it means 'The Table'. The *sūra* belongs to the Medinan period and contains 120 verses; its title is drawn from the Miracle of the Table which is described in vv.112ff. Here Jesus' disciples challenge Jesus and ask if his Lord can send down a table (covered in food) from Heaven. God agrees to send down the requested table at Jesus' prayer, but warns that those who disbelieve thereafter will be severely punished. This *sūra* is a particularly long and rich one: it contains, *inter alia*, a number of prohibitions, instructions on how to perform the prayer, the story of the two sons of **Ādam** (q.v.) and references to the **Ka'ba** (q.v.). (*See* **Diya**; **Gambling**; **Ḥizb Allāh**; **'Īsā**; **al-Janna**; **Qābīl and Hābīl**; **Ṣalāt**.)

Majlis (Ar.) [pl. *majālis*] Meeting place, meeting, gathering, assembly. The word underwent a considerable socio-historical development in Islamic history and the institution often played a major role in Islamic life. One of its important meanings was that of 'public audience' given by the **khalīfa** (q.v.); this sense of *majlis* is not yet defunct in many areas of the Gulf today.

Makhzūm Important and powerful merchant clan of the tribe of **Quraysh** (q.v.). The famous general **Khālid b. al-Walīd** (q.v.) belonged to this clan.

Makka *See* **Mecca.**

Malak *See* **Angel**; **Archangel**.

Mālik Angel who is the chief of the guardians of Hell; he is mentioned in v.77 of **Sūrat al-Zukhruf** (q.v.) of the **Qur'ān**. (*See* **Angel**; **Archangel**; **al-Nār**; **al-Zabāniyya**.)

Mālik b. Anas (*c.* 94/716–179/795) Mālik's full name was Abū 'Abd Allāh Mālik b. Anas. He gave his name to the Mālikī School of law whose real *founders*, strictly speaking, were Mālik's disciples. He is regarded as one of the great jurists of mediaeval Islam. He knew **Abū Ḥanīfa** (q.v.) and also wrote what is considered to be the first major book of law in Islam, *The Smoothed Path* (*al-Muwaṭṭa'*). Mālik is often called the **Imām** (q.v.) of **Medina** (q.v.) since he lived, died and spent most of his life there. Mālik exercised his own 'opinion' (**ra'y** (q.v.)) and championed the 'practice' (*'amal*) of Medina. (*See* **Mālikīs**.)

Mālikīs Adherents of one of the four main law schools (*madhāhib*) of **Sunnī** (q.v.) Islam, named after **Mālik b. Anas** (q.v.). The Mālikī School of law had its origins in the early Medinan school. The Mālikīs, like the **Ḥanafīs** (q.v.), recognized supplementary sources of law. Thus the Mālikīs espoused the principle of **Istiṣlāḥ** (q.v.). Mālikī law gained a dominance in North Africa as well as the West and Centre of that continent. (*See* **Fiqh**; **Ḥanbalīs**; **Madhhab**; **Shāfi'īs**; **Sharī'a**.)

Mamlūks Major dynasty of late mediaeval Islam which flourished between 648/1250 and 922/1517 in Egypt. The Arabic word *mamlūk* means 'one who is owned', 'a slave', and reflected the origins of the dynasty in Circassian and Turkish slave soldiers. The Mamlūks defeated the **Mongols** (q.v.) at the Battle of 'Ayn Jālūt. Their rule in Egypt ushered in a golden age of Egyptian Islamic art and architecture. It is commonly divided into two principal parts: the rule of the *Baḥrī* Mamlūks (so-called because of the military quarters on an island in the Nile, this last word being rendered in Arabic as *Baḥr al-Nīl*) from 648/1250 to

784/1382; and the rule of the *Burjī* Mamlūks (so-called because the first, Barqūq, belonged to a military regiment housed in the Cairo citadel (*al-Burj*)) from 784/1382 to 922/1517. The last really notable Mamlūk sultan, al-Ghawrī (*reg.* 906/1501–922/1516) was overthrown by the **Ottomans** (q.v.) during their conquest of Syria in 922/1516 at the Battle of Marj Dābiq. Egypt fell to the Ottomans soon afterwards. However, this did not mean the extermination of the Mamlūks: they remained as local beys, rulers and princes under Ottoman suzerainty, fought and were defeated by Napoleon at the Battle of the Pyramids in 1213/1798 and their power base was only definitively and fatally undermined by **Muḥammad 'Alī** (q.v.) in 1226/1811. For a survey of the early period, see Irwin's *The Middle East in the Middle Ages: The Early Mamluk Sultanate 1250–1382*. For a fictional account of what the last days of the Mamlūks might have been like, before the coming of the Ottomans, see the brilliant novel entitled *Zayni Barakat* by Gamal al-Ghitani (see back of the *Dictionary* for full bibliographical details). (*See also* **Art and Architecture, Islamic**; **'Ayn Jālūt, Battle of**)

al-Ma'mūn (170/786–218/833) The 7th caliph of the dynasty of the **'Abbāsids** (q.v.); he ruled from 198/813, taking power after a bloody civil war. He is of particular interest in the development of Arabic and Islamic thought because of his foundation in **Baghdād** (q.v.) of a philosophy and translation 'House of Wisdom' (**Bayt al-Ḥikma** (q.v.)). Al-Ma'mūn also espoused the doctrines of the **Mu'tazila** (q.v.) and instituted a **miḥna** (q.v.) to ensure public official adherence to the doctrine of a created **Qur'ān**. (*See* **Aḥmad b. Ḥanbal**; **Hārūn al-Rashīd**.)

Manāf Pre-Islamic deity in ancient Arabia. **Quraysh** (q.v.), and other tribes like **Tamīm** (q.v.), had a great devotion to this goddess before the rise of Islam. One of the most notable in pre-Islam to be named after the goddess was **'Abd Manāf** (q.v.).

Manār (Ar.) Minaret. (*See* **Manāra**.)

Manāra (Ar.) [pl. *manāwir* or *manā'ir*] Minaret, lighthouse. As the former this is one of the great universally recognized symbols of Islam. A minaret is the tower on a mosque from which the call to prayer is made or broadcast. Throughout history its design has provided considerable scope for the skills and tastes of the Islamic architect: minarets range in shape from the square towers of North Africa, to the more ornately decorated minarets of some of the Cairene mosques and the 'finger' minarets of **Istanbul** (q.v.), embracing the very simple and the spiral. An excellent, and unique example of the latter in Egypt, is to be found in the great Mosque of **Ibn Ṭūlūn** (q.v.) in **Cairo** (q.v.). (*See* **Adhān**; **Art and Architecture, Islamic**; **Hilāl**; **Masjid**; **Mu'adhdhin**; **Quṭb Mīnār**; **Ṣawma'a**.)

Manāt Major deity revered in the **Jāhiliyya** (q.v.) by the **Aws** (q.v.) and the **Khazraj** (q.v.) tribes. (*See* **al-Lāt**; **al-'Uzzā**.)

Manslaughter *See* **Murder and Manslaughter**.

Mansūkh *See* **Nāsikh and Mansūkh**.

Manzikert, Battle of Important battle fought in 463/1071 between the **Saljūqs** (q.v.) and the Byzantines. It took place at Manzikert (Malāzgird, Malāsjird) which is near Lake Van. The Byzantines were led by the Emperor Romanus Diogenus while the Saljūqs were commanded by the Sultan Alp Arslan. The battle, which ranks as one of the great decisive battles in history, witnessed the defeat of the Byzantines and the capture of the Byzantine Emperor. The battle meant that Byzantine territories were wide open to future invasion.

Maqāmāt (Ar.) [sing. *maqām*] The Arabic word has a wide range of meanings including 'sites', 'places', 'ranks' and 'saints' tombs'. In **taṣawwuf** (q.v.) the word acquired the specific technical sense of mystical stages in the progress along the **ṣūfī** (q.v.) road which are achievable by man. (*See* **Aḥwāl**.)

Marabout (Fr.) The French word is derived from the Arabic *murābiṭ* meaning 'a holy man', often in a North African context. The Arabic word, especially in its North African usage, also had the military connotation of 'soldier' or 'frontier-soldier'. In Senegal the word *marabout* has a diversity of applications and designates, for example, Muslim religious functionaries as well as leaders. (*see* **Ribāṭ**.)

Marāji' al-Taqlīd (Ar.) [sing. *Marji' al-Taqlīd*] Sources of Imitation. This is an epithet characterizing those Āyatullāhs who bear the rank of Āyatullāh al-'Uẓmā. A supreme or sole *Marji'* is called *Marji' al-Taqlīd al-Muṭlaq*. (*See* **Āyatullāh**.)

Ma'rib Dam Major ancient dam in South Arabia which burst in the 6th century AD and caused, according to Arab tradition, the migration Northwards of the Himyarite peoples. Various reasons have been put forward for the bursting of the dam, the most likely being that it silted up due to political neglect. The dam and its bursting are of particular interest to Islam since they are referred to in the **Qur'ān** under the rubric 'The Flood of the Dam' (*Sayl al-'Arim*). (*See* especially vv.15–17 of **Sūrat Sabā'** (q.v.)).

Ma'rifa *See* **'Ilm**.

Māristān *See* **Bīmāristān**.

Māriya the Copt A Christian slave given to the Prophet **Muḥammad** by an Egyptian notable; she became one of his concubines and was the mother of his son Ibrāhīm. (*See* **Ibrāhīm** (3).)

Marja'-i Taqlīd (Pers.) *See under* **Marāji' al-Taqlīd**.

Marji' al-Taqlīd (Ar.) *See* **Marāji' al-Taqlīd**.

Marj Rāhiṭ, Battle of Major battle which took place on the plain of Marj Rāhiṭ, North of **Damascus** (q.v.) in 65/684 between those who wished Marwān b. al-Ḥakam to be the next Umayyad caliph, on the death of Mu'āwiya II, and their Qaysite opponents. Al-Ḍaḥḥāk b. Qays al-Fihrī, one of the leaders of the latter, was killed on the battlefield and the Marwānid general, 'Abbād b. Ziyād, was victorious. The result of the battle, in the short term, led to Marwān being enthroned as caliph in Damascus; in the long term, the result served to divide the Arabs of Syria and elsewhere. (*See* **Umayyads**.)

Market Inspector *See* **Muḥtasib.**

Marriage *See* **Nikāḥ**; **Mut'a**.

Martyr *See* **Shahīd**; **Sumayya**.

Mārūt *See* **Hārūt and Mārūt**.

Marvels *See* **'Ajā'ib**.

al-Marwa *See* **al-Ṣafā.**

Maryam (1) (Ar.) Mary, the name of the mother of **'Īsā** (q.v.) in the **Qur'ān**. She figures prominently at the beginning of the 19th **sūra** which is named after her **Sūrat Maryam** (q.v.). However, she is also mentioned in many other places, always with great respect. The basic information about the conception of 'Īsā, given in **Sūrat Maryam**, is considerably elaborated by the **tafsīr** (q.v.) literature. It has been pointed out by Geoffrey Parrinder that Maryam 'is the only woman who is called by her proper name in the Qur'ān'. The purity of Maryam has been championed by Muslims from earliest times.

Maryam (2) (Ar.) Mary: the title of the 19th **sūra** of the **Qur'ān**; it is a female name. The *sūra* belongs to the early Meccan period apart from two verses and has a total of 98 verses. The title of the *sūra* is drawn from vv.16–34 which describe the announcement to Maryam, the mother of **'Īsā** (q.v.), by **Jibrīl** (q.v.) of the coming birth of 'Īsā, as well as the actual birth of the latter and the speech of 'Īsā while still a baby in the cradle. The *sūra*, which begins with five of the **Mysterious Letters of the Qur'ān** (q.v.), also refers to **Zakariyyā** (q.v.), his son **Yaḥyā** (q.v.), the story of the prophet **Ibrāhīm** (q.v.) and his idol-worshipping father, **Mūsā** (q.v.), **Hārūn** (q.v.), and **Idrīs** (q.v.). (*See* **Maryam** (1).)

al-Masad (Ar.) The title of the 111th **sūra** of the **Qur'ān**; it means 'The Palm Fibres'. The *sūra* belongs to the Meccan period and has 5 verses. Its title is drawn from the 5th verse which makes reference to the palm fibres round the neck of Abū Lahab's wife. Basically, this entire short *sūra* is a majestic condemnation of an uncle of the Prophet **Muḥammad** called **'Abd al-'Uzzā b. 'Abd al-Muṭṭalib** (q.v.), known as Abū Lahab, who opposed the Prophet. The *sūra* warns that Abū Lahab's riches will not help him and that he and his wife will burn in Hell. (*See* **al-Nār**.)

Maṣḥaf or **Muṣḥaf** (Ar.) [pl. *maṣāḥif*] Copy of the **Qur'ān** (q.v.).

al-Masīḥ (Ar.) Literally, 'The Messiah'. This is a title frequently borne by **'Īsā** (q.v.) in the **Qur'ān**. However, the latter does not explain this title. Some of the commentators identify the word as foreign, and a variety of explanations have been put forward. What is clear is that the Qur'ān does not use the word in the same precise senses of Judaic or Christian usage.

Masjid (Ar.) [pl. *masājid*] Mosque. The word means literally 'a place of bowing down'. The word *masjid* on its own often indicates a fairly simple mosque. A *jāmi'* [pl. *jawāmi'*] or *masjid jāmi'*, on the other hand, indicates a rather larger mosque in a central location which often has a public function as a focus and place for the Friday Prayer. (*See* **al-Aqṣā, al-Masjid**; **Cami**; **al-Fusṭāṭ**; **Ibn Tūlūn**; **al-Kūfa**; **Manāra**; **al-Masjid al-Ḥarām**; **Miḥrāb**; **Minbar**.)

al-Masjid al-Aqṣā *See* **al-Aqṣā, al-Masjid**.

al-Masjid al-Ḥarām (Ar.) The Great Mosque of **Mecca** (q.v.). This is a major focal point for several of the rituals of the **Ḥajj** (q.v.).

Maṣlaḥa *See* **Istiṣlāḥ**.

Maṣr *See* **Cairo**.

Masts, Battle of the There are not many notable sea battles in mediaeval Islamic history by comparison with the great victories which took place on land. However, the Battle of the Masts (called in Arabic *Dhū* [or *Dhāt*] *al-Ṣawārī*) was the *first* great naval victory achieved by Islam; it was fought in 34/655 between the Muslim fleets of **'Uthman b. 'Affān** (q.v.), led by Ibn Abī Sarḥ and Ibn Abī Arṭāh, and a Byzantine fleet commanded by the Emperor Constans II, at Phoenix, off the coast of Lycia. The battle was a major victory for the Muslim fleet which tied its own ships to the enemy's. It marked the continued decline of Byzantine power, at this stage, in the face of Arab Islamic forces. The conflict would not, however, be totally resolved until the fall of Constantinople to the **Ottomans** (q.v.) in 857/1453. (*See* **Istanbul**.)

al-Mas'ūdī, Abū 'l-Ḥasan 'Alī b. al-Ḥusayn (*c.* 283/896–*c.* 345/956) Major early Islamic historian about whose actual life little is known. However, we do know that he was born in **Baghdād** (q.v.) and died in Egypt. He travelled extensively and most probably belonged to the **Ithnā 'Asharīs** (q.v.). He wrote a large number of works but only two have survived. Of these his history entitled *The Meadows of Gold* (*Murūj al-Dhahab*) is the more important and famous. His abilities as an historian, and capacity to combine history with readable narrative or story-telling, have been widely commended. His *Meadows of Gold* is a major Arabic source for mediaeval Islamic history. His writings are also extremely valuable for the insight which they provide into diverse aspects of non-Islamic world history as well. (*See* **al-Ṭabarī; al-Wāqidī.**)

Matn (Ar.) [pl. *mutūn*] The main *text* of a **ḥadīth** (q.v.), distinct from the **isnād** (q.v.).

al-Māturīdī (died 333/944) Very little is known of the life of this Islamic theologian though we do know that he died in **Samarqand** (q.v.). A school of theological thought was named after him known as Māturīdism. However, generally speaking, the school of **al-Ash'arī** (q.v.) has become better known. Māturīdism placed a particular stress on God's justice and fairness.

al-Mā'ūn (Ar.) The title of the 107th **sūra** of the **Qur'ān**; the Arabic word here has been variously translated as 'Charity', 'Benevolence' and 'Alms'. Some of the *sūra*'s 7 verses were revealed in **Mecca** (q.v.) and others in **Medina** (q.v.). The title of the *sūra* is drawn from the 7th verse which refers to the prevention of *al-mā'ūn*. The *sūra* begins with the question: have you seen the man who denies the Judgement to come? (Literally, 'the Islamic faith, *al-Dīn*'.) And it then goes on to identify that man as the one who is cruel to the orphan and the poverty-stricken. Exterior display must mirror an inner piety.

al-Māwardī (364/974–450/1058) Perhaps the most notable political theorist of mediaeval Islam, who propounded his views in a book entitled *Rules of Government* (*al-Aḥkām al-Sulṭāniyya*). Here he lays down, *inter alia*, the qualifications which should be held by a potential or would-be **khalīfa** (q.v.).

Mawḍū' (Ar.) In **ḥadīth** (q.v.) criticism this word has the technical sense of 'invented' when used to describe a *ḥadīth*.

Mawdūdī *See* **Jamā'at-i Islāmī.**

Mawlā (Ar.) [pl. *mawālī*] Client. In early Islamic history this was the technical sense of the word, indicating a non-Arab convert to Islam who became the 'client' of an Arab. Although, in theory, all Muslims in the early Islamic state were supposed to be treated as equals, in practice the *mawālī* or clients were often treated as second-class citizens by comparison with those of Arab stock. This was particularly the case from the point of view of taxation. The word *mawlā* also means 'master' and *al-Mawlā*, that is, 'The Master', is a synonym for God. (*See* **Tax, Taxation.**)

Mawlānā *See* **Mawlawiyya; Rūmī.**

Mawlawiyya (Ar.) or **Mevleviyya** (Turk.) Whirling dervishes. These are an important **ṣūfī** (q.v.) order, originating in Turkey, whose name derives from the title borne by their inspirer, the Persian mystical poet **Rūmī** (q.v.), of *Mawlānā* (Arabic for 'Our Master'; the Turkish form is *Mevlānā*). The whirling dance of the Mawlawiyya which is performed with music during their **dhikr** (q.v.), and for which the order has become famous, attempted to emulate or symbolize the motion of the spheres, according to one interpretation. Like the other orders in Turkey the Mawlawiyya was banned in 1925 by **Atatürk** (q.v.) but it is still possible to witness the **samā'** (q.v.) of the Mawlawiyya on certain occasions in Turkey and elsewhere. (*See* **Baba; Bektāshiyya; Darwīsh.**)

Mawlid (Ar.) [pl. *mawālid*] Birthday, anniversary. The feast of the Prophet **Muḥammad**'s birthday is an occasion of happy celebrations in the Muslim world. (*See* **al-Badawī; 'Īd; Mawlid al-Nabī.**

Mawlid al-Nabī (Ar.) The birthday of the Prophet **Muḥammad**. It is celebrated with much festivity in the Islamic world on the twelfth day of the Islamic lunar month of Rabī' al-Awwal.

Maymūna An widow married by the Prophet **Muḥammad** on his return from pilgrimage in 7/629.

Mecca Called in Arabic *Makka*, this is the holiest city in Islam whose history is inextricably bound up with that of the Prophet **Muḥammad** himself. He lived there for much of his life. Muslims turn towards Mecca in prayer and undertake the pilgrimage (**Ḥajj** (q.v.)) to that city, not only because of its prophetic and historical associations, but because it contains the **Ka'ba** (q.v.). The **Qur'ān** was first revealed to Muḥammad near this city and it was from Mecca that he made his famous migration (**Hijra** (q.v.)) to **Medina** (q.v.) in AD 622. Mecca probably originated and developed as a major city in pre-Islamic times because of its strategic position on the great trade routes running from the Yemen Northwards to the Byzantine and Persian empires. The city today is within the modern Kingdom of Saudi Arabia and the Saudi King likes to refer to himself as 'The Servitor of the Two Sanctuaries' (i.e. Mecca and Medina). Mecca is often characterized as 'The Revered' (*al-Mukarrama*) and also referred to as 'The Mother of Cities' (*Umm al-Qurā*). (*See* **Qibla**).

Medina Anglicized form of the Arabic *al-Madīna* meaning 'The City'. This is the second holiest city in Islam after **Mecca** (q.v.). Its early name was Yathrib. Medina is frequently characterized by the epithet 'The Radiant' (*al-Munawwara*). Like the city of Mecca the early history of Medina is closely bound up with that of the Prophet **Muḥammad**. It was to this city that he made his famous **Hijra** (q.v.) in AD 622. It was here that, very early on, the 'Constitution of Medina' was formulated. And it is here that the Prophet Muḥammad lies buried. The city today is part of the modern Kingdom of Saudi Arabia. (*See* **al-Anṣār**; **al-Aws**; **al-Khazraj**; **al-Muhājirūn**; **al-Naḍīr**; **Qaynuqā'**; **Qurayẓa**.)

Mehmet II 'The Conqueror' (835-6/1432–886/1481) The Ottoman conqueror of Constantinople in 857/1453. He reigned twice, from 848/1444 until 850/1446 and 855/1451 until 886/1481. (*See* **Istanbul**; **Ottomans**.)

Menstruation As in Judaism, menstruation renders a woman ritually impure. Thus, she should not touch a copy of the **Qur'ān** nor perform the **ṣalāt** (q.v.) among a variety of other restrictions. At the end of her period a woman becomes ritually pure again by undertaking the major ritual washing of **ghusl** (q.v.). Sexual intercourse with a menstruating woman is prohibited by the Qur'ān. (*See* **'Idda; Ṭalāq.**)

Merciful, The *See* **al-Raḥmān** (1).

Messenger *See* **Rasūl.**

Mevlānā *See* **Mawlawiyya; Rūmī.**

Mevleviyya *See* **Mawlawiyya.**

Michael *See* **Mīkā'īl.**

Mīḍa'a or **Mīḍā'a** (Ar.) Ablution fountain, area or receptacle found in a mosque for ritual washing before prayers. Considerable artistry often went into the design of the mediaeval *mīḍa'a*; its modern counterpart is frequently wrought in a similar beautiful fashion. (*See* **Ṣalāt; Wuḍū'.**)

Mi'dhana or **Ma'dhana** (Ar.) [pl. *ma'ādhin*] Place from which the call to prayer is made, minaret. (*See* **Adhān; Manāra; Mu'adhdhin; Ṣalāt; Ṣawma'a.**)

Midian *See* **Madyan.**

Migration *See* **Hijra.**

Miḥna (Ar.) Inquisition. The most famous *miḥna* in mediaeval Islam was that instituted by **al-Ma'mūn** (q.v.) in an attempt to impose public adherence to the Mu'tazilite doctrine of a created **Qur'ān.** (*See* **Aḥmad b. Ḥanbal; Mu'tazila.**)

Miḥrāb (Ar.) [pl. *maḥārīb*] Indented niche within a mosque indicating the direction of the prayer (**qibla** (q.v.)) towards **Mecca** (q.v.). *Miḥrāb*s are frequently decorated with beautiful calligraphy, tiles and mosaics and constitute an area of the mosque where the artist feels free to give full expression to his combined religious fervour and artistic zeal. Scholars disagree as to exactly when the *miḥrāb* became a formal part of the mosque. In the **Qur'ān** the word *miḥrāb* often has a sense other than that outlined above. In v.11 of **Sūrat Maryam** (q.v.), for example, **Zakariyyā** (q.v.) comes out to his people from a *miḥrāb* which is clearly not the prayer niche of a mosque but rather a kind of sanctuary. (*See* **Masjid**; **Ṣalāt**.)

Mīkā'īl (Ar.) Michael, one of the great Islamic angels. He is mentioned once in the **Qur'ān** in the company of **Jibrīl** (q.v.). (*See* v.98 of **Sūrat al-Baqara** (q.v.)). Tradition shows him and Jibrīl instructing **Muḥammad** and both were characterized as **wazīr** (q.v.) (literally, 'minister') by the Prophet. Mīkā'īl watches over places of worship. (*See* **Angel**; **Archangel**.)

Mīlād *See* **Mawlid**.

Minā Small town about three miles from **Mecca** (q.v.). On the tenth day of the Islamic lunar month of **Dhū 'l-Ḥijja** (q.v.), an animal is sacrificed at Minā during the **Ḥajj** (q.v.) as the climactic event of the pilgrimage. This is done in emulation of the actions of Ibrāhīm. Indeed, Islamic tradition holds that Minā is the actual place where Ibrāhīm sacrificed a ram instead of his son Ismā'īl. Stones are also cast in the valley of Minā, in emulation again of Ibrāhīm, this time of the great patriarch's rejection of Satan. (*See* **Ibrāhīm** (1); **'Īd al-Aḍḥā**; **Ismā'īl** (1); **al-Jamra**.)

Minaret *See* **Manāra**.

Minbar (Ar.) [pl. *manābir*] Pulpit. This is a key piece of furniture in the mosque, from which the Friday **khuṭba** (q.v.) or sermon is preached by the mosque **Imām** (q.v.). The *minbar* in a large mosque is often a very high and ornate structure, intricately carved from beautiful woods. The period of the **Mamlūks** (q.v.) in Egypt produced many beautifully wrought *minbars*. The *minbar* is usually sited in the mosque fairly close to the **miḥrāb** (q.v.). (*See* **Dikka**; **Masjid**.)

Minor Pilgrimage *See* **Ḥajj**.

Mīqāt (Ar.) [pl. *mawāqīt*] Literally, 'time of appointment', or 'meeting point'. In the technical terminology of the **Ḥajj** (q.v.) the word *mīqāt* has the specialist sense of the place where, or the time at which, pilgrims to **Mecca** (q.v.) gather.

Mi'rāj (Ar.) Ascension, specifically that of the Prophet **Muḥammad** from **Jerusalem** (q.v.) through the Seven Heavens, after the **Isrā'** (q.v.) or Night Journey from **Mecca** (q.v.) to Jerusalem. In Paradise Muḥammad entered God's presence. The Night Journey and Ascension into Paradise are covered in some detail in the **Qur'ān**, in **Sūrat al-Isrā'** (q.v.) and **Sūrat al-Najm** (q.v.). The latter, in vv.13–18, relates how Muḥammad saw **Jibrīl** (q.v.) by **Sidrat al-Muntahā** (q.v.) and also beheld God's 'greatest signs' at the climax of his *mi'rāj*. (*See* **al-Aqṣā, al-Masjid**; **al-Burāq**; **al-Janna**; **Laylat al-Mi'rāj**; **Qubbat al-Ṣakhra**.)

Moghuls *See* **Mughals**.

Monastery The nearest equivalent to this Christian and Indian religious institution in Islam is the **ṣūfī** (q.v.), **khānagāh** (q.v.), **ribāṭ** (q.v.), **tekkē** (q.v.) or **zāwiya** (q.v.).

Mongols In 602-3/1206, having been united by Genghis Khan, the Mongol tribes began a devastating advance across East and Central Asia, creating a massive empire. They sacked **Baghdād** (q.v.) in 656/1258, thereby ending the 'Abbāsid caliphate. They were only halted by the decisive Battle of 'Ayn Jālūt in 658/1260. The Mongols at first were Shamanists, Buddhists or Nestorian Christians before converting to Islam. (*See* **'Abbāsids; 'Ayn Jālūt, Battle of; Mughals; Tīmūr-i Lang; William of Rubruck.**)

Morals *See* **Akhlāq.**

Moses *See* **Mūsā.**

Moslem Brotherhood, Brethen *See* **al-Bannā'; Ikhwān; al-Ikhwān al-Muslimūn.**

Mosque *See* **Masjid.**

Mosque of 'Umar *See* **Qubbat al-Ṣakhra.**

Moulid, Muulid (Ar.) Egyptian colloquial word for **mawlid** (q.v.) which is variously transliterated in English.

Mozarab Word deriving from the Arabic *musta'rib* which means literally 'one who has become Arabised'. The Mozarabs were Christians living under Muslim Arab rule in mediaeval Islamic Spain who adopted the *mores* of their masters but maintained, nonetheless, their Christian faith. (*See* **al-Andalus.**)

Mu'adhdhin (Ar.) The person who gives the call to prayer (**adhān** (q.v.)) from the minaret of a mosque. In the Islamic world, particularly in large cities like **Cairo** (q.v.), it is becoming more infrequent for this to be done in person, loudspeakers having replaced in many mosques the need for a *mu'adhdhin*'s physical presence. The first *mu'adhdhin* was **Bilāl b. Rabāḥ** (q.v.), appointed by the Prophet **Muḥammad** himself. The Arabic word *mu'adhdhin* has been anglicized as muezzin. (*See* **Manāra; Masjid; Ṣalāt.**)

Mu'āmalāt *See under* **'Ibāda.**

Mu'āwiya b. Abī Sufyān (died 60/680) Governor of Syria and later, founder of the dynasty of the **Umayyads** (q.v.). He was a member of the Umayyad family in the **'Abd Shams** (q.v.) clan of the **Quraysh** (q.v.) tribe. After the murder of **'Alī b. Abī Ṭālib** (q.v.), Mu'āwiya ruled from 41/661 until 60/680. (*See* **Abū Sufyān**; **Fitna**; **al-Ḥasan b. 'Alī**; **al-Ḥusayn b. 'Alī**; **Ṣiffīn, Battle of**)

Muḍāraba (Ar.) Technical term in Islamic business and banking indicating limited or silent partnership. In practical terms, *muḍāraba* operates as follows: an Islamic bank will agree to lend money to a customer so that the latter can, for example, build up a business. The bank will receive annually a certain per cent of that business's profits over a specified time. In this way the loan is repaid and some profit is earned. (*See* **Islamic Banking**.)

al-Muddathir (Ar.) The title of the 74th **sūra** of the **Qur'ān**; it means 'The Shrouded One'. The *sūra* belongs to the Meccan period and has 56 verses. Its title is taken from the 1st verse in which the Prophet **Muḥammad** (q.v.) is addressed formally as 'Oh Shrouded One'. This is one of the most important *sūras* of the Qur'ān for it constitutes the initial command to Muḥammad to begin preaching the Revelation. It warns too, of the torments of **Saqar** (q.v.) (=Hell), guarded by nineteen keepers, whose inhabitants will include those who did not pray nor feed the poor.

Muezzin *See* **Mu'adhdhin**.

Mufassir (Ar.) [pl. *mufassirūn*] Exegete, interpreter, especially of the **Qur'ān**. Three of the most famous and best-loved exegetes in Islam were – and are – **al-Bayḍāwī** (q.v.), **al-Ṭabarī** (q.v.) and **al-Zamakhsharī** (q.v.), though there were and are many others as well. (*See* **Tafsīr**.)

Muftī (Ar.) One who delivers, or is qualified to deliver, a **fatwā** (q.v.). He may or may not hold the rank of **qāḍī** (q.v.).

The *muftī* constitutes a living bridge from pure Islamic jurisprudence to everyday Islamic life. In some cities and countries there exists (or has existed) the office of Grand *Muftī*. (*See* **Fiqh**; **Sharī'a**.)

Mughals Important dynasty which flourished in India between 932/1526 and 1274/1858. The word 'Mughal' is a form of the word 'Mongol'. The age of the early or great Mughals inaugurated a period of great cultural and artistic effervescence in India and heralded a Golden Age of Muslim Indian art and architecture. The six most famous Mughal emperors were, chronologically, **Bābur** (q.v.), **Humāyūn** (q.v.), **Akbar** (q.v.), **Jahāngīr** (q.v.), **Shāh Jahān** (q.v.) and **Aurangzeb** (q.v.). After the death of the latter, a gradual decline set in culminating in the overthrow of the last Mughal by the British in 1274/1858. (*See* **Mongols**; **Tīmūr-i Lang**.)

al-Muhājirūn (Ar.) The migrants or emigrants. These were the people who fled from **Mecca** (q.v.) to **Medina** (q.v.) and assisted the Prophet **Muḥammad** there. (*See* **al-Anṣār**; **al-Hijra**.)

Muḥammad (1) (*c.* AD 570–11/632) Muḥammad b. 'Abd Allāh was the Prophet and Founder of Islam and that faith's most important and significant messenger. He is referred to on numerous occasions in the body of this *Dictionary*: only an outline, therefore, of his life will be given here. Muḥammad received the first revelation of the Holy **Qur'ān** via the angel **Jibrīl** (q.v.) when he was about forty years old. He began to preach the messages which he received – messages of the Oneness of God, the need for repentance, the certainty of a Day of Judgement – and encountered much opposition in his native city of **Mecca** (q.v.), especially from the merchant classes who perceived a triple threat to their selfish *mores*, trade and polytheistic religion. Muḥammad was eventually forced to make his famous **Hijra** (q.v.) to the city of **Medina** (q.v.) in 1/622 where he was welcomed. He set about establishing himself here, achieved a position of power, fought three major battles with the Meccans – **Badr** (q.v.), **Uḥud** (q.v.) and **al-Khandaq** (q.v.) – and finally returned in triumph to Mecca in 8/630. He died two years later in 11/632. W. M. Watt has emphasized that Muḥammad, a human being who never claimed divinity, was both a prophet *and* a statesman and these two epithets neatly sum up the two principal features of his life. Through his prophethood he founded a great religion, that of Islam; through his statesmanship he laid the foundations for what would later become a great Islamic empire under such dynasties as those of the **Umayyads** (q.v.) and the **'Abbāsids** (q.v.). Muḥammad is buried in Medina and his tomb is frequently visited by Muslim pilgrims after the **Ḥajj** (q.v.). Books about the Prophet Muḥammad are many. However, two useful introductions are Martin Lings' *Muḥammad: His Life Based on the Earliest Sources*, which, as the title implies, has the merit of being based on very early historical sources like **Ibn Isḥāq** (q.v.) and **al-Wāqidī** (q.v.); and W. M. Watt's succinct and classic summary *Muḥammad, Prophet and Statesman* (see back of this *Dictionary* for full bibliographical details). (*See also*, among other relevant entries, **'Abd Allāh b. 'Abd al-Muṭṭalib; Abraha; al-Anṣār; al-Aws; Baḥīrā; Barēlwīs; Deobandis; al-Khazraj; al-Muhājirūn; Nabī; Rasūl; Sīra; Sunna.**)

Muḥammad (2) The title of the 47th **sūra** of the **Qur'ān**; Muḥammad is a proper name in Arabic. The *sūra* belongs to the Medinan period and has 38 verses. Its title is drawn from the 2nd verse which talks about belief in what has been revealed to the Prophet Muḥammad. The *sūra* begins by warning that the deeds of the unbelievers will be in vain. However, the reverse is true of the deeds of those killed in the path of God: they will enter Paradise. God will protect the believer but the unbeliever will have no protector. Paradise contains rivers of milk, wine and honey by contrast with the boiling water which will be fed to the wicked in Hell. (*See* **al-Janna; al-Nār.**)

Muḥammad al-Bāqir (57/676– died between 114/732 and 126/743) Fifth Shī'ite Imām. He was the grandson of the Second Shī'ite Imām, **al-Ḥasan b. 'Alī** (q.v.). Muḥammad al-Bāqir was not politically active but his imāmate saw the development of certain Shī'ite rituals and legal attitudes. Tradition has it that Muḥammad al-Bāqir debated with the Umayyad caliph **Hishām** (q.v.). Shī'ite tradition also holds that al-Bāqir was martyred. He is buried in **Medina** (q.v.). (*See* **Imām**; **Shī'ism**; **Umayyads**.)

Muḥammad 'Alī (*c.* 1193/1769–1265/1849) Albanian soldier and commander who came to power in Egypt (after the incursion of Napoleon) in 1226/1811. His rule represents a transition from the declining and often corrupt rule of the Mamlūk beys or overlords of preceding centuries to a dynasty which, though often no less despotic, marked the entry of Egypt into the modern world. In 1233/1818 his son defeated the **Wahhābīs** (q.v.) in Arabia. Muḥammad 'Alī himself fought at various times both for the **Ottomans** (q.v.) and against them. (*See* **Mamlūks**; **al-Ṭahṭāwī**.)

Muḥammad al-Qā'im, al-Mahdī, al-Muntaẓar (*c.* 255/868–*ghayba* 260/874) Twelfth Shī'ite Imām of the **Ithnā 'Asharīs** (q.v.); his return is expected and for this reason he is called 'The Mahdi' (**al-Mahdī** (q.v.)) and 'The Awaited (or Expected) One' (*al-Muntaẓar*). He was the son of the Eleventh Shī'ite Imām Ḥasan al-'Askarī (q.v.). At his father's funeral, as a young boy, he made a single appearance and then, according to Shī'ite belief, entered a state of **ghayba** (q.v.). The returning figure of the Twelfth Imām is identified by the Shī'ites with the eschatological figure of the *Mahdī* whose return will signal the approaching Day of Judgement. (*See* **Imām**; **Ishārāt al-Sā'a**; **Shī'ism**; **Yawm al-Qiyāma**.)

Muḥammad al-Taqī (195/810–220/835) Ninth Shī'ite Imām of the **Ithnā 'Asharīs** (q.v.). He was the son of **'Alī al-Riḍā** (q.v.). Born in **Medina** (q.v.) he assumed the title of Imām on the death of his father: the new young Imām was only seven years old but he is said to have been endowed with unusual and precocious knowledge. He lived for a time in **Baghdād** (q.v.) marrying while there a daughter of the 'Abbāsid calph **al-Ma'mūn** (q.v.). After a further period in Medina, Muḥammad al-Taqī returned to Baghdād in the last year of his life. Shī'ite tradition has it that he was poisoned by his wife. Muḥammad al-Taqī lies buried in Baghdād. (*See* **Imām**; **Kāẓimayn**.)

Muḥammad b. Ismā'īl (2nd/8th century) Seventh Imām for the **Ismā'īlīs** (q.v.). Before **Ja'far al-Ṣādiq** (q.v.) died, many of his followers championed the claims to the imāmate of Ja'far's son Ismā'īl. However, Ismā'īl had died before Ja'far and so these followed Ismā'īl's son Muḥammad as Imām. These were the group later to be called Ismā'īlīs. Others, however, supported the claims of Ismā'īl's brother **Mūsā al-Kāẓim** (q.v.) to be Ja'far's successor. These are the group later to be known as Twelvers or **Ithnā 'Asharīs** (q.v.). (*See* **Imām**; **Ismā'īl** (2).)

al-Muḥarram (Ar.) First month of the Islamic lunar calendar. Al-Muḥarram is often called the Muslim 'Month of Mourning' because of the commemoration of the martyrdom of **al-Ḥusayn b. 'Alī** (q.v.) at the Battle of Karbalā', on the tenth day of the month. (*See* **'Āshūrā'**; **Karbalā', Battle of**; **Ta'ziya**.)

Muḥkamāt (Ar.) [sing. *muḥkam*] Literally 'strengthened', 'precise'. The word has the technical sense, in the exegesis of the **Qur'ān**, as an epithet applied to those words or passages in the Qur'ān which are 'clear' and 'intelligible', as opposed to the **mutashābihāt** (q.v.). The Qur'ān itself divides its verses into the dual categories of *muḥkamāt* and *mutashābihāt* in v.7 of **Sūrat Āl 'Imrān** (q.v.). The former are described as 'The Essence of the Book' (*Umm al-Kitāb*). (*See* **Tafsīr**.)

Muḥtasib (Ar.) This term has been loosely translated as 'Market Inspector'. The *muḥtasib* was charged with the exercise of *ḥisba*, that is, making sure that the religious and moral injunctions of the **Sharī'a** (q.v.) were carried out, especially in the markets of Islamic cities and towns. The *muḥtasib* checked weights and measures and exercised a kind of quality control over cloth, brass etc. The concept and term do not appear in the **Qur'ān**.)

al-Mujādila (Ar.) The title of the 58th **sūra** of the **Qur'ān**; it means 'The Woman who Disputes'. The *sūra* belongs to the Medinan period and contains 22 verses. Its title is drawn from the 1st verse which states that God has heard the speech of the woman who disputes with you in the matter of her husband. The reference here, and in the following verses, is to a pre-Islamic prelude to divorce, and concerns an actual case brought to the attention of the Prophet Muḥammad. The remainder of the *sūra* threatens dire punishments to those who are unbelievers and hypocrites. (*See* **Ḥizb Allāh**; **Ṭalāq**.)

Mujtahid (Ar./Pers.) One entitled to give an independent judgement on a point of theology or law. In Iran the title of **Āyatullāh** (q.v.) has been applied to *mujtahids* in recent times. In the absence of the **Imām** (q.v.), the Iranian *mujtahid* has a particular power and religious authority and significance. (*See* **Ijtihād**; **Muḥammad al Qā'im**.)

al-Mulk (Ar.) The title of the 67th **sūra** of the **Qur'ān**; it means 'The Sovereignty'. The *sūra* belongs to the Meccan period and has 30 verses. Its title is drawn from the 1st verse in which blessing is called down upon God in whose hand is 'the sovereignty'. He is the Creator of the Seven Heavens. Unbelievers will be tormented in **Jahannam** (q.v.) but those who fear God will be well rewarded. Those who are cast into Hell will be asked whether or not a warner came to them. They will respond in the affirmative but admit that they rejected such warners. (*See* **al-Nār**.)

Mulla, Mullah Word deriving from the Arabic **mawlā** (q.v.), a word meaning 'master'. It was borne as a title of respect by religious figures and jurists in Iran and other parts of Asia. (*See* **Faqīh**; **'Ulamā'**.)

Mulla Ṣadra (979/1571–1050/1640) Persian philosopher, theologian and mystic whose actual name was Muḥammad b. Ibrāhīm Ṣadr al-Dīn al-Shīrāzī. His thought was much influenced by that of Aristotle as well as that of his predecessors like **Ibn Sīnā** (q.v.) and Shihāb al-Dīn Abū 'l-Futūḥ Yaḥyā **al-Suhrawardī** (q.v.). Mulla Ṣadra famously held a doctrine of different levels of Being. One of his best-known works is *The Four Journeys*.

Mu'min (Ar.) [pl. *mu'minūn*] Believer.

al-Mu'minūn (Ar.) The title of the 23rd **sūra** of the **Qur'ān**; it means 'The Believers'. The *sūra* belongs to the Meccan period and has 118 verses. Its title is taken from the 1st verse which proclaims the triumph of the believers. God has created man from clay and ultimately fashioned him into a human being. The early verses recall God's blessings which he has showered on his creation before proceeding to outline in some detail the histories of **Nūḥ** (q.v.), **Mūsā** (q.v.) and **Hārūn b. 'Imrān** (q.v.); **Maryam**(q.v.) and her son **'Īsā** (q.v.), we are told, have been made a sign by God, who has led them to a safe place.

al-Mumtaḥana (Ar.) The title of the 60th **sūra** of the **Qur'ān**; it means 'The Woman who is Tested'. The *sūra* is Medinan and contains 13 verses. Its title comes from the 10th verse which advises that believing females among new **muhājirūn** (q.v.) should be tested as to their true beliefs. The *sūra* deals with some of the problems which arose after the Treaty of **al-Ḥudaybiyya** (q.v.).

Mumtāz Maḥal *See* **Tāj Maḥal**.

Munāfiqūn (Ar.) [sing. *munāfiq*] Hypocrites. They are roundly condemned throughout the **Qur'ān**. The latter warns, in v.145 of

Sūrat al-Nisā' (q.v.), that the hypocrites will be in the lowest level of Hell, unless they repent. (*See* **Sūrat al-Munāfiqūn**.)

al-Munāfiqūn (Ar.) The title of the 63rd **sūra** of the **Qur'ān**; it means 'The Hypocrites'. The *sūra* belongs to the Medinan period and contains 11 verses. Its title is drawn from the 1st verse which tells the Prophet **Muḥammad** that God is well aware that the hypocrites do not mean what they say when they acknowledge Muḥammad as the prophet of God. The hypocrites do not understand that God is the real owner of all wealth and treasure in Heaven and on earth.

Munkar and Nakīr The Angels of the Grave. These two angels, who play a significant role in the afterlife of man, are described principally in the tradition literature and do not appear in the **Qur'ān** by name, although it is possible that the Qur'ān does refer to the Punishment of the Grave. (*See* **'Adhāb al-Qabr**; **Sūrat Muḥammad** (v.27); *see also* **Angel**; **Archangel**; **Rūmān**.)

al-Muntaẓar *See* **Muḥammad al-Qā'im**.

Muqarnaṣ (Ar.) Term used in Islamic architecture to denote the honeycomb or hanging decoration which often appears within a mosque or mausoleum dome, or at the top of a **miḥrāb** (q.v.), window or large door. (*See* **Masjid**.)

al-Murābiṭūn *See* **Almoravids**.

Murder and Manslaughter Modern legislation differs from country to country today where Islam is the dominant religion; such legislation will not be dealt with here. This entry will concentrate rather on the Qur'ānic legislation. The **Qur'ān** enjoins just retaliation (**qiṣāṣ** (q.v.)): a life for a life; (*see* v.178 of **Sūrat al-Baqara**). The same verse indicates that if the murderer is pardoned by the brother of the slain, a blood fine may be paid instead. The importance of the Qur'ānic legislation is that it limits the life forfeited (i.e. the killer's) to one, rather than many as often happened in pre-Islam. Punishment for murder, however, remained the province of the victim's relatives who could ask for the death penalty, accept blood money or even issue a total pardon. There was also a further punishment in the next life: v.93 of **Sūrat al-Nisā'** (q.v.) mentions that the wilful murderer will be punished in Hell in great torment for all eternity. The previous verse, which deals with manslaughter, imposes as a punishment for this lesser offence the freeing of a believing slave and the payment of blood money to the victim's family, unless they absolve him from payment. (*See* **Diya**.)

al-Murji'a (Ar.) Those who adhered to a belief in 'postponement' (*irjā'*). These were people in early Islam who, while differing on other points, agreed that the Muslim who committed grave sin did not cease to be a Muslim (contrary to the view of the **Khārijites** (q.v.)). For the *Murji'a*, sometimes called Murji'ites in English, any decision about the grave sinner was postponed and left to God. It must be noted here that the concept of postponement (*irjā'*) had profoundly political origins and connotations as well. The word *Murji'a* is sometimes translated into English as 'quietists', a word which by no means fully reflects their theology.

al-Mursalāt (Ar.) The title of the 77th **sūra** of the **Qur'ān**; it means 'Those who have been Sent'. The *sūra* belongs to the Meccan period and has 50 verses. Its title is drawn from the 1st verse which commences by swearing by 'Those who have been sent'. These have been interpreted as angels but also as winds or rain clouds. The *sūra* begins with a description of the Last Day and goes on to issue dire warnings to those who have made accusations of lying. The good, however, will be well rewarded in Paradise. (*See* **al-Janna**; **Yawm al-Qiyāma**.)

Mūsā (Ar.) Moses. He is a major prophet and messenger in the **Qur'ān**. He is portrayed in several places proclaiming his mission in front of Pharaoh. Of particular interest is the meeting of Mūsā and the sage identified as **al-Khaḍir** (q.v.). The Qur'ān records Mūsā as performing nine signs or miracles, including the division of the sea. The text also presents Mūsā's religion as that of the Prophet **Muḥammad**; the former is thus a precursor of the latter. (*See* **Fir'awn**; **Ghāfir**; **Hārūn b. 'Imrān**.)

Mūsā al-Kāẓim (*c.* 128/745–183/799) Seventh Imām for the **Ithnā 'Asharīs** (q.v.), and a younger son of **Ja'far al-Ṣādiq** (q.v.). After the latter's death, his claims to the imāmate were supported by those Shī'ites who later became called **Ithnā 'Asharīs** (q.v.). Others (the **Ismā'īlīs** (q.v.)) followed Ja'far's grandson **Muḥammad b. Ismā'īl** (q.v.). During his life Mūsā encountered considerable hostility from the **'Abbāsids** (q.v.). He was eventually arrested and poisoned, probably at the instigation of the Barmakid **wazīr** (q.v.) Yaḥyā b. Khālid. (*See* **Barmakids**; **Imām**; **Ismā'īl** (2); **Kāẓimayn**; **Shī'ism**.)

Musaylima (died 12/633) Rival Arabian prophet to **Muḥammad**; his real name was Maslama. (Musaylima, an Arabic diminutive of the latter, was a name of contempt given to him by Muslims.) He claimed that he had received revelations from God. Musaylima was defeated and killed at the extremely bloody Battle of 'Aqrabā' by a Muslim force led by **Khālid b. al-Walīd** (q.v.). A story portrays Musaylima writing to Muḥammad a letter in which he dignified both Muḥammad and himself by the title of 'Messenger of God'. Muḥammad replied, reserving the latter designation for himself, and characterizing Musaylima as 'the liar'. (*See* **'Aqrabā', Battle of**)

Mushrikūn (Ar.) [sing. *mushrik*] Polytheists. (*See* **Shirk**.)

Music *See* **Dhikr**; **Haḍra**; **Mawlawiyya**; **Samā'**.

Muslim (Ar.) [masc. pl. *muslimūn*] Literally, 'submitter', 'one who submits (i.e. to the will of God)'. A Muslim is one who professes and practises the faith of **Islām** (q.v.). (*See* **Shahāda**.)

Muslim b. al-Ḥajjāj, Abū 'l-Ḥusayn (*c.* 202/817–261/875) Very famous compiler of **ḥadīth** (q.v.). His collection, called the *Ṣaḥīḥ*, is almost as famous as that of **al-Bukhārī** (q.v.). Indeed, the two collections together are called 'The Two *Ṣaḥīḥs*' (*al-Ṣaḥīḥān*). Muslim's collection of *ḥadīth* ranks among the six major collections. However, unlike other collectors of traditions, Muslim did not sub-divide the books of his work into chapters. (*See* **Ṣaḥīḥ**.)

Muslim Brotherhood, Brethren *See* **al-Bannā'**; **Ikhwān**; **al-Ikhwān al-Muslimūn**.

Muslim League Political group, founded on the Indian sub-continent in 1324/1906, which supported demands for constitutional reform and, ultimately, for an independent Pakistan. (*See* **Jinājḥ**.)

Muslim World League International Muslim organization with a particular interest, among other things, in education. It opened an office in London in 1984.

Musnad (Ar.) Literally, 'based', 'founded'. The word is much used as a technical term in **ḥadīth** (q.v.) criticism to characterize a tradition whose complete **isnād** (q.v.) links it directly, usually to the Prophet **Muḥammad**. The *Musnad* was also the name of the principal work by **Aḥmad b. Ḥanbal** (q.v.).

Musta'lians Adherents of a branch of the **Ismā'īlīs** (q.v.). In 487/1094 the **wazīr** (q.v.) al-Afḍal (who was the son of Badr al-Jamālī) supported as candidate for the Fāṭimid Egyptian caliphate al-Musta'lī (younger son of **al-Mustanṣir** (q.v.)), instead of the oldest son Nizār. This split the Ismā'īlīs with some following one son and others the other. Today Musta'lians exist mainly in the Yemen, and also in India under the name **Bohorās** (q.v.). (*See* **Fāṭimids**; **Nizārīs**.)

al-Mustanṣir (420/1029–487/1094) The 8th caliph of the dynasty of the **Fāṭimids** (q.v.) who ruled in Egypt from 427/1036 until 487/1094, acceding to the throne at the age of seven. His reign witnessed a great famine in Egypt in 446/1054 during which the Fāṭimids were obliged to seek food from the Byzantines. Although al-Mustanṣir was proclaimed as caliph in **Baghdād** (q.v.) itself, for a brief year, this success was shortlived and Baghdād was retaken by the **Saljūqs** (q.v.) in 451/1060. In 466/1073 al-Mustanṣir tried to solve his domestic problems by calling in the Syrian general Badr al-Jamālī to take control of the situation. Al-Mustanṣir is notable for the longevity of his reign. It may be noted, in passing, here that the name al-Mustanṣir was also borne by rulers from other dynasties like the **'Abbāsids** (q.v.).

Musta'rib *See* **Mozarab.**

Mut'a (Ar.) [pl. *muta'*] Temporary marriage. This is permitted by the law of the **Ithnā 'Asharīs** (q.v.) but not sanctioned elsewhere in Islam. The temporary marriage is contracted for a fee (*ujra*), rather than a dowry (**mahr** (q.v.)), which the woman receives. *Mut'a* also has the further technical sense of compensation received by a divorced wife. (*See* **Nikāḥ**.)

al-Muṭaffifīn (Ar.) The title of the 83rd **sūra** of the **Qur'ān**; it means 'Those who give Short Measure'. The *sūra* belongs to the Meccan period and has 36 verses. It is considered that this was the last *sūra* to have been revealed in **Mecca** (q.v.) before the **Hijra** (q.v.) took place. The title of the *sūra* is taken from the 1st verse which threatens woe to those who give short measure. The *sūra* condemns unfair business and trading practices and promises the joys of Paradise to the pious. Mention is also made of **Tasnīm** (q.v.). (*See* **al-Janna**.)

Mutashābihāt (Ar.) [sing. *mutashābih*] Literally, 'ambiguous', 'unclear. The word has the technical sense, in the exegesis of the **Qur'ān**, as an epithet applied to those words and passages in the Qur'ān which are not clear or which are obscure, as opposed to those which may be characterized as **muḥkamāt** (q.v.). (*See* **Tafsīr**.)

al-Mutawakkil (206/821–247/861) Notable 'Abbāsid caliph who acceded aged 26 in 232/847. He renounced the **Mu'tazila** (q.v.) and the **miḥna** (q.v.) and tried to introduce sweeping changes in the army. In particular, he split up the army of **Sāmarrā** (q.v.) but his attempt to integrate the latter into his new army backfired. Al-Mutawakkil's murder resulted in several years anarchy. (*See* **'Abbāsids**.)

Mutawātir (Ar.) Literally, 'successive'. The word is used as a technical term in **ḥadīth** (q.v.) criticism to characterize a tradition which has a very large number of reliable transmitters. (*See* **Isnād**.)

Muṭawwif (Ar.) Pilgrim guide in **Mecca** (q.v.) whose function is to guide the visiting pilgrim through the complex rituals of the **Ḥajj** (q.v.). (*See* **Ṭawāf**.)

Mu'tazila (Ar.) Literally, 'Seceders'. The word derives from the Arabic verb 'to withdraw, to secede' (*i'tazala*) but the origins of the group which took this name are a matter of scholarly dispute and it is clear that the Mu'tazila underwent a number of different stages of development. A popular story portrays a meeting held by **al-Ḥasan al-Baṣrī** (q.v.) from which one of those present withdraws. Al-Ḥasan comments: 'He has withdrawn' (*I'tazala*). The meeting, if it actually took place, is of some relevance since it was a discussion about the position of the grave sinner in the Islamic community: the man who withdrew maintained that such a sinner was in an 'intermediate position', and an 'intermediate' stance came to be a characteristic of the Mu'tazila. *Mu'tazila*, in effect, was an umbrella term covering diverse scholars who were divided on a number of points but united on others. Among those on which many agreed were the doctrine of a created **Qur'ān**, God's absolute Oneness (which they believed the doctrine of a created Qur'ān reflected) where God's principal attributes were identical with His Divine Essence, God's justice and man's free will, and an allegorical attitude towards the *physical* attributes of God mentioned in the Qur'ān. (*See* **Aḥmad b. Ḥanbal; al-Amr bi 'l-Ma'rūf; Bishr b. al-Mu'tamir; Kalām; al-Kindī; Miḥna; al-Murji'a; al-Wa'd wa 'l-Wa'īd; Wāṣil b. 'Aṭā'**.)

Mu'tazilite Anglicized adjective meaning 'of or pertaining to the **Mu'tazila** (q.v.)'.

Muttaṣil (Ar.) Literally, 'continuous', 'adjacent'. The word is used as a technical term in **Ḥadīth** (q.v.) criticism to characterize an **isnād** (q.v.) which is unbroken back to its source, either the Prophet **Muḥammad** himself or one of the companions. (*See* **Ṣaḥāba**.)

al-Muwaḥḥidūn *See* **Almohads**; **Wahhābīs**.

al-Muwaṭṭa' (Ar.) *The Smoothed Path*: the title of the major work of **Mālik b. Anas** (q.v.).

al-Muzammil (Ar.) The title of the 73th **sūra** of the **Qur'ān**; it means 'The Mantled One'. The *sūra* belongs mainly to the Meccan period and has 20 verses. Its title is taken from the 1st verse which translates as 'Oh Mantled One' (i.e. **Muḥammad**). The reference is to Muḥammad's request to his wife **Khadīja bint Khuwaylid** (q.v.) to wrap him up in a mantle after his receiving the vision of **Jibrīl** (q.v.). The *sūra* praises God as Lord of the East and the West and stresses that Muḥammad has been sent to his people in the same way that **Mūsā** (q.v.) was sent to Pharaoh. (*See* **Fir'awn**.)

Muzdalifa A place near **Mecca** (q.v.) between the Plain of **'Arafa** (q.v.) and **Minā** (q.v.). Most pilgrims, except the sick, weak and the women, spend the night here after the running (*ifāḍa*) from 'Arafa. (*See* **Ḥajj**; **Sa'y**.)

Mysterious Letters of the Qur'ān, The Twenty-nine **sūras** of the **Qur'ān** begin with single letters, or groups of letters, from the Arabic alphabet. They occur after the **Basmala** (q.v.) but before any other words. A large number of theories, over the centuries, have been put forward by Muslim and non-Muslim scholars in an endeavour to explain these letters. Such theories include the idea that each letter is the first of an epithet characterizing God (e.g. K=*Karīm* (Noble)), and the idea that each letter has a numerical (mystical) value, among many others. M. S. Seale in his book *Qur'ān and Bible* advances the interesting thesis that 'the standing puzzle posed to Islamic scholarship by the initial letters . . . may be explained by reading them as mnemonics or as abbreviated tables of contents'. However, the comment in the mediaeval *Exegesis* (*Tafsīr*) of al-Jalālayn is one of the most telling as well as one of the most succinct. Following the citation of the five Arabic letters with which **Sūrat Maryam** (q.v.) commences, the authors of the *Exegesis* comment: 'God knows best what is meant by this'.

Mysticism, Islamic *See* **Taṣawwuf**.

al-Nabā' (Ar.) The title of the 78th **sūra** of the **Qur'ān**; it means 'The News'. The *sūra* belongs to the Meccan period and has 70 verses. The title comes from the 2nd verse which refers to 'the great news'. The *sūra* begins with physical references to the earth and the Heavens created by God and this is followed by a description of the Day of Judgement. The wicked will drink foul things in Hell while the good will enjoy the physical delights of Paradise. (*See* **al-Janna**; **al-Nār**; **Yawm al-Qiyāma**.)

Nabī (Ar.) [pl. *nabiyyūn* or *anbiyā'*] Prophet. Islam teaches that **Muḥammad** was the Last or Seal of the Prophets (**Khātam al-Nabiyyīn** (q.v.)). A total of 28 prophets are named in the **Qur'ān**. Several are mentioned in **Sūrat Maryam** (q.v.) where each is characterized as a *nabī* or **rasūl** (q.v.) or both. Every *rasūl* is necessarily a *nabī*; however the reverse is not true.

Nabîdh (Ar.) [pl. *anbidha*] Wine. More specifically, this is wine made from dates, raisins, barley or honey. Despite the prohibition in Islam on wine-drinking, the consumption of *nabīdh* was permitted by the **Ḥanafīs** (q.v.), if drunk moderately, for a variety of reasons. (*See* **Ḥadd**; **Khamr**; **Khayyām**.)

al-Naḍīr One of three major Jewish clans in **Medina** (q.v.); the other two were **Qaynuqā'** (q.v.) and **Qurayẓa** (q.v.). Since their settlement in Medina in pre-Islamic times the Naḍīr had become much Arabized. The Prophet **Muḥammad** ultimately expelled them from Medina: many went to **Khaybar** (q.v.) or Syria.

Nafīsa, al-Sayyida (died 208-9/824) Great grand-daughter of **al-Ḥasan b. 'Alī** (q.v.). She migrated to Egypt and gained a reputation as a miracle worker. Her Mosque-Shrine in **Cairo** (q.v.) is much visited today by petitioners and pilgrims. The City of the Dead in Cairo also contains a small retreat (*khalwa*) of Nafīsa.

Nafs (Ar.) [pl. *nufūs* or *anfus*] Soul, spirit, human being, person, self, mind. The individual usages of this word need to be examined with care in their respective contexts. (*See* **Rūḥ**.)

al-Naḥl (Ar.) The title of the 16th **sūra** of the **Qur'ān**; it means 'The Bees'. The vast majority of the *sūra* belongs to the late Meccan period; it contains 128 verses. The title of the *sūra* is drawn from v.68 which refers to God's advice to the bees that they should find dwellings in the mountains and trees and building materials. The *sūra* lauds God's blessings on His creation, proclaims His Oneness, and describes the Paradise awaiting the pious. Much pain awaits those who do not believe in the signs, or verses. (*āyāt*) of God. The *sūra* also forbids the consumption of pork, dead meat, blood, and what has been killed in a name other than God's name. Towards the end of this *sūra*, **Ibrāhīm** (q.v.) is described as a **ḥanīf** (q.v.) who was not one of the polytheists. (*See* **Āya**; **al-Janna**; **al-Nār**; **Slaughter, Ritual**)

al-Nahrawān, Battle of Fought between **'Alī b. Abī Ṭālib** (q.v.) and the **Khārijites** (q.v.) (who had left 'Alī's army), at al-Nahrawān, East of the Tigris River, in 38/658. The Khārijite leader Ibn Wahb was killed with most of his followers, and the Khārijites were for the time being defeated. It was, however, a kind of Pyrrhic victory; 'Alī himself was later assassinated by a Khārijite and Khārijite insurrections continued under the rule of the **Umayyads** (q.v.).

al-Najaf Iraqi city, very near **al-Kūfa** (q.v.), where **'Alī b. Abī Ṭālib** (q.v.) lies buried accordiing to Shī'ite tradition. A shrine, sometimes destroyed and then rebuilt over the centuries, has stood over the tomb of 'Alī since the days of **Hārūn al-Rashīd** (q.v.). 'Alī's shrine is a place of great veneration for the **Shī'ites** (q.v.) and paralleled only by such places as the shrine of **al-Ḥusayn b. 'Alī** (q.v.) at **Karbalā'** (q.v.) (which contains his body), the Mosque of Sayyidnā 'l-Ḥusayn in **Cairo** (q.v.) (which contains his head), and the shrine at **Kāẓimayn** (q.v.) in **Baghdād** (q.v.). The Shī'ites characterize al-Najaf as 'The Most Noble' *(al-Ashraf)*.

al-Najm (Ar.) The title of the 53th **sūra** of the **Qur'ān**; it means 'The Star'. The *sūra* is Meccan and has 62 verses. The title comes from an oath in the 1st verse. The early verses of the *sūra* (vv.13–18) are a major source of detail about the famous **Mi'rāj** (q.v.) of **Muḥammad**. Reference is also made to **al-Lāt** (q.v.), **al-'Uzzā** (q.v.), and **Manāt** (q.v.). A number of major prophets like **Mūsā** (q.v.). **Ibrāhīm** (q.v.) and **Nūḥ** (q.v.) are also mentioned, as is the fate which overtook **'Ād** (q.v.) and **Thamūd** (q.v.). (*See* **Sūrat al-Isrā'**.)

Nakīr *See* **Munkar and Nakīr**.

al-Naml (Ar.) The title of the 27th **sūra** of the **Qur'ān**; it means 'The Ants'. The *sūra* is Meccan and has 93 verses. Its title is drawn from the 18th verse which portrays an ant advising his brethren to seek refuge in their homes lest they be inadvertently crushed by **Sulaymān** (q.v.) and his armies. The *sūra* begins with two of the **Mysterious Letters of the Qur'ān** (q.v.), makes reference to the staff of **Mūsā** (q.v.) being turned into a snake, and then goes on to relate the story of Sulaymān who can speak the language of the birds. The hoopoe bird brings him news of the ruler of Sheba and Sulaymān has a notable encounter with her. This *sūra* is full of prophetic history and it goes on to give details of the stories of **Ṣāliḥ** (q.v.) and **Lūṭ** (q.v.). (*See* **Bilqīs**; **Sūrat Sabā'**.)

Namrūd (Ar.) Nimrod. He is a king identified with the figure in the **Qur'ān** who cast **Ibrāhīm** (q.v.) into a blazing fire in vv.68–70 of **Sūrat al-Anbiyā'** (q.v.). Later Arabic writings considerably developed the story of Namrūd. (*See* **Jibrīl**.)

Naqshabandiyya Major **ṣūfī** (q.v.) order which became popular in Central Asia, Kurdistan and the Indian subcontinent but much less so in the Arab world. The order derives its name from Bahā' al-Dīn al-Naqshabandī (died 791/1389) who is not, however, considered to be the founder. Naqshabandīs emphasize a mental **dhikr** (q.v.) and adhere to a rule of eleven major principles. (*See* **Riḍā**; **Taṣawwuf**.)

al-Nār (Ar.) Hell: literally, 'The Fire'. This commonest of all names for Hell appears many times in the **Qur'ān** where Hell is always described in very physical terms. The eternity of Hell, especially for wicked Muslims, has been questioned by some theologians who have pointed to verses in the Qur'ān and the **Ḥadīth** (q.v.) literature to support their views. (*See* **al-Hāwiya**; **al-Ḥuṭama**; **Jahannam**; **al-Jaḥīm**; **Laẓā**; **Sa'īr**; **Saqar**; **al-Zabāniyya**; **al-Zaqqūm**.)

al-Nās (Ar.) The title of the 114th and last **sūra** of the **Qur'ān**; it means 'The People' or 'Mankind'. The *sūra* belongs to the Meccan period and has 6 verses. Its title comes from the 1st verse which counsels that one should say 'I seek refuge with the Lord of mankind'. The remaining 5 verses are a completion of the invocation. They describe God as the King and God of mankind and then specify that the evil from which refuge is sought is that of the Devil, called here 'The Tempter' and 'The one who leaves when God's name is mentioned', who whispers in men's hearts, as well as the evil of the **Jinn** (q.v.) and men. (See **Iblīs**.)

al-Nasā'ī (died 303/915) Compiler of one of the six major compilations of **Ḥadīth** (q.v.). He travelled widely to collect traditions, lived in both **Damascus** (q.v.) and Egypt and is buried in **Mecca** (q.v.). His collection of traditions gives a prominent place to the *'ibādāt* (*See* **'Ibāda**.)

Nāsikh and Mansūkh (Ar.) Doctrine of abrogation in the **Qur'ān** according to which a verse revealed later may abrogate one revealed earlier; this resolves the problem of any apparent conflict etc. The Arabic word *nāsikh* designates the 'abrogating' verse while *mansūkh* indicates that the verse has been 'abrogated'. The Qur'ān itself refers to this very principle of abrogation in v.106 of **Sūrat al-Baqara** (q.v.) and v.101 of **Sūrat al-Naḥl** (q.v.). It must be stressed here that the abrogated verses still remain a part of the Qur'ān.

Naskh *See* **Nāsikh and Mansūkh**.

al-Naṣr (Ar.) The title of the 110th **sūra** of the **Qur'ān**; it means 'The Help'. The *sūra* belongs to the Medinan period and has 3 verses. It was the last Qur'ānic *sūra* to be revealed to the Prophet **Muḥammad** and is characterized as Medinan by commentators despite its revelation during the **Ḥajj al-Wadā'** (q.v.). The title is taken from the 1st verse which speaks of when God's help and victory arrive. At that time God is to be praised and His forgiveness sought.

Naṣrids *See* **Alhambra**.

Naṣṣ (Ar.) [pl. *nuṣūṣ*] Literally, 'text', 'expression'. The word also has the technical sense among the **Ithnā 'Asharīs** (q.v.) and **Ismā'īlīs** (q.v.) of 'designation'; that is, the **Imām** (q.v.) designates his successor.

Nāṭiq (Ar.) [pl. *nuṭaqā'*] Literally, 'speaker'. In the early cyclical history of the **Ismā'īlīs** (q.v.), each of the seven eras began with a prophetic 'Speaker' (*Nāṭiq*) beaing a revelation.

al-Nawawī (631/1233–676/1277) Syrian scholar from Nawā most famous for his short collection of **Ḥadīth** (q.v.) known in English as *Forty Hadith*. It is worth noting, however, that he produced many other major writings as well. Al-Nawawī was held in particular reverence by the **Shāfi'īs** (q.v.).

al-Nāzi'āt (Ar.) The title of the 79th **sūra** of the **Qur'ān**; it means 'The Removers'. The *sūra* belongs to the Meccan period and has 46 verses. The title comes from an oath in the 1st verse; the 'removers' are the angels who remove evil men's souls. The *sūra* begins with a series of five formal oaths and goes on to stress the doctrine of the resurrection of the body on the Last Day. **Al-Jaḥīm** (q.v.) awaits the wicked. The *sūra* concludes by underlining that only God knows when the Last Day will be. (*See* **Angel**; **Yawm al-Qiyāma**.)

Neoplatonism, Islamic The thought of Plotinus (AD 204-5–AD270) with its classical emphasis on eternal emanation and hierarchy, an unknowable Divinity and a number of major emanated hypostases like Intellect and Soul, was known from early times in the Middle East. Notable vehicles for Neoplatonic thought included the city of **Alexandria** (q.v.) as well as a book, the so-called *Theology of Aristotle* (*Theologia Aristotelis*). In the thought of many of the classical Islamic philosophers, *creatio ex nihilo* was replaced by emanation (**fayḍ** (q.v.)) to the dismay of mainstream theologians. Among whole groups or sects of Muslims who were influenced by Neoplatonic thought were the

Ismā'īlīs (q.v.). It must be stressed, however, that Neoplatonism, as it developed in the Middle East, was often very different from the versions which Europe encountered. (*See* **Aristotelianism, Islamic; Falsafa; al-Fārābī; al-Ḥāmidī; Ibn al-'Arabī; Ibn Sīnā; Ikhwān al-Ṣafā'; al-Kirmānī; Platonism, Islamic; al-Sijistānī; al-Suhrawardī.**)

Nifāq (Ar.) Hypocrisy. (*See* **Munāfiqūn; Sūrat al-Munāfiqūn.**)

Night Journey of Muḥammad *See* **Isrā'**; *see also* **al-Aqṣā, al-Masjid; al-Burāq; Mi'rāj; Qubbat al-Ṣakhra; Sūrat al-Isrā'.**

Night of (Divine) Decree *See* **Laylat al-Qadr.**

Night of Power *See* **Laylat al-Qadr.**

Nikāḥ (Ar.) Marriage, marriage contract. The **Qur'ān** permits a Muslim male to marry up to four wives, provided that he feels able to treat them all equitably. However, as a result of the interpretation of certain verses of the Qur'ān, polygamy is now banned in countries like Tunisia. The Qur'ān also specifies certain forbidden degrees of kindred within which a Muslim may not marry. The marriage need not be contracted in a mosque nor does it *have* to be in the presence of a religious official. It is thus more a civil than a religious affair. The dowry (**mahr** (q.v.)) is an important part of the marriage contract. (*See* **Mut'a; Sūrat al-Nisā'; Ṭalāq.**)

Ni'matullāhiyya Major **ṣūfī** (q.v.) Shī'ite order named after Shāh Ni'matullāh Walī (730/1330–834/1431). It gained particular popularity in Iran and also in India. The order has become divided into a number of branches, one of which flourishes in London. (*See* **Shī'ism; Taṣawwuf.**)

Nimrod *See* **Namrūd.**

al-Nisā' (Ar.) The title of the 4th **sūra** of the **Qur'ān**; it means 'The Women'. The *sūra* belongs to the Medinan period and has 176 verses. Its title reflects much of the subject matter of the *sūra* which was revealed around the time of the Battle of Uḥud and its aftermath. Orphans are to be treated fairly, women may receive the dowry and rules for inheritance are prescribed. Punishment is also prescribed for sexual sin and a list of the forbidden degrees of kindred is given. Wilful murder will be punished forever in Hell. Much of this *sūra* may fairly be described as a 'women's rights document' in view of its concern for females. Towards the end of the *sūra* a firm statement denies that **'Īsā** (q.v.) was killed or crucified: this is one of the key texts in any understanding of the Islamic view of the crucifixion. (*See* **Murder and Manslaughter**; **al-Nār**; **Uḥud, Battle of**)

Niyya (Ar.) [pl. *niyyāt*] Intention. Islamic moral theology, and, indeed, Islamic ritual, places considerable emphasis on a man's intention. A well-known **ḥadīth** (q.v.) states that actions are judged by the intentions associated with them and that every man will receive what he intended.

Nizārīs Members of branch of **Ismā'īlīs** (q.v.) which supported the claims of Nizār, eldest son of the Fāṭimid caliph **al-Mustanṣir** (q.v.), as successor. (*See* **Āghā Khān**; **Assassins**; **Fāṭimids**; **Khojas**; **Musta'lians**.)

Noah *See* **Nūḥ**.

Noble Sanctuary, The *See* **al-Ḥaram al Sharīf**.

Noe *See* **Nūḥ**.

Nūḥ (1) (Ar.) Noah (Noe): Qur'ānic messenger (*rasūl*) sent to warn his people who reject him. They are drowned in a great flood while Nūḥ is saved in the ark (*al-fulk*). The story of Nūḥ is related at some length in the **Qur'ān** in **Sūrat Hūd** (q.v.).

Nūḥ (2) (Ar.) Noah (Noe): the title of the 71st **sūra** of the **Qur'ān**; it is a proper name. The *sūra* belongs to the Meccan period and has 28 verses. The title is drawn from the 1st verse in which God states that He has sent Nūḥ to his people. The *sūra* is devoted almost entirely to the story of Nūḥ: he comes to warn his people and tells them to seek forgiveness from God. Nūḥ is refused and the wicked are drowned in the Flood. The *sūra* concludes with Nūḥ praying to God that the Latter should not leave one unbeliever on the earth. (*See* **Nūḥ** (1).)

al-Nu'mān, al-Qāḍī (died 363-4/974) Major theoretician and jurist of the **Fāṭimids** (q.v.). He was a prolific author whose best-known work is perhaps his *The Pillars of Islam* (*Da'ā'im al-Islām*). Al-Nu'mān is of particular importance for the development of **fiqh** (q.v.) and the recorded history of the Fāṭimids. (*See* **Ismā'īlīs**.)

al-Nūr (Ar.) The title of the 24th **sūra** of the **Qur'ān**; it means 'The Light'. The *sūra* is Medinan and has 64 verses. Its title is taken from v.35 which describes God as the Light of the Heavens and the earth in one of the most famous and mystically beautiful of all the Qur'ānic verses, called 'The Light Verse' (*Āyat al-Nūr*). The *sūra* lays down a number of legal and other injunctions: for example, 100 lashes are prescribed for adultery; women are to dress modestly; prayer (**ṣalāt** (q.v.)) is to be performed; **zakāt** (q.v.) is to be paid and the Messenger of God is to be obeyed. These are just a few of the regulations which are laid down in what is a very wide-ranging *sūra* from the point of view of its legal content. (*See* **'Ā'isha bint Abī Bakr**.)

Nuṣayrīs Members of syncretic group also called 'Alawīs (i.e. those who follow **'Alī b. Abī Ṭālib** (q.v.)). Their name Nuṣayrīs derives from one of their important early leaders Muḥammad b. Nuṣayr (*c.* 3rd/9th century). Their beliefs have much in common with those of the **Ismā'īlīs** (q.v.). There are Nuṣayrīs in Syria, Turkey and Lebanon. In Turkey they are known as Alevis.

Obscurities (Qur'ānic) *See* **Mutashābihāt**.

Observance, Religious *See* **'Ibāda**.

Occasionalism *See* **Atomism**.

Occultation *See* **Ghayba**.

Old Man of the Mountain *See* **Ḥasan-i Ṣabbāḥ**.

Oneness of God *See* **Tawḥīd**.

Order, Ṣūfī *See* **Ṭā'ifa**; **Ṭarīqa**.

Organization of the Islamic Conference *See* **Islamic Conference Organization**.

Ottomans Major dynasty which occupied a prominent position in the Near and Middle East from 680/1281 until 1342/1924 and founded a great empire. They took their name from an early leader in the 7th/13th century called 'Uthmān (Osman). The Ottomans successively established capitals at **Bursa** (q.v.), Edirne (Adrianople) and, after its conquest in 857/1453 by **Mehmet II 'The Conqueror'** (q.v.), at **Istanbul** (q.v.). Under such sultans as Selīm the Grim and **Süleymān 'The Magnificent'** (q.v.) the Ottoman empire reached its heyday in the 10th/16th century. Thereafter its history was one of gradual decline. Turkey entered the First World War siding with Germany and the Central Powers, thus precipitating the loss of Arab lands and, ultimately, at the instigation of **Atatürk** (q.v.), the abolition of the Ottoman sultanate and the caliphate after the War. The last Ottoman, 'Abd al-Majīd II, was deposed in 1342/1924. (*See* **'Abd al-Ḥamīd II**; **Sinān**.)

Paradise *See* **al-Janna**.

Passion Play *See* **Ta'ziya**.

Pbuh 'Peace be upon him'. This set of initials, or the entire phrase, is used after the name of the Prophet **Muḥammad** in English, as a mark of respect. The equivalent Arabic letters are ṢL'M (=*Ṣallā Allāh 'alayhi wa sallam*, usually translated as 'May God bless him and grant him salvation').

Peace be with you! *See* **al-Salāmu 'alaykum**.

People of the Book *See* **Ahl al-Kitāb**.

People of the Cave *See* **Aṣḥāb al-Kahf**.

Permission *See* **al-Aḥkām al-Khamsa**; **Ḥalāl**.

Pharaoh *See* **Fir'awn**.

Philosophy *See* **Falsafa**.

Pilgrimage *See* **Ḥajj**; *see also* **'Arafa**; **Arkān**; **al-Jamra**; **al-Marwa**; **Minā**; **Muzdalifa**; **al-Ṣafā**; **Sa'y**; **Wuqūf**.

Pilgrimage of Farewell *See* **Ghadīr al-Khumm**; **Ḥajj al-Wadā'**; **Muḥammad**.

Pillars of Islam, Five *See* **Arkān**.

Pīr (Pers.) Wise guide, spiritual master, saint, old man.

Platonism, Islamic Generally speaking, the thought of Plato had less impact on the development of Islamic Philosophy than that of Aristotle or Plotinus. Plato's greatest areas of influence were perhaps those of ethics and morals, and in such classifications as the tripartite division of the soul. The Islamic philosopher upon whom Platonic thought probably made the greatest impact was **al-Fārābī** (q.v.). Plato's *Republic* was translated into Arabic in the 3rd/9th century. The Platonic themes of the body as a prison for the soul and Socrates as a hero who knows how to die bravely, appear in such Arabic works as the *Epistles* of the **Ikhwān al-Ṣafā'** (q.v.). The Platonic doctrine of the Forms, however, received little attention or approval either here, or in other Arabic texts. (*See* **Aristotelianism, Islamic**; **Falsafa**; **Neoplatonism, Islamic**)

Poitiers, Battle of Battle between the Arabs and Charles Martel, fought between Tours and Poitiers, in 114/732 which is alleged finally to have halted the Muslim advance into Europe. The Arab forces were commanded by 'Abd al-Raḥmān al-Ghāfiqī, and the Christian army by Martel. The battle, sometimes called the Battle of Tours, was one in which the Arabs were defeated. The historian Edward Gibbon believed that this battle was so decisive that, had the Arabs not been defeated, 'the Arabian fleet might have sailed without a naval combat into the mouth of the Thames' and that 'Perhaps the interpretation of the Koran would now be taught in the schools of Oxford . . .' However, some historians believe that Gibbon created something of a major myth when he imbued the battle with so much significance and they claim that the whole affair, in reality, was little more than a skirmish. (*See* **Hishām**; **Qur'ān**.)

Poll Tax *See* **Jizya.**

Polygamy *See under* **Nikāḥ**.

Polytheism *See* **Shirk.**

Polytheists *See* **Mushrikūn**; **Shirk**.

Pool, The *See* **Ḥawḍ**.

Pork The **Qur'ān** prohibits the consumption of pork. The latter is considered to be **ḥarām** (q.v.). See v.3 of **Sūrat al-Mā'ida** (q.v.). (*See also* **Sūrat al-Naḥl**.)

Potiphar *See* **Qiṭfīr**.

Prayer *See* **Ṣalāt**; **Tarāwīḥ**; **Witr**.

Prayer Beads *See* **Subḥa**.

Prayer Carpet, Prayer Rug *See* **Sajjāda**.

Predestination *See* **Taqdīr**; *see also* **Qadar**; **Qadariyya**.

Pre-Islam *See* **Jāhiliyya**.

Preserved Tablet *See* **al-Lawḥ al-Maḥfūẓ**.

Prince of the Believers *See* **Amīr al-Mu'minīn**; **Khalīfa**.

Principles of Law *See* **Uṣūl al-Fiqh**; *see also* **Subsidiary Principles of Law**.

Profession of Faith *See* **Shahāda**.

Prohibition *See* **al-Aḥkām al-Khamsa**; **Ḥarām**.

Promise and the Threats, The *See* **al-Wa'd wa 'l-Wa'īd**.

Prophet *See* **Nabī**.

Prostration, Ritual *See* **Sujūd**.

Pulpit *See* **Minbar**.

Punishment of the Grave *See* **'Adhāb al-Qabr**.

Punishments, Islamic *See* **Ḥadd**.

Purdah A word deriving from the Urdu and Persian word *pardah* meaning 'veil' or 'curtain'. The concept of purdah embraces the whole idea of the general seclusion of women. (*See* **Ḥijāb**.)

Purification, Ritual *See* **Ṭahāra**; *see also* **Ghusl**; **Mīḍa'a**; **Tayammum**; **Wuḍū'**.

Purity, Ritual *See* entries cited above.

Qabḍ (Ar.) Literally, 'contraction', 'gripping'. This is a technical term used in **taṣawwuf** (q.v.). *Qabḍ* is the mystical opposite of **basṭ** (q.v.). It is a time of spiritual desolation perhaps akin to the state in Christian mysticism known as 'the Dark Night of the Soul'. *See* v.245 of **Sūrat al-Baqara** (q.v.) in the **Qur'ān**.

Qābīl and Hābīl The Arabic names for Cain and Abel. These two sons of **Ādam** (q.v.) are mentioned, though not by these names, in the **Qur'ān** which tells the well-known story of the first murder. (*See* vv.27–31 of **Sūrat al-Mā'ida** (q.v.).)

Qaḍā' (Ar.) Divine decree, divine judgment, divine will, the function of God as Judge (**Qāḍī** (q.v.)). The word has a variety of other senses in the **Qur'ān**. (*See* **Qadar**.)

Qadar (Ar.) Often translated as 'destiny', 'fate', 'divine predestination', 'divine determination', *qadar* specifically is the divine application of **qaḍā'** (q.v.) in time, according to the most widespread interpretations. (*See* **Kasb**.)

Qadariyya School of theology in early Islam which championed the idea of man's free will. The **Qur'ān** contains verses which both back the idea of predestination and that of man's free will. The Qadariyya arose in early Islam as a result of the debates about man's exact freedom to act. The partisans of a free will doctrine received what was, in effect a nickname, *Qadarīs*, because they talked about **qadar** (q.v.), its opposite! The whole question of free will became one of the key issues in mediaeval

Islamic theology. It was discussed, for example, by the **Mu'tazila** (q.v.); the solution, in so far as it may really be termed a solution, was formulated eventually by theologians according to the doctrine of **kasb** (q.v.). In answer to the idea that Arabic had no word which exactly paralleled or translated the Greek *autoexousios*, that is, 'free will', M. S. Seale in his *Muslim Theology* (see back of this *Dictionary* for full bibliographical details) has maintained that this was not the case, and suggested that *tafwīḍ* (delegation), from the verb *fawwaḍa*, was a good equivalent. He notes: 'Fawwaḍa means the entrusting by God to man of the power to act and choose through *tafwīḍ*, that is delegation. It is significant that one of the seven Qadarī groups . . . was called the *Mufawwiḍa*, because they believed that they were empowered to act without God's help or guidance'. (*See* **Kalām**; **Taqdīr**.)

Qadhf (Ar.) False accusation of unchastity. (*See* **Ḥadd**.)

Qāḍī (Ar.) [pl. *quḍāt*] Judge. Some people refused to become judges in early and mediaeval Islam lest their judgements lead them to condemnation in Hell fire. The institution dates from the time of the **Umayyads** (q.v.).

Qādianīs *See* **Aḥmadiyya** (1).

Qādiriyya Major **ṣūfī** (q.v.) order named after 'Abd al-Qādir **al-Jīlānī** (q.v.) who, when more than fifty years old, established a reputation by his preaching in **Baghdād** (q.v.). He is buried in that city. The order has been described as the first major one in the history of **taṣawwuf** (q.v.). Although never the *most* popular of the orders, the Qādiriyya none the less spread widely all over the Near and Middle East and also established itself in parts of India.

al-Qādisiyya, Battle of Major battle which took place near the present site of **al-Najaf** (q.v.) between the Muslim army and that of the Sāsānian King Yazdagird III; various dates for this battle are given between 15/636 and 16/637. The Persians were led by Rustam, who was killed in the battle, and the Arab army was commanded by Sa'd b. Abī Waqqāṣ. The battle was noteworthy for the use of elephants by the Persian side. The Muslim army defeated the Persians in what was a vital victory, opening as it did the path to the eventual Muslim conquest of Persia.

al-Qadr (Ar.) The title of the 97th **sūra** of the **Qur'ān**; it means 'The Power' or 'The Decree'. The *sūra* belongs to the Meccan period and has 5 verses. Its title is drawn from the reference to **Laylat al-Qadr** (q.v.) in the 1st verse.

Qāf (Ar.) The title of the 50th **sūra** of the **Qur'ān**; *qāf* is one of the letters of the Arabic alphabet. The *sūra* belongs to the Meccan period and contains 45 verses. Its title is drawn from the first letter of v.1, the whole of which reads: '*Qāf*, by the Glorious Qur'ān'. The *sūra* retails some of God's blessings and mentions various peoples to whom God has sent His messengers. Hell awaits the sinners and Paradise the pious. In a famous statement in v.16, which underlines His immanence, God declares that He is nearer to man than the latter's jugular vein. (*See* **al-Janna**; **Mysterious Letters of the Qur'ān**; **al-Nār**.)

Qāf, Mount A mountain range in Islamic cosmology which circles the whole earth.

al-Qāhira *See* **Cairo**.

Qā'id A'ẓam *See* **Jināḥ**.

Qājārs Major dynasty which succeeded the **Ṣafavids** (q.v.) in Persia and, gradually gaining in power from 1133/1721, ruled from 1193/1779 until 1342/1924 when Sulṭān Aḥmad Shāh was deposed; the latter was succeeded by Riḍā Shāh Pahlavī. Towards the end of the Qājār period, Persian power gradually declined and the area was both wooed and squeezed by the Great Powers of the age like Russia, France and Britain.

al-Qalam (Ar.) The title of the 68th **sūra** of the **Qur'ān**; it means 'The Pen'. The *sūra* belongs to the Meccan period and has 52 verses. Its title is drawn from an oath in the 1st verse 'By the Pen'. The *sūra* begins by reassuring **Muḥammad** that he is not mad and, after telling the story of the selfish owners of the garden, whose desire to gather its fruit is frustrated, the *sūra* concludes with a reference to the story of **Yūnus** (q.v.).

al-Qamar (Ar.) The title of the 54th **sūra** of the **Qur'ān**; it means 'The Moon'. The *sūra* belongs mainly to the Meccan period and contains 55 verses. Its title is drawn from the 1st verse which refers to the Hour approaching and the moon splitting. This is interpreted either as a reference to the end of the world, or to an eclipse. A number of disbelieving peoples, like those of **Nūḥ** (q.v.), **'Ād** (q.v.) and **Thamūd** (q.v.), who ignored the warnings of God's messengers and in consequence were punished by God, are mentioned. The wicked will burn in **Saqar** (q.v.) (=Hell) while the pious enjoy the delights of Paradise. (*See* **al-Janna**; **al-Nār**; **al-Sā'a**; **Yawm al-Qiyāma**.)

Qarāmiṭa (Ar.) [sing. *Qarmaṭī*] Carmathians. At first this was a revolutionary movement of early Ismā'īlī inspiration, deriving its name from an Ismā'īlī leader called Ḥamdān Qarmaṭ (disappeared *c*. 286/899). There were groups of Qarāmiṭa in the Syrian desert, **al-Kūfa** (q.v.) and Bahrain. Their most audacious and sacriligious act, from a theological perspective, was to seize the Black Stone from the **Ka'ba** (q.v.) in 317/930, only returning it some 22 years later in 339/951. (*See* **al-Ḥajar al-Aswad**; **Ismā'īlīs**.)

al-Qāri'a (Ar.) The title of the 101st **sūra** of the **Qur'ān**; it means 'The Sudden Misfortune' and the reference here is to the time of the Last Judgement. The *sūra* belongs to the Meccan period and has 11 verses. Its title is drawn from the first 2 verses which may be translated as 'The Misfortune! What is the Misfortune?'. The *sūra* goes on to provide a brief description of the end of the world and the Judgement with scales. For the person whose scales are light, **al-Hāwiya** (q.v.) (=Hell) awaits. (*See* **al-Ḥisāb**; **al-Nār**; **Yawm al-Qiyāma**.)

al-Qaṣaṣ (Ar.) The title of the 28th **sūra** of the **Qur'ān**; it means 'The Story'. The *sūra* belongs to the Meccan period and has 88 verses. The title of the *sūra* is drawn from the reference to a story in v.25. The *sūra* begins with three of the **Mysterious Letters of the Qur'ān** (q.v.), and then tells the story of **Mūsā** (q.v.) in considerable detail, referring to Pharaoh several times. At the end of the *sūra* which also covers a variety of other matters, man is warned not to be an idolater, and told that all things will perish except the face of God who will judge all men. (*See* **Fir'awn**.)

al-Qāsim Son of the Prophet **Muḥammad** and **Khadīja bint Khuwaylid** (q.v.), who died in infancy aged two. It was because of him that Muḥammad was sometimes called Abū 'l-Qāsim. (*See* **'Abd Allāh b. Muḥammad**; **Ibrāhīm** (3).)

Qāsim Amīn *See* **Amīn, Qāsim**.

Qaynuqā' Major Jewish clan in **Medina** (q.v.), ultimately expelled by the Prophet **Muḥammad** from that city. It is said that they went to Syria. (*See* **al-Naḍīr**; **Qurayẓa**.)

Qayrawān Tunisian city, often transliterated into English as Kairouan, founded in 43/663-4 or 50/670 by 'Uqba b. Nāfi', the great Muslim conqueror of North Africa. The city became a great cultural centre under the **Aghlabids** (q.v.) and a focus for Mālikī jurisprudence. During the period of the **Umayyads** (q.v.), one of the earliest North African mosques was erected in Qayrawān. (*See* **Hilāl, Banū**; **Mālikīs**.)

al-Qayyūm (Ar.) The Eternal, i.e. God. (*See* **Āyat al-Kursī; Sūrat al-Baqara**.)

Qibla (Ar.) Direction of prayer towards the **Ka'ba** (q.v.) in **Mecca** (q.v.). This is indicated in a mosque by the **miḥrāb** (q.v.). Originally, the direction of prayer was towards **Jerusalem** (q.v.) but it was changed towards Mecca after the **Hijra** (q.v.). This change is recorded in the **Qur'ān** in **Sūrat al-Baqara** (q.v.) which notes that the original *qibla* towards Jerusalem was designed as a test for the faithful, and specifically urges them to turn towards 'the Sacred Mosque' (*al-Masjid al-Ḥarām*) in Mecca. At the time of revelation this phrase would have indicated simply the *Ka'ba*; **al-Masjid al-Ḥarām** (q.v.) now means the whole Great Mosque of Mecca. (*See* **Ṣalāt**.)

Qiṣāṣ (Ar.) Retaliation. Pre-Islamic blood revenge (*tha'r*) was replaced by the concept of just retaliation in Islam, as Coulson observes (see back of this *Dictionary* for full bibliographical details). (*See* **Diya**; **Murder and Manslaughter**.)

Qiṭfīr (Ar.) Potiphar. In the **Qur'ān**, in **Sūrat Yūsuf** (q.v.), the Egyptian purchaser of Yūsuf is not named. However the exegetes identify him as Potiphar, and Qiṭfīr is just one of the Arabic forms by which this name is rendered.

al-Qiyāma (Ar.) The title of the 75th **sūra** of the **Qur'ān**; it means 'The Resurrection'. The *sūra* belongs to the Meccan period and has 40 verses. Its title is drawn from the 1st verse which contains an oath 'by the Day of Resurrection'. Some of the signs of this day are itemized. At the end man is reminded of God's power to raise the dead. (*See* **Ishārāt al-Sā'a**; **Yawm al-Qiyāma**.)

Qiyās (Ar.) Analogy, analogical reasoning. This was one of the four main sources of law for **al-Shāfi'ī** (q.v.). It has been described as a type of **ijtihād** (q.v.) and implies an extension or elaboration of the basic guidelines and principles which may be derived from the three other major sources of law enunciated by al-Shāfi'ī, namely, **Qur'ān**, **Sunna** (q.v.) and **ijmā'** (q.v.). (*See* **Uṣūl al-Fiqh**.)

Qubba (Ar.) [pl. *qibāb* or *qubab*] Dome, cupola. This is a major architectural feature in Islamic mosque and shrine building. It may often be beautifully decorated in golden coloured copper alloy sheeting, or, alternatively, coloured tiles. An excellent example of the first is to be seen on the Regents Park Mosque in London; examples of beautiful coloured tile domes are scattered throughout Iran. Interestingly, the Iraqi city of **al-Baṣra** (q.v.) bears the title 'The Dome of Islam' (*Qubbat al-Islām*). (*See* **Art and Architecture, Islamic**; **Hilāl**; **Muqarnaṣ**; **Qubbat al-Ṣakhra**.)

Qubbat al-Ṣakhra (Ar.) The Dome of the Rock. This is the principal Islamic shrine in **Jerusalem** (q.v.) built over the area of rock on the Temple Mount from which the Prophet **Muḥammad** made his famous **Mi'rāj** (q.v.). The Dome of the Rock is frequently, but inaccurately, called 'The *Mosque* of 'Umar'. (*See* **'Abd al-Malik b. Marwān**; **al-Aqṣā, al-Masjid**; **al-Burāq**; **Isrā'**; **Qubba**.)

al-Quds *See* **Jerusalem**.

Quietists *See* **al-Murji'a**.

Qur'ān (Ar.) Often spelled in English as Koran. Literally this word means 'Recitation'. The Qur'ān is Islam's holiest book, being the *uncreated* word of God revealed through **Jibrīl** (q.v.) to the Prophet **Muḥammad**. The text consists of 114 chapters, each called a **sūra** in Arabic, arranged so that the longest ones come first. Each *sūra* is classified as Meccan or Medinan according to whether that *sūra* was revealed to Muḥammad in **Mecca** (q.v.) or **Medina** (q.v.). Each *sūra* is divided into verses, a single one of which is called in Arabic an **āya** (q.v.). It is a particular feature of this *Dictionary* that every single one of the 114 *sūras* is described separately under its own Arabic *sūra* title. Diverse other *Dictionary* entries also refer to other aspects of the Qur'ān and the reader is referred to some of these at the end of this entry. Muslims believe that the Qur'ān is inimitable. Stylistically, much of the text resembles a kind of rhymed prose called *saj'* in Arabic. Books about the Holy Qur'ān abound in many different languages. A useful introduction to both structure and content is Bell's *Introduction to the Qur'ān*, revised by W. M. Watt; Khatib's *The Bounteous Koran* provides a beautifully produced and scholarly Arabic-English edition of the sacred text. The Arabic Text used is that of The Royal Cairo Edition and the work has the additional merit of having been authorized by **al-Azhar** (q.v.) in 1984. For a concordance to the Qur'ān, (based on the English rendition by A. J. Arberry entitled *The Koran Interpreted*) see Kassis, *A Concordance of the Qur'ān*. (Full bibliographical details of all the above-mentioned works will be found at the back of this *Dictionary*.) Of course, no modern commentary on the Qur'ān can beat the great classics by such scholars as **al-Bayḍāwī** (q.v.), **al-Ṭabarī** (q.v.), and **al-Zamakhsharī** (q.v.) and the reader able to understand Arabic is referred to these. *Complete* English translations of most commentaries have yet to be made; a start has been made on that by al-Ṭabarī, (*see* vol. 1 of *The Commentary on the Qur'ān*, translated and edited by J. Cooper). (*See also*, among other relevant entries in this *Dictionary*, **Āyat al-Kursī**; **Bāṭin**; **Ḥusayn, Ṭāhā**; **I'jāz**; **Ismā'īlīs**; **al-Lawḥ al-Maḥfūẓ**; **Light Verse**; **Muḥkamāt**; **Mutashābihāt**; **Mu'tazila**; **Mysterious Letters of the Qur'ān**; **Nāsikh and Mansūkh**; **al-Shāfi'ī**; **Tafsīr**; **Ta'wīl**; **'Uthmān b. 'Affān**; **Ẓāhir**; **Zayd b. Thābit**.)

Quraysh (1) Major tribe in **Mecca** (q.v.), of which the clan of **Hāshim** (q.v.), to which the Prophet **Muḥammad** belonged, was a part. The word Quraysh means 'shark'. Muḥammad descended from that branch of Quraysh which came to be called 'Quraysh of the Hollows' (*Quraysh al-Baṭā'iḥ*) who occupied the hollow within which was the **Ka'ba** (q.v.), The whole tribe of Quraysh descended from a common ancestor called Fihr or Quraysh. (*See* **Hāshim** (2).)

Quraysh (2) The title of the 106th **sūra** of the **Qur'ān**; Quraysh is a proper name. The *sūra* belongs to the Meccan period and has 4 verses. It takes its title from the reference to the tribe of Quraysh in the 1st verse. The *sūra* orders Quraysh to serve God who has fed them and protected them. (*See* **Quraysh** (1).)

Qurayẓa Major Jewish clan in **Medina** (q.v.), accused by the Prophet **Muḥammad** of treachery after the Siege and Battle of **al-Khandaq** (q.v.). The males were executed while the women and children were enslaved. (See **al-Naḍīr**; **Qaynuqā'**.)

Qurbān (Ar.) This word has the specialist ritual sense of sacrifice, and denotes in particular what is sacrificed on **'Īd al-Aḍḥā** (q.v.). The latter feast is known in Turkish as Büyük Bayram or Kurban Bayramı.

Quṣayy 5th century AD father of **'Abd Manāf** (q.v.) and **'Abd al-'Uzzā** (q.v.), and ancestor of the Prophet **Muḥammad**.

Quṭb (Ar.) [pl. *aqṭāb*] In the technical terminology of **taṣawwuf** (q.v.) this word means 'pole', 'pivot' or 'axis' and designates the Head of the saints (*awliyā'*), although other saints have been honoured by the title as well. Popular belief holds that the idea of a *quṭb* originated with the famous Egyptian **ṣūfī** (q.v.) **Dhū 'l-Nūn** (q.v.). (*See* **Walī**.)

Quṭb, Sayyid (1324/1906–1386/1966) A major thinker and ideologue of the Muslim Brotherhood in Egypt, executed in 1386/1966, having been accused of a variety of terrorist charges including a plot to kill President Nasser of Egypt. His most notable and influential piece of writing was his book of the early fifties, *Signposts on the Road*. In this he divided society into 'the Ignorant Order' and 'The Islamic Order'. (*See* **al-Bannā'**; **al-Ikhwān al-Muslimūn**.)

Quṭb Mīnār Literally, 'the Minaret of Quṭb'. This is a famous, and very tall, minaret in **Delhi** (q.v.), reaching a height of 238 feet, built *c.* 627/1230. It was originally built as a victory tower, begun by Quṭb al-Dīn Aybak (died 607/1210) and continued by the Sultan Shams al-Dīn Iltutmish (died 633/1236) who lies buried nearby; however, the Quṭb was also used as a minaret. It has been damaged by earthquake and restored at least twice. The Quṭb dominates the whole region in which it stands and may be seen from miles away. It is now the oldest standing tower in the entire subcontinent. (*See* **Manāra**.)

Qūṭifar *See* **Qiṭfīr**.

al-Rabb (Ar.) The Lord. Strictly speaking, this title should only be applied to God who is also called 'The Lord of the Worlds' (*Rabb al-'Ālamīn*) in the **Fātiḥa** (q.v.). The **ḥadīth** (q.v.) literature forbids a slave calling his master 'My lord' (*Rabbī*).

Rābi'a al-'Adawiyya (95/713-4 or 99/717–185/801) Perhaps the most famous of all female ṣūfīs. She spent her entire life in **al-Baṣra** (q.v.). Enslaved as a child, she began an ascetical life on regaining her freedom. She attracted many disciples and became famous for her mystical teachings and emphasis on love of God. She refused marriage preferring instead to be the beloved of God. Perhaps her most famous saying was that in which she prayed to God that, if she worshipped Him out of fear of Hell, then He should consign her there; and if she worshipped Him hoping for Paradise, then He should exclude her from there; but if she worshipped Him for His own sake alone, then He should not keep His eternal beauty from her. (*See* **Ṣūfī**; **Taṣawwuf**.)

al-Ra'd (Ar.) The title of the 13th **sūra** of the **Qur'ān**; it means 'The Thunder'. The *sūra* belongs to the Medinan period and has

43 verses. Its title is drawn from v.13 where the thunder is described as praising God. The *sūra* beings with four of the **Mysterious Letters of the Qur'ān** (q.v.) and has much to say about the wonders of God's creation. There is a stress on the unity of God and Paradise is promised for the virtuous with Hell as the abode of the wicked and the infidels. (*See* **al-Janna**; **al-Nār**; **Taqdīr**; **Tawḥīd**.)

Rāfiḍī (Ar.) [pl. *arfāḍ* or *rawāfiḍ*] Rejector. General term of abuse used by Sunnīs of Shī'ites, especially in mediaeval times. The Shī'ites reject the legitimacy of the calphates of **Abū Bakr** (q.v.). **'Umar b. al-Khaṭṭāb** (q.v.) and **'Uthmān b. 'Affān** (q.v.) and hold that the first correct successor of the Prophet **Muḥammad** was **'Alī b. Abī Ṭālib** (q.v.). (*See* **Rāshidūn**; **Shī'ism**; **Sunnī**.)

al-Raḥīm (Ar.) The Compassionate. This is one of the 99 Beautiful Names of God. An example of its usage in the **Qur'ān** is to be found in v.143 of **Sūrat al-Baqara** (q.v.). (*See* **Basmala**.)

al-Raḥmān (1) (Ar.) The Merciful. This is one of the 99 Beautiful Names of God. An example of its usage in the **Qur'ān** is to be found in v.1 of **Sūrat al-Raḥmān** (q.v.) which draws its title from this verse. (*See* **Basmala**; **al-Raḥmān** (2).)

al-Raḥmān (2) (Ar.) The title of the 55th **sūra** of the **Qur'ān**; it means 'The Merciful' and the reference, of course, is to God. The *sūra* belongs to the Medinan period and has 78 verses. Its title is drawn from the 1st verse which reads 'The Merciful'. The *sūra* goes on to say that God has taught the Qur'ān and created man. It describes God's blessings to man and also the **jinn** (q.v.), provides a vivid description of Paradise and its delights, and threatens Jahannam (=Hell) for the wicked. (*See* **al-Janna**; **al-Nār**; **al-Raḥmān** (1).)

Rā'īl *See* **Zulaykhā**.

al-Rajīm (Ar.) An epithet of **Iblīs** (q.v.) which may be translated both as 'The Accursed' and 'The Stoned'. The first translation reflects the **Qur'ān** where, in v.34 of **Sūrat al-Ḥijr** (q.v.), Iblīs is described as *rajīm*. The second translation reflects the stoning ritual at **Minā** (q.v.) during the **Ḥajj** (q.v.). (*See* **al-Jamra**; **al-Janna**.)

Rak'a (Ar.) [pl. *raka'āt*] Literally, 'bowing'. The *rak'a* is a 'unit of prayer' in which the worshipper recites a number of ritual prayers and invocations while standing, bowing, prostrating and sitting. The number of *raka'āt* performed varies from prayer time to prayer time, as does the recitation being silent or said out loud. The fivefold **ṣalāt** (q.v.) follows the following pattern:

1st *ṣalāt*: 2 *raka'āt* (r) said out loud.
2nd *ṣalāt*: 4 silent r.
3rd *ṣalāt*: 4 silent r.
4th *ṣalāt*: 3 r.: 2 said out loud, 1 said silently.
5th *ṣalāt*: 4 r.: 2 said out loud, 2 said silently.

Thus the observant Muslim must perform a minimum of 17 *raka'āt* every day. For the names of the various prayers, see the entry **Ṣalāt**. (*See also* **Adhān**; **Arkān**; **Masjid**; **Mu'adhdhin**; **Tarāwiḥ**.)

Ramaḍān (Ar.) The ninth month of the Muslim lunar calendar and also the Muslim month of fasting. Because the Islamic calendar is lunar rather than solar, Ramaḍān falls at different times every year. By fasting (**ṣawm** (q.v.)) in Ramaḍān – and fasting at this time is one of the five **arkān** (q.v.) – Muslims mark the revelation of the **Qur'ān** in that month. The fast lasts every day technically, according to the Qur'ān, from the time when a believer can distinguish between a white and a black thread (or, according to another interpretation, when he can perceive the first white streak of dawn on a black sky). During the fast the believer must abstain from food, drink and sexual intercourse. Those who are sick, women who are pregnant and those making long journeys are exempted from fasting. The evenings of Ramaḍān –

when the fast has ended for the day – are particularly joyful in the great cities of the Islamic world: the streets are full of vendors, coloured lights and lanterns (*fawānīs*) and throngs of people, especially in such areas as the quarter of the Sayyidnā 'l-Ḥusayn Mosque in **Cairo** (q.v.). The mosques in Ramaḍān are also full of worshippers performing extra prayers. The month concludes with one of the great feast days of the Muslim calendar, **'Īd al-Fiṭr** (q.v.). (*See* **Calendar**; **al-Ḥusayn b. 'Alī**; **Ifṭār**; **Laylat al-Qadr**; **Saḥūr**; **Tarāwīḥ**.)

Rāshidūn (Ar.) An epithet applied to the first four 'Rightly Guided Caliphs' (*al-Khulafā' al-Rāshidūn*) who led the Islamic community in its early days after the death of the Prophet **Muḥammad**. Their names were **Abū Bakr** (q.v.), **'Umar b. al-Khaṭṭāb** (q.v.), **'Uthmān b. 'Affān** (q.v.) and **'Alī b. Abī Ṭālib** (q.v.). The Arabic title *Rāshidūn* meaning 'rightly guided' constitutes a deliberate contrast with the more secular rulers of the succeeding dynasties of the **Umayyads** (q.v.) and **'Abbāsids** (q.v.). (*See* **Khalīfa**.)

Rasūl (Ar.) [pl. *rusul*] Messenger, envoy, apostle. **Muḥammad** is called in the **Shahāda** (q.v.), the **Qur'ān** (see v.40 of **Sūrat al-Aḥzāb** (q.v.)) and elsewhere, 'The Messenger of God' (*Rasūl Allāh*). His absolute humanity is stressed in the Qur'ān in terms of his being a *Rasūl* and it is stressed in the same verse that there were other messengers before him. (*See* v.144 of **Sūrat Āl 'Imrān** (q.v.).) (*See also* **Nabī**.)

Rāwī (Ar.) [pl. *ruwāt*] Story-teller, transmitter of **ḥadīth** (q.v.) or old Arabic poetry.

Ra'y (Ar.) [pl. *ārā'*] Opinion, idea. In Islamic law *ra'y* has the sense of personal opinion, individual judgment, or speculation not based on a recognized source of law. It may be compared with **ijtihād** (q.v.) and contrasted with **taqlīd** (q.v.). (*See* **Fiqh**; **Ijmā'**; **Qiyās**; **Qur'ān**; **Sharī'a**; **Sunna**.)

Rayḥāna bint Zayd (died 10/632) Concubine of the Prophet **Muḥammad**.

Reckoning *See* **al-Ḥisāb**.

Recording Angels *See* **Kirām al-Kātibīn**.

Red Crescent Islamic and Middle Eastern counterpart to the Red Cross. (*See* **Hilāl**.)

Religion *See* **Dīn**; **Islām**.

Renunciation *See* **Zuhd**.

Repentance *See* **Tawba**.

Resignation (to the Will of God) *See* **Islām**.

Resurrection *See* **Ba'th**; **Sūrat al-Ṣāffāt**; **Yawm al-Dīn**; **Yawm al-Qiyāma**.

Retaliation *See* **Qiṣāṣ**.

Retreat *See* **Khalwa**; **Tahannuth**.

Revelation *See* **Qur'ān**; **Tanzīl**.

Revenge, Blood *See under* **Qiṣāṣ**.

Ribā (Ar.) Usury, the charging of interest on a loan. This is forbidden by Islam and condemned in the **Qur'ān**, for example in **Sūrat al-Baqara** (q.v.), in no uncertain terms. Despite this the course of history shows that the observance of this prohibition has often fallen short of the ideal. (*See* **Ḥiyal**; **Islamic Banking**; **Muḍāraba**.)

Ribāṭ (Ar.) [pl. *rubuṭ*] Literally, 'ribbon', 'band'. However, this is a word in Arabic which has assumed a large number of disparate meanings including 'frontier post'. In the technical terminology of **taṣawwuf** (q.v.) a *ribāṭ* is often considered to be synonymous with a **zāwiya** (q.v.). However, those who lived in an Egyptian *ribāṭ* were not necessarily all ṣūfīs. (*See* **Almoravids**; **Khānagāh**; **Marabout**; **Ṣūfī**; **Tekkē**.)

Riḍā, Muḥammad Rashīd (1281-2/1865–1353-4/1935) Major modern thinker. Attracted in his youth to **taṣawwuf** (q.v.) – he joined the **Naqshabandiyya** (q.v.) – he grew away from his early mysticism and came under the influence of **al-Afghānī** (q.v.) and **'Abduh** (q.v.). After leaving Syria in 1314-5/1897 for **Cairo** (q.v.) he established a journal called *The Lighthouse* (*al-Manār*) which contained reformist ideas in line with 'Abduh's thought.

Ridda (Ar.) Apostasy from the Islamic faith. After the death of the Prophet **Muḥammad** a War of the *Ridda* or Apostasy War broke out in Arabia, many tribes believing that their contract and contact with Islam had ended with the death of the Prophet. The majority of these tribes were defeated during the rule of Muḥammad's successor, **Abū Bakr** (q.v.). Other tribes too, which had not formally embraced Islam in the time of Muḥammad, were also subdued. (*See* **'Aqrabā', Battle of**; **Fitna**; **Irtidād**; **Musaylima**.)

Riḍwān Angel in charge of **al-Janna** (q.v.). At the Last Judgement it will be his task to adorn Paradise and set out robes of honour for the Prophet **Muḥammad**. On the same occasion Riḍwān will also feed the blessed fasters as they are resurrected from their graves. (*See* **al-Ḥisāb**; **Yawm al-Qiyāma**.)

Rifā'iyya Major **ṣūfī** (q.v.) order named after Aḥmad b. 'Alī al-Rifā'ī (499-500/1106–577-8/1182). Aḥmad passed most of his life in the marsh area of Southern Iraq where he attracted many disciples who became famous for their extreme practices like eating live snakes and various feats with fire. **Ibn Baṭṭūṭa** (q.v.) encountered a large group of Rifā'ī dervishes during his **Riḥla**

(q.v.) and commented with horrified fascination on such practices. The early Rifā'iyya was an extremely widespread order, found in Egypt, Syria, Palestine, Asia Minor and even as far afield as the Maldives. The order spawned a very large number of sub-groups or associated branches under a variety of names.

Right Path, The *See* **al-Ṣirāṭ al-Mustaqīm.**

Riḥla (Ar.) Travel, journey, travelogue. A well-known **ḥadīth** (q.v.) attributed to the Prophet **Muḥammad** urges the believer to seek knowledge even as far as China. This provided the religious impetus in mediaeval Islam for the tradition, undertaken by many of the great **ḥadīth** collectors and scholars, of travel *in search of knowledge* (*ṭalab al-'ilm*). A primary impulse also in undertaking a *riḥla* was the performance of the **Ḥajj** (q.v.) and this gave rise to a whole genre of travel or *riḥla* literature. Perhaps the best known of all the exponents of the *riḥla*, both in terms of actual journey and literary tradition, was **Ibn Baṭṭūṭa** (q.v.). (*See* **'Ilm**; **Maḥfūẓ**;)

Ritual Slaughter *See* **Slaughter, Ritual.**

Riwāq (Ar.) [pl. *arwiqa*] Literally, 'tent', 'tent-flap', 'porch'. The Arabic word also has the specialist sense of living and working areas for students of **al-Azhar** (q.v.). Each *riwāq* was allocated to, and named after, a particular nationality or region.

Rosary *See* **Subḥa.**

Rūḥ (Ar.) [pl. *arwāḥ*] Spirit, soul, life breath. **Jibrīl** (q.v.) in **Sūrat Maryam** (q.v.) is described as 'Our (i.e. God's) Spirit' (*Rūḥanā*) in v.17. (*See* **Nafs.**)

al-Rūm (Ar.) The title of the 30th **sūra** of the **Qur'ān**; it means 'The Byzantine Greeks'. The *sūra* belongs to the Meccan period and has 60 verses. Its title is taken from the 2nd verse which reads: 'The Byzantine Greeks have been defeated'. This is probably a reference to the Persian capture of **Jerusalem** (q.v.) from the Byzantines in AD 614. This is one of the very few references in the Qur'ān to contemporary history. The *sūra* begins with three of the **Mysterious Letters of the Qur'ān** (q.v.) and goes on to talk of the Hour and God's signs. (*See* **al-Sā'a**.)

Rūmān Interrogating angel who, according to some traditions, visits the deceased in the grave even before **Munkar and Nakīr** (q.v.) and tells the dead person to write down his or her good and evil acts. The latter will use his saliva, finger and shroud as ink, pen and paper. Rūmān's face is said to be bright like the sun. (*See* **Angel**; **Archangel**.)

Rūmī, Jalāl al-Dīn (604/1207–672/1273) One of the greatest of Persia's mystics and poets, and principal inspiration behind the **ṣūfī** (q.v.) order, the **Mawlawiyya** (q.v.) which many claim he founded. He became well-known as 'Our Master' (Ar. *Mawlānā*; Turk. *Mevlānā*). Born in Balkh, Jalāl al-Dīn later came to **Konya** (q.v.) in 626/1228, where he met, and formed his famous relationship with, the itinerant ṣūfī Shams al-Dīn Muḥammad Tabrīzī (died 645/1247). Rūmī died in Konya in 672/1273. His best known literary work is his lengthy poem known simply as the *Mathnawī*.

Running *See* **Muzdalifa**; **Sa'y**.

Ruqayya The name of one of the daughters of **Muḥammad** and **Khadīja bint Khuwaylid** (q.v.). Ruqayya's first marriage was to one of the sons of **Abū Lahab** (q.v.); later she married **'Uthmān b. 'Affān** (q.v.). This Ruqayya should be distinguished from the Sayyida Ruqayya who was a daughter of **'Alī b. Abī Ṭālib** (q.v.) by a wife other than **Fāṭima** (q.v.). This Sayyida Ruqayya, although buried in **Damascus** (q.v.), also has a shrine, where intercession is made, in **Cairo** (q.v.).

Rushdie, Salman *See* **Satanic Verses, The.**

Ru'yat Allāh (Ar.) Vision of God, sight of God, in Paradise. The possibility and modality of the Beatific Vision gave rise to considerable controversy in mediaeval Islam. **Al-Ash'arī** (q.v.) for example, taught that the vision of God in Paradise was a reality, though its modality was beyond man's comprehension, thereby vehemently opposing the idea of the **Mu'tazila** (q.v.) that God would not be visible in a literal sense to men. (*See* **Bilā Kayf**; **al-Janna**.)

al-Sā'a (Ar.) The Hour. This word is used to designate the Last Day, the Hour of Resurrection. In the **Qur'ān**, v.107 of **Sūrat Yūsuf** (q.v.) talks of 'The Hour' taking the unwary unbeliever by surprise. Islamic eschatology has elaborated a profusion of detail about 'The Hour' and the portents or 'Signs of the Hour' (**Ishārāt al-Sā'a** (q.v.)) which signal its imminent coming. (*See* **Ba'th**; **al-Ḥisāb**; **Yawm al-Qiyāma**.)

Sabā' (Ar.) The title of the 34th **sūra** of the **Qur'ān**; *Sabā'* is one of the Arabic forms of the place name known in English as Sheba. It was a major seat of South Arabian civilization in ancient times. The *sūra* belongs to the Meccan period and has 54 verses. Its title is drawn from vv.15 ff which relate the story of the destruction of the great **Ma'rib Dam** (q.v.). The *sūra* goes on to stress that **Muḥammad** has been sent as a herald (*bashīr*) and a warner (*nadhīr*). (*See* **Sabaeans**.)

Sabaeans At least three distinct groups have borne this name in Middle Eastern history: (1) The pagan sect which flourished in **Ḥarrān** (q.v.), Northern Syria, whose transcendent theology may be characterized as both astral and Neoplatonic; (2) The inhabitants of the South Arabian pre-Islamic Kingdom of *Sabā'* (Sheba); (3) The Sabaeans (*Ṣābi'ūn*) of the **Qur'ān** mentioned in v.62 of **Sūrat al-Baqara** (q.v.), v.17 of **Sūrat al-Ḥajj** (q.v.) and v.69 of **Sūrat al-Mā'ida** (q.v.). This last group may originally have been the Mandaeans of South Iraq. Some scholars maintain that the Sabaeans of Ḥarrān cleverly tried to identify themselves with the Sabaeans of the Qur'ān to give themselves some legitimacy as 'People of the Book' (**Ahl al-Kitāb** (q.v.)). (*See* **Neoplatonism, Islamic**; **Sūrat Sabā'**.)

Sabīl (Ar.) [pl. *asbila*] Public drinking fountain, sometimes with a Qur'ānic School (**Kuttāb** (q.v.)) attached on an upper storey. Many were the result of endowments. Charming examples of the *sabīl-kuttāb*, mainly in a state of decay, are to be found in cities like **Cairo** (q.v.). Many here illustrate facets of the glorious architecture of the Mamlūk period. The first *sabīl* to be built in Cairo was in 726-7/1326 and from then on, despite changes in architecture and decoration, the *sabīl* served the function of free water provision and often, educational provision as well. (*See* **Art and Architecture, Islamic**; **Qur'ān**; **Mamlūks**; **Waqf**.)

Sacred Tradition *See* **Ḥadīth Qudsī**.

Ṣād (Ar.) The title of the 38th **sūra** of the **Qur'ān**; it is the name of one of the letters of the Arabic alphabet. The *sūra* belongs to the Meccan period and has 88 verses. It takes its title from the letter *Ṣād* which appears in the 1st verse and which, in this context, is one of the **Mysterious Letters of the Qur'ān** (q.v.). The *sūra* surveys some of those people who have disbelieved the messengers sent to them. It tells at some length the story of **Dāwūd** (q.v.) who is asked to give judgement between two disputants, provides information from the life of **Sulaymān** (q.v.) and refers to some of the trials of **Ayyūb** (q.v.). Several other prophets are mentioned as well. Towards the end of the *sūra* the story of **Iblīs** (q.v.) is told with his refusal to bow down to God's new creation **Ādam** (q.v.). (*See* **Dhū 'l-Kifl**; **Khalīfa**.)

Ṣadaqa (Ar.) [pl. *ṣadaqāt*] Voluntary almsgiving. Compare **zakāt** (q.v.).

al-Ṣafā Small hill now enclosed within the Great Mosque at **Mecca** (q.v.). It is 1247 feet from another similarly enclosed hill called **al-Marwa**. During the minor pilgrimage (*'umra*) and the major pilgrimage (**Ḥajj** (q.v.)) the ritual of the **Sa'y** (q.v.) takes place between these two small hills. This ritual of *sa'y* is undertaken following the **ṭawāf** (q.v.) of the **Ka'ba** (q.v.) during the pilgrimage. The hills of al-Ṣafā and al-Marwa are both mentioned in the **Qur'ān** in v.158 of **Sūrat al-Baqara** (q.v.). (*See* **Ismā'īl** (1).)

Ṣafavids Major dynasty which ruled in Persia from 907/1501 until 1145/1732. They drew their name from the founder of the Ṣafawiyya order of dervishes, Shaykh Ṣafī al-Dīn (died 735/1334). Ṣafavid rule was established in Persia in 907/1501 by Ismā'īl b. Ḥaydar (=Ismā'īl 1). It was under the Ṣafavids that Ithnā 'Asharī **Shī'ism** (q.v.) became the official branch of Islam in Persia. Although there were nominal Ṣafavid rulers after 1145/1732, to all intents and purposes the dynasty effectively ceased to have any real power by that date. (*See* **Ithnā 'Asharīs**; **Qājārs**.)

al-Ṣaff (Ar.) The title of the 61st **sūra** of the **Qur'ān**; it means literally 'The Row' or 'The Rank'. The *sūra* belongs to the Medinan period and has 14 verses. Its title is drawn from the 4th verse which notes that God must love those who fight in His way 'in rank(s)'. The *sūra* condemns hypocrisy among the believers, goes on to quote **'Īsā** (q.v.) prophesying the coming of **Muḥammad**, and urges men to strive or fight for God (literally, in the way of God).

al-Saffāḥ (died 136/754) First ruler of the dynasty of the **'Abbāsids** (q.v.) which succeeded that of the **Umayyads** (q.v.). His full name was 'Abd Allāh b. Muḥammad Abū 'l-'Abbās; al-Saffāḥ means both 'the generous' and 'the bloodthirsty'. He ruled as caliph from 132/749 until 136/754.

al-Ṣāffāt (Ar.) The title of the 37th **sūra** of the **Qur'ān**; it means 'The Rangers', i.e. the angels ranged in front of God. The *sūra* belongs to the Meccan period and contains 182 verses. Its title is drawn from the 1st verse which takes the form of an oath: 'By the rangers in lines'. The *sūra* goes on to stress the Oneness of God and His ability to raise bodies from the dead at the end of time. The torments of Hell await the wicked while the blessed will enjoy the delights of Paradise. **Nūḥ** (q.v.) called on God and was saved by Him while others drowned. **Ibrāhīm** (q.v.) is flung into the flames and also asked to sacrifice his son **Ismā'īl** (q.v.). In both cases he is rescued or reprieved by God. Reference is also made to the blessings received by **Mūsā** (q.v.) and **Hārūn** (q.v.), and the stories of **Ilyās** (q.v.) and **Yūnus** (q.v.) are recounted too. The whole *sūra*, as can be seen, is full of prophetic history. (*See* **Angel**; **al-Janna**; **al-Nār**.)

Ṣafiyya bint Ḥuyayy One of the wives of the Prophet **Muḥammad**. She was a Jewess, captured at **Khaybar** (q.v.), but was freed on conversion to Islam.

Ṣaḥāba (Ar.) [sing. *ṣāḥib*] Companions, i.e. of the Prophet **Muḥammad**. The word is used variously to denote both the Prophet's close friends and associates, and, more loosely, anyone who saw the Prophet while the latter was alive. (*See* **Salafiyya**; **Tābi'ūn**.)

Ṣaḥīfa (Ar.) [pl. *ṣuḥuf*] Literally, 'page', 'paper'. The word in a more technical sense designates any revealed writings to the prophetic predecessors of **Muḥammad**.

Ṣaḥīḥ (Ar.) Sound. Technical term in **ḥadīth** (q.v.) criticism indicating the highest level of trustworthiness in a tradition. The compilations of traditions by **al-Bukhārī** (q.v.) and **Muslim b. al-Ḥajjāj** (q.v.) each bore the title *The Sound* (or *The True*, *The Authentic*) (*al-Ṣaḥīḥ*). Together they are known as 'The Two *Ṣaḥīḥ*s' (*al-Ṣaḥīḥān*): they are pre-eminent in both importance and authority among all the *ḥadīth* collections.

al-Ṣaḥīḥān *See* **al-Bukhārī**; **Muslim b. al-Ḥajjāj**; **Ṣaḥīḥ**.

Ṣaḥn (Ar.) [pl. *ṣuḥūn*] Dish, yard, courtyard. In Islamic architecture this word bears the specific sense of a mosque's central courtyard. (*See* **Art and Architecture, Islamic**)

Saḥūr (Ar.) Last meal eaten before the day's fasting begins in **Ramaḍān** (q.v.). (*See* **Ifṭār**.)

Saint *See* **Walī**.

Sa'īr (Ar.) One of the seven ranks of Hell. According to tradition Sa'īr is the blazing inferno in which **Sabaeans** (q.v.) will burn. Although not as common a word for Hell in the **Qur'ān** as **Jahannam** (q.v.), the word Sa'īr used to designate Hell occurs 16 times. (*See* **Hell**; **al-Nār**.)

al-Sajda (Ar.) The title of the 32nd **sūra** of the **Qur'ān**; it means 'The Prostration'. The *sūra* belongs to the Meccan period and has 30 verses. Its title is drawn from v.15 where reference is made to those believers in God's signs who prostrate themselves in prayer before God when reminded of them. The *sūra* begins with three of the **Mysterious Letters of the Qur'ān** (q.v.) and goes on to refer to God's creative power and might. Those who believe and do good works will abide in Paradise while the wicked will burn in Hell. (*See* **'Izrā'īl**; **al-Janna**; **al-Nār**.)

Sajjāda (Ar.) [pl. *sajjād*] Carpet, prayer rug, prayer carpet. The word acquired an extra dimension in **taṣawwuf** (q.v.) where the head of a **ṭarīqa** (q.v.) might bear a title like 'Master of the Prayer Rug' (*Shaykh al-Sajjāda*), i.e. Master of the Prayer Rug previously owned by the order's founder. (*See* **Shaykh**.)

Saladin Anglicized form of **Ṣalāḥ al-Dīn** (q.v.).

Salafiyya (Ar.) This Arabic word has borne a considerable number of cultural and religious meanings over the years. It derives from an Arabic word *salaf* meaning basically 'ancestors', 'predecessors'. In a religious sense, these were the early generation after **Muḥammad**, i.e. such groups as the **ṣaḥāba** (q.v.) and the **tābi'ūn** (q.v.), whose example constituted a religious paradigm for later generations. *Al-Salafiyya* was also the name borne by an Egyptian reformist movement whose founders were **'Abduh** (q.v.) and **al-Afghānī** (q.v.). The *Salafiyya* tried, among other things, to identify a *via media* between the strict tenets of Islam and the ideas of secular society and modern science. 'Abduh extended the compass of the word *salaf* to embrace later generations of theologians like **al-Ash'arī** (q.v.). Today the word *salafiyya* has been used as one of the attempts in Arabic to render the word 'fundamentalism' and it is in this sense a synonym of *uṣūliyya*. (*See* **Fundamentalism, Islamic**)

Ṣalāḥ al-Dīn (532/1138–589/1193) Saladin, also spelled Saladdin. He is esteemed as one of the great heroes of Arab and Islamic history and also a figure around whom much legend has been woven by and in the West, because of his interaction with King Richard the Lionheart of England. Of Kurdish origin, Ṣalāḥ al-Dīn later assumed his uncle's command, brought the dying rule of the **Fāṭimids** (q.v.) in Egypt to a final end in 567/1171, and took **Damascus** (q.v.) in 570/1174. He is justly famed for his defeat of the Crusaders at the Battle of Ḥaṭṭīn in 583/1187, and following conquest of **Jerusalem** (q.v.). King Richard of England captured Acre from him in 589/1191. (*See* **Ayyūbids; Crusades; Ḥaṭṭīn, Battle of**)

al-Salāmu 'alaykum (Ar.) Peace be with you! Peace be upon you! A traditional and much used Muslim greeting. (*See* **Kirām al-Kātibīn**.)

Ṣalāt (Ar.) often transliterated *Ṣalāh* [pl. *ṣalawāt*] The Prayer and its accompanying ritual, performed by the practising Muslim five times a day. This should not take place at the time of the actual rising or setting of the sun. Although the **Qur'ān** mentions prayer many times, the obligation to pray *five* times per day derives from **ḥadīth** (q.v.) rather than the Qur'ān. The Prayer Ritual is one of the five **arkān** (q.v.) or Pillars of Islam. The times of prayer, with their Arabic names, are as follows:

(1) The Morning Prayer (*Ṣalāt al-Ṣubḥ*, also called *Ṣalāt al-Fajr*).
(2) The Midday Prayer (*Ṣalāt al-Ẓuhr*).
(3) The Afternoon Prayer (*Ṣalāt al-'Aṣr*).
(4) The Evening or Sunset Prayer (*Ṣalāt al-Maghrib*).
(5) The Night Prayer (*Ṣalāt al-'Ishā'*).

(*See* **al-Fātiḥa**; **Ka'ba**; **Khuṭba**; **Rak'a**; **Sajjāda**; **Sujūd**; **Sūrat al-Isrā'**; **Tarāwīḥ**; **Witr**.)

Ṣāliḥ Arabian prophet sent to warn the tribe of **Thamūd** (q.v.). The latter not only reject Ṣāliḥ's message but they hamstring the she-camel which has been sent as a 'proof' and a 'sign' from God, i.e. of friendship and covenant. Thamūd are consequently destroyed in an earthquake. (*See* **Shu'ayb**; **Sūrat al-A'rāf**; **Sūrat Hūd**.)

Saljūqs The Seljuks. This was a major dynasty in mediaeval Islamic history whose name is sometimes transliterated, less accurately, as Seljuks. The Saljūqs originally came from the steppe country to the North of the Caspian Sea. They established themselves in Persia in 429/1038 and gradually extended their rule over Persia and Iraq, gaining control of **Baghdād** (q.v.) in 447/1055. Control of Iraq and Western Persia lasted until 590/1194 at which date the Saljūq Sultan Toghrīl b. Arslan was killed waging war against the Khwārazm-Shāh Tekish. Saljūq dynasties also ruled in Syria and Kirmān. The most famous Saljūq victory was the defeat of the Byzantines at the Battle of Manzikert in 463/1071. (*See* **Manzikert, Battle of**)

Salmān al-Fārisī Early Persian convert to Islam and companion of the Prophet **Muḥammad**, who suggested the digging of a ditch or trench to Muḥammad before the Siege and Battle of **al-**

Khandaq (q.v.). Salmān probably died in the early years of the rule of **'Uthmān b. 'Affān** (q.v.). Salmān al-Fārisī is a very popular figure in **ṣūfī** (q.v.) circles. (See **Sūrat al-Aḥzāb**; **Taṣawwuf**.)

Salsabīl (Ar.) Famous spring (*'ayn*) or fountain in Paradise; the word means literally 'easy to swallow'. It occurs only once in the **Qur'ān**, in v.18 of **Sūrat al-Insān** (q.v.). Some traditions have interpreted Salsabīl more as a river flowing through Paradise rather than just a spring. (*See* **al-Janna**; **Kāfūr**; **al-Kawthar**; **Tasnīm**.)

Samā' (Ar.) Literally, 'audition', 'hearing'. The word has the technical sense in **taṣawwuf** (q.v.) of a mystical or spiritual concert. (*See* **Dhikr**; **Ḥaḍra**; **Mawlawiyya**.)

Samarkand *See* **Samarqand.**

Samarqand City now situated in the Republic of Uzbekistān and, like **Bukhārā** (q.v.), famous for its Islamic monuments. The mausoleum of **Tīmūr-i Lang** (q.v.) is to be found in Samarqand and the beauty of this mausoleum has been much admired.

Sāmarrā New city founded in 221/836 by the 'Abbāsid caliph al-Mu'taṣim (*reg*. 218/833–227/842); it lay about 60 miles North of his old capital **Baghdād** (q.v.). Apart from its mediaeval political and military significance in Islamic history, Sāmarrā is of considerable Islamic interest on two other counts: the Tenth and Eleventh Shī'ite Imāms, **'Alī al-Hādī** (q.v.) and **Ḥasan al-'Askarī** (q.v.) were buried there in two shrines called the *'Askariyayn*; secondly, Sāmarrā was the site of the largest mosque ever built, the Great Mosque of **al-Mutawakkil** (q.v.) with its famous huge spiral minaret (*al-manāra al-malwiyya*). The 'Abbāsid capital remained at Sāmarrā until 279/892 when it returned to Baghdād. (*See* **'Abbāsids**; **Ibn Ṭūlūn**; **Imām**; **Manāra**; **Shī'ism**.)

Sanad *See* **Isnād**.

Sanctuary *See* **Ḥaram**; **al-Ḥaramān**; **al-Masjid al-Ḥarām**.

Sanūsī, The Grand *See* **Sanūsiyya**.

Sanūsiyya Major **ṣūfī** (q.v.) revivalist order named after Sayyid Muḥammad b. 'Alī al-Sanūsī (1202?/1787?–1276/1859) who is often referred to as the Grand Sanūsī. He was born at al-Wāsiṭa in Algeria but his order, which was basically a puritanical summons to real Islam, based on the **Qur'ān** and **Sunna** (q.v.) was, properly speaking, begun in Libya. The Grand Sanūsī was much influenced by the thought of **Ibn Taymiyya** (q.v.) despite the hostility of the latter to **taṣawwuf** (q.v.). The Sanūsī **dhikr** (q.v.) does not seek to induce any kind of ecstatic state though an attempt is made to achieve some kind of identification with the Prophet **Muḥammad**. The grandson of the Grand Sanūsī, Sayyid Idrīs, who was the then head of the Sanūsī order, became the King of an independent Libya from 1371/1951 until 1389/1969 when he was overthrown. The Sanūsiyya achieved their greatest popularity in Libya, but also gained a following in the Sudan.

Saqar (Ar.) One of the seven ranks of **Hell** (q.v.). Saqar is the scorching fire to which tradition assigns the Zoroastrians. (The Arabic verb *saqara* was used of the sun and means 'to scorch'.) The word *Saqar* is used to indicate Hell four times in the **Qur'ān**. (*See* **al-Nār**; **Sūrat al-Muddathir**; **Sūrat al-Qamar**.)

Saqīm (Ar.) Literally, 'sick', 'infirm'. This is a technical term used in **ḥadīth** (q.v.) criticism to indicate the lowest level of trustworthiness in a tradition.

Sariqa (Ar.) Theft. The prescribed punishment in the **Qur'ān** (in v.38 of **Sūrat al-Mā'ida** (q.v.)) is the amputation of the hand. **Sharī'a** (q.v.) law prescribes the corroborating testimony of witnesses or the thief's own confession, and insists that the property have some value. In practice, the usual punishment has often been imprisonment rather than a strict application of the Qur'ānic law. This will, of course, depend on the country in which the theft takes place. (*See* **Ḥadd**.)

Sāsānians Dynasty of kings who ruled in Persia prior to the Arab conquests and who were overthrown by the Muslim armies. The last Sāsānian king, Yazdagird III, was assassinated in 31/651-2. (*See* **al-Qādisiyya, Battle of**)

Satan *See* **Iblīs**.

Satanic Verses, The Title of a novel by the author Salman Rushdie (born in 1947 in Bombay) which was published in 1988. The work aroused massive hostility in the Islamic world resulting in riots, deaths and public burnings of the book. The author was condemned to death in a **fatwā** (q.v.) issued by the Āyatullāh **Khumaynī** (q.v.), shortly before the latter's own death. Salman Rushdie went into immediate hiding. The original Satanic Verses, which gave their name to Rushdie's novel, were allegedly transmitted by the Prophet **Muḥammad** as part of the Qur'ānic revelation. They appeared to permit some kind of veneration and respect being paid towards **al-Lāt** (q.v.), **Manāt** (q.v.) and **al-'Uzzā** (q.v.). This strange story goes on to allege that Muḥammad later realized that he had been tricked by Satan and, in consequence, he withdrew the verses, transmitting others in their place (*see* vv.19–23 of **Sūrat al-Najm** (q.v.) in the **Qur'ān**). However, it is now recognized that the *ḥadīth*s on which the story of the Satanic Verses is based are, in fact, later forgeries. Thus it must be concluded and stressed that the original Satanic Verses were never, even temporarily, accepted as part of the genuine Qur'ānic revelation. (*See* **Ḥadīth**; **Iblīs**.)

Sawda bint Zam'a A wife of the Prophet **Muḥammad** and a member of the tribe of **Quraysh** (q.v.). She married the Prophet having been widowed from al-Sakrān b. 'Amr who was an early convert to Islam. A well-known tradition from the *Ṣaḥīḥ* of **al-Bukhārī** (q.v.) portrays some of the wives of the Prophet asking him which of them would be the quickest to join him (i.e. in death). The response was: She who has the longest hand. This proved to be Sawda whose generosity (= length of hand) was well known.

Ṣawm (Ar) Fasting, one of the five **arkān** (q.v.) or Pillars of Islam. (*See* **Ramaḍān**.)

Ṣawma'a (Ar.) [pl. *ṣawāmi'*] Minaret. This word was popularly used for the square minarets found in Spain and the Maghreb. The word originally meant a monk's cell. (*See* **al-Maghrib**; **Manāra**.)

Sa'y (Ar.) Sevenfold 'running' (mainly walking) between **al-Ṣafā** (q.v.) and al-Marwa during the **Ḥajj** (q.v.). (*See* **Ismā'īl** (1); **Muzdalifa**.)

Sayl al-'Arim *See* **Ma'rib Dam**.

Sayyid Aḥmad Khān *See* **Khān, Sayyid Aḥmad**.

Sayyid Ameer Ali *See* **Amīr 'Alī, Sayyid**.

Sayyid Quṭb *See* **Quṭb, Sayyid**.

Scales, Judgement with *See* **al-Ḥisāb**.

School *See* **Madrasa**.

School of Law *See* **Madhhab**.

Seal of the Prophets *See* **Khātam al-Nabiyyīn**.

Searching for Knowledge *See* **Ibn Baṭṭūṭa**; **'Ilm**; **Riḥla**; **Ṭalab al-'Ilm**.

Seeking Knowledge *See entry above.*

Seljuks *See* **Saljūqs**.

Sermon *See* **Khuṭba**.

Servant (of God) *See* **'Abd**.

Seveners *See* **Ismā'īlīs**.

Shab-i Miraj *See* **Laylat al-Mi'rāj**.

Shādhiliyya Major **ṣūfī** (q.v.) order named after Abū 'l-Ḥasan 'Alī al-Shādhilī (593/1196–656/1258). The order, which achieved popularity in North Africa, Arabia and Syria, gave rise to numerous offshoots and sub-groups. (*See* **Burhāniyya**; **Ḥizb**.)

Shafā'a (Ar.) Intercession, mediation. While many Muslim theologians, particularly under the influence of Wahhābī teachings, have disapproved of the idea of the invocation of, or intercession with or via, the saints, popular Islam, with its cult of the saints and veneration at their tombs, has never lost the idea. **Muḥammad** will intercede with God for sinners on the Day of Judgement. (*See* **Baraka**; **Ḥawḍ**; **Wahhābīs**; **Walī**; **Yawm al-Qiyāma**.)

al-Shāfi'ī, Muḥammad b. Idrīs (150/767–205/820) Outstanding Muslim jurist, widely recognized in Islam as 'the Father of Islamic Jurisprudence'. He later gave his name to the Shāfi'ī School of jurisprudence founded by his disciples. His key methodological significance was to found the law upon four points: **Qur'ān**, **Sunna** (q.v.) – which was now to be considered as divinely inspired, – **Ijmā'** (q.v.) (i.e. of the whole Muslim community), and **Qiyās** (q.v.). Al-Shāfi'ī's principal work enshrining his thought was called 'The Epistle' (*al-Risāla*). His huge tomb is a focus of pilgrimage and petition in **Cairo** (q.v.). (*See* **Istiḥsān**; **Shāfi'īs**; **Uṣūl al-Fiqh**.)

Shāfi'īs Adherents of one of the four main law schools (*madhāhib*) of **Sunnī** (q.v.) Islam, named after 'The Father of Islamic Jurisprudence', **al-Shāfi'ī** (q.v.). The Shāfi'ī School of law was supported and developed by those who championed the doctrines of al-Shāfi'ī, particularly with regard to his views on the function of traditions. The Shāfi'ī School of law became popular in Eastern Africa, Southeast Asia, Malaya, and parts of Southern Arabia like Yemen. (*See* **Ḥadīth**; **Ḥiyal**.)

Shahāda (Ar.) Profession of Faith. This is one of the five **arkān** (q.v.). The Profession runs as follows: 'There is no god but God and **Muḥammad** is the Messenger of God'. (*See* **Nabī**; **Rasūl**.)

Shahīd (Ar.) [pl. *shuhadā'*] Martyr. Islam assures the believers that those who die as martyrs in battle fighting the infidel and in defence of their faith will go to Paradise. (*See* **al-Janna**; **Jihād**.)

Shāh Jahān (1000/1592–1076/1666) Mughal emperor who ruled in India from 1038/1628 until his deposition in 1068/1658. He was the father of **Aurangzeb** (q.v.) who interned Shāh Jahān and later succeeded him. Shāh Jahān had earlier rebelled against *his* father **Jahāngīr** (q.v.). Jahān's reign was notable for its building, particularly in marble. Although he inherited an empire which was stable, his further imperialist dreams never came to fruition. In the popular mind, however, Shāh Jahān will forever be associated with the building of the **Tāj Maḥal** (q.v.) where he lies buried beside his wife. (*See* **Mughals.**)

al-Shahrastānī, Muḥammad b. 'Abd al-Karīm (479/1086–548/1153) Together with **Ibn Ḥazm** (q.v.) al-Shahrastānī is one of Islam's best-known historians of religion. His most famous work was *The Book of Religions and Sects* (*Kitāb al-Milal wa 'l-Niḥal*). This work is characterized by considerable fairness towards all the religions with which it deals.

Shaikh *See* **Shaykh**.

al-Shams (Ar.) The title of the 91st **sūra** of the **Qur'ān**; it means 'The Sun'. The *sūra* belongs to the Meccan period and has 15 verses. Its title comes from the 1st verse which begins with the oath 'By the sun . . .'. The *sūra* continues with a series of oaths and then briefly tells the story of the people of **Thamūd** (q.v.) (visited by the prophet **Ṣāliḥ** (q.v.)) who hamstrung the she-camel sent to them by God as a sign. Their end is briefly noted.

al-Sharḥ (Ar.) The title of the 94th **sūra** of the **Qur'ān**; it means 'The Laying Open' or 'The Expanding'. The *sūra* belongs to the Meccan period and has 8 verses. Its title is taken from the 1st verse which asks: 'Did We not lay open your heart for you?'. Some commentators suggest that this refers to the incident in the childhood of the Prophet **Muḥammad** during which the Prophet's heart was laid open by angels and a clot of sin was removed. The *sūra* seeks to console the Prophet by reminding him that he has a high reputation and that the difficulty he has suffered will bring its rewards. (*See* **Angel**.)

Sharī'a (Ar.) The Holy Law of Islam. (*See* **Fiqh**; **Ḥiyal**; **Madhhab**; **Uṣūl al-Fiqh**.)

Shaykh (Ar.) [pl. *shuyūkh*] Old man, chief, title of respect for Islamic religious leader, tribal head, master of a **ṣūfī** (q.v.) order. (*See* **Imām**; **Sajjāda**; **Ṭarīqa**.)

al-Shayṭān *See* **Iblīs**.

Sheba *See* **Bilqīs**; **Sulaymān**; **Sūrat al-Naml**; **Sūrat Sabā'**.

Shī'a (Ar.) Party, i.e. of **'Alī b. Abī Ṭālib** (q.v.); those who follow and accept the claims of 'Alī. For fuller descriptions of the principal sub-divisions of the *Shī'a*, the reader is directed to the entries listed s.v. **Shī'ism**. Here, a general outline follows of some of the principal tenets of this important branch of Islam: adherents of the *Shī'a* differ from the Sunnīs on a variety of matters, principal of which are the questions of succession, authority and law. Shīʻites believe that ʻAlī b. Abī Ṭalib, rather than **Abū Bakr** (q.v.) should have succeeded **Muḥammad** as **Khalīfa** (q.v.). The role of the **Imām** (q.v.) in Shīʻite political theory is much more powerful than that of the Sunnī *Khalīfa*. Legal differences between Sunnīs and Shīʻites include matters of inheritance and marriage, Shīʻite law among the **Ithnā ʻAsharīs** (q.v.) for example, permitting **mutʻa** (q.v.) or temporary marriage. There are, moreover, minor distinctions of ritual, as in the Call to Prayer, between Sunnīs and Shīʻites. The majority of the world's Shīʻites today are concentrated in Iran and Southern Iraq. (*See* **Adhān**; **Ghadīr al-Khumm**; **Sunnī**.)

Shīʻism *See* **Hāshimiyya**; **Ismāʻīlīs**; **Ithnā ʻAsharīs**; **Zaydīs**.

Shīʻite Anglicized form of the Arabic word *shīʻī* meaning a member of the **Shīʻa** (q.v.) branch of Islam.

Shīrāz Major historic city of South West Iran, famous both for its Islamic architecture and late mediaeval school of miniature painting. Shīrāz was also the home of two of Iran's greatest poets, Saʻdī (died 690/1291) and Ḥāfiẓ (*c.* 720/1320–792/1390). In the mid and later 12th/18th century Shīrāz also became a Zand tribal capital for a period. (*See* **Iṣfahān**; **Ṣafavids**.)

al-Shīrāzī *See* **Mulla Ṣadra**.

Shirk (Ar.) Idolatry, polytheism. This is a heinous sin condemned in the **Qur'ān**. The Arabic word means literally 'sharing': man is forbidden to share his worship of God with that of any other creatures, and to ascribe partners to God as sharers of His Divinity. Polytheism is the one sin which the Qur'ān tells us cannot and will not be forgiven. This is because it denies God's very existence. (*See* v.116 of **Sūrat al-Nisā'** (q.v.).) **Ibrāhīm** (q.v.) is presented as a pure monotheist who 'was not among the polytheists' (*wa mā kāna min al-mushrikīn*): *see* v.67 of **Sūrat Āl ʻImrān** (q.v.). (*See also* **Mushrikūn**.)

al-Shu'arā' (Ar.) The title of the 26th **sūra** of the **Qur'ān**; it means 'The Poets'. The *sūra* belongs mainly to the Meccan period and has 227 verses. Its title is drawn from vv.224 ff which refer to local Arab poets. The *sūra* begins with three of the **Mysterious Letters of the Qur'ān** (q.v.) and provides considerable detail about the stories of **Mūsā** (q.v.) and Pharaoh, **Ibrāhīm** (q.v.), **Nūḥ** (q.v.), **Hūd** (q.v.), **Ṣāliḥ** (q.v.), **Lūṭ** (q.v.), and **Shu'ayb** (q.v.). It is thus a *sūra* which concentrates overwhelmingly on prophetic history. (*See* **Fir'awn**.)

Shu'ayb Arabian prophet sent to warn the people of **Madyan** (q.v.) to worship the one true God and against sharp business practices; they reject his message and are punished accordingly in an earthquake. The story of Shu'ayb and his message appears in some detail in **Sūrat al-A'rāf** (q.v.) and also **Sūrat Hūd** (q.v.). It follows a similar pattern to that of **Ṣāliḥ** (q.v.). Shu'ayb has sometimes been identified with Jethro.

Shūrā (Ar.) Consultation, counsel, consultative body, council. **'Uthmān b. 'Affān** (q.v.) was elected by a *shūrā* of six eminent **muhājirūn** (q.v.), appointed by **'Umar b. al-Khaṭṭāb** (q.v.).

al-Shūrā (Ar.) The title of the 42nd **sūra** of the **Qur'ān**; it may be translated as 'The Counsel' (but see other translations in the entry above). The *sūra* belongs mainly to the Meccan period and contains 53 verses. Its title comes from v.38 which refers to those who organize themselves by *shūrā*. The *sūra* begins with five of the **Mysterious Letters of the Qur'ān** (q.v.) (spread over two verses), goes on to emphasize God's power and omniscience, and makes reference to such great figures as **Nūḥ** (q.v.), **Ibrāhīm** (q.v.), **Mūsā** (q.v.) and **'Īsā** (q.v.). His mercy to His creation and His signs are mentioned and the *sūra* concludes by noting that all things return to God.

Shu'ūbiyya (Ar.) The word derives from the Arabic word *sha'b* [pl. *shu'ūb*] meaning 'people', 'nation', 'race'. The

Shu'ūbiyya movement championed the idea of the basic equality of Arabs and non-Arabs, and had a literary as well as a political dimension. (*See* **Dhimmī**.)

al-Ṣiddīq (Ar.) The Righteous, The Upright, The Honest, The True, The Truthful One. This was a title borne both by **Abū Bakr** (q.v.) and **Yūsuf** (q.v.). *See* v.46 of **Sūrat Yūsuf** (q.v.) where the latter is called *al-Ṣiddīq*. (*See also* **Idrīs**.)

Sidrat al-Muntahā (Ar.) The furthest lote or lotus tree, located in Paradise. It is mentioned in the **Qur'ān** in v.14 of **Sūrat al-Najm** (q.v.). (*See* **al-Janna**; **Mi'rāj**.)

Ṣifāt Allāh (Ar.) The attributes of God. Muslim theology classically distinguished between the basic attributes of the Essence (*al-Dhāt*) (like God's eternity, self-subsistence and permanence), and others. Much mediaeval theological debate concerned itself with the exact relationship between all the attributes and God's Essence: were they identical with the Essence or separate? If the latter were the case, what were the implications for the doctrine of God's unity? One conclusion to the debate was that God's attributes were eternal and subsisted in His Essence, but they were not God nor other than God! (*See* **Aḥmad b. Ḥanbal**; **al-Ash'arī**; **Bilā Kayf**; **Istawā**; **Khān, Sayyid Aḥmad**; **Mu'tazila**; **Tanzīh**; **Tashbīh**; **Ta'ṭīl**; **Tawḥīd**.)

Ṣiffīn, Battle of Significant event in early Islamic history. The battle and the immediate events surrounding it lasted over a period of three months up to 37/657 at a plain called Ṣiffīn which is South of the River Euphrates. The conflict was between **'Alī b. Abī Ṭālib** (q.v.) and the governor of Syria, **Mu'āwiya** (q.v.). No sooner was actual battle commenced than an appeal for more talks was made by some of the Syrians who fixed copies of the **Qur'ān** to their spears. The result was a protracted arbitration but in 40/661 'Alī was assassinated and the way was open for Mu'āwiya to inaugurate Islam's first dynasty, that of the **Umayyads** (q.v.).

Sight of God *See* **Ru'yat Allāh.**

Sign (of God) *See* **Āya.**

Signs of the Hour *See* **Ishārāt al-Sā'a.**

al-Sijistānī Name borne by two famous mediaeval thinkers: (1) Abū Sulaymān al-Sijistānī (*c.* 300-02/913-4–*c.* 376-8/987-8) was called 'The Logician' and became one of the intellectual leaders of the **Baghdād** (q.v.) of his day. His thought is characterized by a strong Neoplatonic tinge. His best-known work is his *Cupboard of Wisdom* (*Ṣiwān al-Ḥikma*). (2) Abū Ya'qūb Isḥāq b. Aḥmad al-Sijistānī (died *c.* 360-1/971–392-4/1002-3) was an early Ismā'īlī Neoplatonist. He produced a number of important books including *The Book of the Springs* (*Kitāb al-Yanābī'*). (*See* **Ismā'īlīs; Neoplatonism, Islamic**; *see also* **Abū Dā'ūd**.)

Silsila (Ar.) Literally, 'chain'. In **taṣawwuf** (q.v.) this word has the technical sense of a chain of spiritual authorities or leaders, whereby the present **shaykh** (q.v.) of a **ṭarīqa** (q.v.) with whom the *silsila* ends, receives legitimacy and authority. The *silsila* is traced back from the present *shaykh* to some great spiritual figure of the past like **'Alī b. Abī Ṭālib** (q.v.) or the Prophet **Muḥammad** himself. The word *silsila* has been neatly translated as 'a mystical *isnād*'. (*See* **Isnād**.)

Sin *See* **Dhanb; Ḥadd; Shirk.**

Sinān Pasha (895/1488–996/1588) Architectural genius of the high Ottoman age, responsible for the construction of many of Turkey's greatest mosques. (*See* **Istanbul; Masjid; Ottomans; Süleymān 'The Magnificent'**.)

Sīra (Ar.) Biography, particularly that of the Prophet **Muḥammad**. The most famous exponent of this genre was **Ibn Isḥāq** (q.v.).

Ṣirāṭ al-Jaḥīm (Ar.) The Bridge of Hell. This bridge over Hell is mentioned in v.23 of **Sūrat al-Ṣāffāt** (q.v.) of the **Qur'ān**. **Al-Jaḥīm** (q.v.) is one of the names in Arabic for Hell. Islamic tradition goes into considerable detail about the nature of, and the imagery and rituals associated with, this bridge. For example, it has seven arches and is extraordinarily thin and sharp. (*See* **al-Nār**.)

al-Ṣirāṭ al-Mustaqīm (Ar.) The Straight Path, the Right Path. (In Islamic eschatology *ṣirāṭ* can also mean a bridge: *see* **Ṣirāṭ al-Jaḥīm**.) The phrase *al-Ṣirāṭ al-Mustaqīm* is Qur'ānic and occurs most notably in v.5 of the **Fātiḥa** (q.v.). (*See also* v.52 of **Sūrat al-Shūrā** (q.v.)). The phrase has been interpreted as indicating the Islamic Faith or that which pleases God. (*See* **Qur'ān**.)

Siyāsa Shar'iyya (Ar.) Governing in accordance with the **Sharī'a** (q.v.). This is a technical term indicating the ruler's discretionary right to supplement the law as defined by the jurists. The criminal law provided many cases where this happened.

Slaughter, Ritual Animals for human consumption by Muslims should be *ritually* slaughtered. Components of this ritual include the recitation of the phrase 'In the name of God; God is Most Great' over the animal and the draining of the blood as much as possible. The slaughterer should be a Muslim himself. (*See* **Ḥalāl**.)

Slave *See* **'Abd**.

Sleepers of the Cave *See* **Aṣḥāb al-Kahf**; **Sūrat al-Kahf**.

ṢL'M *See* **Pbuh**.

Solomon *See* **Sulaymān**.

Soul *See* **Nafs**; **Rūḥ**.

Spain, Islamic *See* **al-Andalus**.

Spirit *See* **Nafs**; **Rūḥ**.

Standing (at ʻArafa) *See* **ʻArafa**; **Wuqūf**.

States, Spiritual *See* **Aḥwāl**; **Basṭ**; **Maqāmāt**; **Qabḍ**; **Taṣawwuf**.

Stoning *See* **Āyat al-Rajm**; **al-Jamra**; **Minā**; **al-Rajīm**.

Straight Path, The *See* **al-Ṣirāṭ al-Mustaqīm**.

al-Ṣubḥ, Ṣalāt (Ar.) The Morning Prayer. (*See* **Ṣalāt**.)

Subḥa (Ar.) [pl. *subuḥāt*] Rosary. A *full* Islamic rosary comprises 99 beads, each indicating one of the 99 beautiful names of God. However, rosaries can be smaller. (*See* **al-Asmā' al-Ḥusnā**.)

Submission (to the Will of God) *See* **Islām**.

Subsidiary Principles of Law *See* **Istiḥsān**; **Istiṣḥāb**; **Istiṣlāḥ**.

Substance (as philosophical term) *See* **Jawhar**.

Ṣūfī (Ar.) Islamic mystic. The term should not be used, or appropriated, by those mystics who are not Muslims or who do not root their mysticism in the **Qur'ān**. A variety of possible etymologies for the word *ṣūfī* have been put forward: the most likely, and most generally agreed by scholars, is that it derives from the Arabic word *ṣūf* meaning 'wool', in reference to the garments of the early Muslim ascetics. (*See* **Taṣawwuf**.)

Ṣūfī House *See* **Khānagāh**; **Ribāṭ**; **Tekkē**; **Zāwiya**.

Ṣūfism *See* **Taṣawwuf**.

al-Suhrawardī Name borne by at least three well-known persons in mediaeval times. They should not be confused: (1) The most famous was the great 'Master of Illumination', Shihāb al-Dīn Abū 'l-Futūḥ Yaḥyā al-Suhrawardī (547-8/1153–587/1191) who is also designated 'The Executed' and 'The Martyr' because of his mysterious end. This philosophical mystic's greatest work was his *Ḥikmat al-Ishrāq*, usually translated as *The Wisdom of Illumination*. Theologically al-Suhrawardī is important for his conception of God as 'The Light of Lights' (*Nūr al-Anwār*). (2) 'Abd al-Qāhir Abū Najīb al-Suhrawardī (died 564/1168) was a disciple of Aḥmad (brother of the famous Abū Ḥāmid Muḥammad **al-Ghazālī** (q.v.)). 'Abd al-Qāhir was the inspiration behind the **Suhrawardiyya** (q.v.) **ṣūfī** (q.v.) order, and he wrote a book called *The Manners of the Novices*. (3) Shihāb al-Dīn Abū Ḥafs 'Umar al-Suhrawardī (540/1145–632/1234) was the nephew of the above 'Abd al-Qāhir. He was the author of *The Gifts of Mystical Knowledge* and probably the real founder of the Suhrawardiyya. (*See* **Barzakh**; **Čishtiyya**.)

Suhrawardiyya Major **ṣūfī** (q.v.) order whose origins go back to 'Abd al-Qāhir Abū Najīb al-Suhrawardī and Shihāb al-Dīn Abū Ḥafs 'Umar al-Suhrawardī. (*See* above entry). The mediaeval Islamic traveller **Ibn Baṭṭūṭa** (q.v.) was affiliated to the Suhrawardiyya while in **Iṣfahān** (q.v.) and the Suhrawardiyya also became an important **ṭarīqa** (q.v.) in India with a variety of branches. (*See* **Čishtiyya**; **al-Suhrawardī**.)

Sujūd (Ar.) Ritual prostration, with the forehead touching the ground, during the **ṣalāt** (q.v.). (*See* **Rak'a**.)

Sulaymān Solomon. He is a prophet and king, epitome of wisdom and arcane knowledge, frequently mentioned in the **Qur'ān**. Here he is portrayed as knowing the language of the birds and the insects, and dealing with the Queen **Bilqīs** (q.v.). Reference is also made to his death in **Sūrat Sabā'** (q.v.) and this is elaborated in tradition: the **jinn** (q.v.) continue to build the

Temple after he dies, and only realise he is dead when the staff on which his dead body leans is eaten through by a worm, and King Solomon's body falls over. (*See* **Sūrat al-Naml**; **Sūrat Ṣād**.)

Süleymān 'The Magnificent' (900/1494–974/1566) Major Ottoman sultan who acceded in 926/1520 and whose reign saw the peak of the Ottoman dynasty's power. He patronized the arts and employed, for example, the great architect **Sinān** (q.v.). Süleymān thus has some importance in the history of Islamic architecture. Islamic history also bestowed on him the title of 'The Lawgiver'. (*See* **Istanbul**; **Ottomans**.)

Sulṭān (Ar.) [pl. *salāṭīn*] Sultan, ruler, title borne by the Ottoman rulers. (*See* **Ottomans**.)

Sumayya bint Khubbāṭ Woman much revered as Islam's first martyr; she was killed by **Abū Jahl** (q.v.).

Sunna (Ar.) [pl. *sunan*] Literally, this word means 'trodden path'. It developed from meaning 'customary practice' to indicating the specific actions and sayings of the Prophet **Muḥammad** himself. **Al-Shāfi'ī** (q.v.) established *sunna* as one of his four major sources of law. (*See* **Ḥadīth**; **Uṣūl al-Fiqh**.)

Sunnī (Ar.) One who adheres to the **sunna** (q.v.) or customary practice of the Prophet **Muḥammad** himself. The word is used to designate the mainstream or majority branch of Islam, and contrasted with **Shī'ism** (q.v.). The word *sunnī* is sometimes loosely translated as 'orthodox' but this should not be taken to disparage the Shī'ite branch of Islam.

Supplementary Sources of Law *See* **Subsidiary Principles of Law.**

Sūra (Ar.) [pl. *suwar*] Chapter of the **Qur'ān**. Each chapter is divided into a number of verses (*see* **Āya**) and the chapters are characterized as either Meccan or Medinan according to their place of revelation. The Qur'ān is arranged so that, after the **Fātiḥa** (q.v.), the longest chapters appear first. Each of the 114 chapters of the Qur'ān is described individually in this *Dictionary under its title heading*. For example, to look up **Sūrat al-Anfāl**, see under **al-Anfāl**. (*See* **Mecca**; **Medina**.)

al-Suyūṭī, Jalāl al-Dīn (849/1445–911/1505) Egyptian polymath, historian, belletrist, grammarian and commentator on the **Qur'ān** who is credited with having written well over 500 books. Among his more important books were compilations of **ḥadīth** (q.v.) and his *History of the Caliphs*. He is particularly well known for his part in writing the famous *Qur'ānic Commentary by the Two Jalāls*. (*See* **Tafsīr**.)

Swine *See* **Pork**.

al-Ṭabarī, Abū Ja'far Muḥammad b. Jarīr (*c.* 224-5/839–310/923) Major early Islamic historian and exegete of the **Qur'ān**. Born in Ṭabaristān in Northern Iran, he travelled to many of the great centres of the Islamic world. He was erudite in a large variety of subjects of which three stand out: history, Qur'ānic exegesis and law. He wrote an extremely important world history; his great commentary on the Qur'ān is used to this day; and he actually founded a School of law which became known as the *Jarīriyya*. This, however, seems to have owed much theoretically to the **Shāfi'īs** (q.v.) and fell into disuse. (*See* **Tafsīr**.)

Tābi'ūn (Ar.) [sing. *tābi'*] Followers; the next generation after the **Ṣaḥāba** (q.v.) or Companions (who actually knew the Prophet **Muḥammad**). (*See* **Salafiyya**.)

Tabūk Town in the Northern Arabian peninsula, about 250 miles from **Medina** (q.v.), near the Gulf of al-'Aqaba, to which the Prophet **Muḥammad** led his greatest expedition in 9/630.

Tadlīs (Ar.) Literally, 'fraud'. In the technical terminology of **ḥadīth** (q.v.) criticism, this word assumed the sense of interfering with, or disguising defects in, the **isnād** (q.v.).

Tafsīr (Ar.) [pl. *tafāsīr*] Exegesis, interpretation, commentary, especially relating to the **Qur'ān**. Classical Qur'ānic *tafsīr* concentrated on such matters as grammar, identification or provision of proper names, textual ambiguities, provision of more information on central characters, lexicography, philology etc., all with the intention of clarifying the Qur'ānic words themselves. Ismā'īlī exegesis differed somewhat in its desire to seek a hidden (**bāṭin** (q.v.)) sense beneath the apparent (**ẓāhir** (q.v.)) sense. The great classical exegetes were **al-Bayḍāwī** (q.v.), **al-Ṭabarī** (q.v.) and **al-Zamakhsharī** (q.v.). (*See* **Ismā'īlīs**; **Ta'wīl**.)

al-Taghābun (Ar.) The title of the 64th **sūra** of the **Qur'ān**; it means 'The Mutual Disillusion' or 'The Mutual Cheating'. The *sūra* belongs to the Medinan period and has 18 verses. Its title comes from v.9 which refers to the Day of Resurrection as 'The Day of Mutual Disillusion' (*Yawm al-Taghābun*). On this day men's expectations will be turned upside down. The believers will enter Paradise while the disbelievers who denied God's signs will enter Hell. The believers are warned to beware of enemies even among their wives and children. (*See* **al-Janna**; **al-Nār**; **Yawm al-Qiyāma**.)

Ṭāhā [Ṭā' Hā'] (Ar.) The title of the 20th **sūra** of the **Qur'ān**; it consists of two letters of the Arabic alphabet Ṭ and H. The *sūra* belongs to the Meccan period and contains 135 verses. The title is drawn from the 1st verse which comprises simply the above-mentioned letters. The early part of the *sūra* has much to say about **Mūsā** (q.v.), Pharaoh, the Children of Israel and **Hārūn** (q.v.). Later, reference is made to the terrors of the Day of Judgement, the rebellion of **Iblīs** (q.v.), and the temptation of **Ādam** (q.v.) and Eve. (*See* **Fir'awn**; **Mysterious Letters of the Qur'ān**; **Yawm al-Qiyāma**.)

Ṭāhā Ḥusayn *See* **Ḥusayn, Ṭāhā**.

Taḥannuth (Ar.) Devotional or pious practice of some kind. The Prophet **Muḥammad** used to occupy himself with *taḥannuth* in a cave on Mount **Ḥirā'** (q.v.) around the time of the revelation of the **Qur'ān**. (*See* **Khalwa**.)

Ṭahāra (Ar.) Ritual purification, ritual purity, ritual cleanliness. Islam places much stress on the concepts of inner and outer purity. The first is expressed in such forms as the pure **niyya** (q.v.); the latter in **ghusl** (q.v.), **iḥrām** (q.v.), **wuḍū'** (q.v.) etc. Books of **fiqh** (q.v.) frequently have a chapter devoted to purity in all its aspects. (*See* **Menstruation**; **Mīḍa'a**; **Ṣalāt**; **Tayammum**.)

Taḥrīf (Ar.) Corruption, distortion, alteration, especially as applied to sacred texts. Muslims invoke the concept of *taḥrīf* to account, for example, for the disparity between the data about Jesus in the New Testament and that in the **Qur'ān**: Islam believes that Christians have altered the original text of a proto-Gospel (**al-Injīl** (q.v.)) now lost. In v.13 of **Sūrat al-Mā'ida** (q.v.) the Jews are also accused of textual corruption. (*See* **'Īsā**.)

al-Taḥrīm (Ar.) The title of the 66th **sūra** of the **Qur'ān**; it means 'The Prohibition'. The *sūra* belongs to the Medinan period and has 12 verses. It draws its title from the 1st verse which asks the Prophet **Muḥammad** why he has forbidden to himself something lawful in the eyes of God, i.e. honey. The *sūra* goes on to warn both believers and disbelievers of the pains of Hell and concludes by surveying a number of disbelieving and believing women. **Maryam** (q.v.) is among the latter. (*See* **Jibrīl**; **al-Nār**.)

al-Ṭahṭāwī, Rifā'a (1215-6/1801–1289-90/1873) Egyptian translation expert who spent five years in Paris as **Imām** (q.v.) to an Egyptian student mission and who, thereafter, attempted to interpret in various ways the West to the East. On his return to

Egypt he directed, during the rule of **Muḥammad 'Alī** (q.v.), a new School of Languages and also, a little later, a translation bureau attached to that School. Despite his stay in Paris al-Ṭahṭāwī remained a conventional Muslim who, none the less, opened a window on Western culture and thought, looked through it and caused others to do the same.

al-Ṭā'if Town about forty miles from **Mecca** (q.v.) whose people resisted with stones the early attempts by the Prophet **Muḥammad** to establish contacts. During his return to Mecca, one night after his visit to al-Ṭā'if, Muḥammad converted a company of **jinn** (q.v.). (*See* **Thaqīf**.)

Ṭā'ifa (Ar.) [pl. *ṭawā'if*] This word has the specialist technical sense of a **ṣūfī** (q.v.) order. (*See* **Ṭarīqa**; **Taṣawwuf**.)

Tāj Maḥal This is perhaps the most spectacular, as well as the best-known, Islamic mausoleum in the world. Built in white marble at **Āgra** (q.v.) on the River Yamunā (Jumna) by **Shāh Jahān** (q.v.) as a loving tribute to his beloved wife Mumtāz Maḥal who died in childbirth in 1040/1631, the Tāj is one of the great glories of Islamic Mughal architecture. There appears to be no truth in the tradition that the architect of the Tāj was a Venetian. The words 'Tāj Maḥal' are a corrupted form of Mumtāz Maḥal. (*See* **Mughals**.)

al-Takāthur (Ar.) The title of the 102nd **sūra** of the **Qur'ān**; it means literally 'The Growth' or 'The Multiplication' but the title has also been rendered as 'The Rivalry' or 'The Worldly Gain'. The *sūra* belongs to the Meccan period and has 8 verses. Its title is drawn from v.1 where it is stated that 'Multiplication preoccupies you'. According to one interpretation this is directed at clans which have boasted about their numbers, one even enumerating the dead in its calculations.

Takbīr (Ar.) Praise, glorification, the declaration or expression 'God is Most Great' (*Allāhu Akbar*). The latter is a much used part of the **ṣalāt** (q.v.).

Takiyya *See* **Tekkē; Zāwiya.**

al-Takwīr (Ar.) The title of the 81st **sūra** of the **Qur'ān**; it means 'The Winding Up' or 'The Darkening'. The *sūra* belongs to the Meccan period and has 29 verses. Its title is drawn from the 1st verse which begins a description of the Day of Resurrection with the words 'When the sun is wound up/darkened'. The *sūra* refers to the occasion when **Muḥammad** saw the angel **Jibrīl** (q.v.) in his glory, standing on the horizon, for the first time. There is also an interesting reference in vv.8–9 to the pre-Islamic custom of burying female children alive.

Ṭalab al-'Ilm (Ar.) The search for knowledge. (*See* **Ibn Baṭṭūṭa; 'Ilm; Riḥla.**)

Ṭalāq (Ar.) Divorce. There is a saying by the Prophet **Muḥammad** that of all things which are permitted, divorce is the most hateful in the eyes of God. Divorce, therefore, is clearly permitted in Islam but it is not encouraged. The two principal **sūras** of the **Qur'ān** which deal with the subject are **Sūrat al-Baqara** (q.v.) and **Sūrat al-Ṭalāq** (q.v.). Classically a divorce repudiation was followed by a waiting period (**'idda** (q.v.)) of three menstrual cycles to give a chance for a reconciliation to take place between the spouses, and also to determine whether the wife was pregnant. **Sunnī** (q.v.) jurists also classified divorce as 'approved' or 'reprehensible' according to the way in which it was pronounced. An example of the latter 'reprehensible' type was three repudiations said all at one time. Today, in some Islamic countries like Tunisia, divorce has been institutionalized and removed from the competence of the individual. In Tunisia, therefore, divorce *outside the jurisdiction of a court of law* has no legal validity. (*See* **Mut'a; Nikāḥ.**)

al-Ṭalāq (Ar.) The title of the 65th **sūra** of the **Qur'ān**; it means 'The Divorce'. The *sūra* belongs to the Medinan period and contains 12 verses. Its title is drawn from the first verses which deal with the subject of divorce and supplement the data in **Sūrat al-Baqara** (q.v.). The *sūra* concludes by linking good deeds with entry to Paradise and wicked deeds to a parallel end in Hell. (*See* **al-Janna**; **al-Nār**.)

Talfīq (Ar.) Literally, 'concoction', 'fabrication', 'piecing together'. In modern jurisprudence this word acquired the sense of piecing together views from different Schools of law to formulate a legal principle or rule. (*See* **'Abduh**.)

Ṭalḥa b. 'Ubaydullāh al-Taymī (died 36/656) A very early convert to Islam and companion of the Prophet **Muḥammad**, Ṭalḥa belonged to the Taym (q.v.) clan of the tribe of **Quraysh** (q.v.). He fought against **'Alī b. Abī Ṭālib** (q.v.) at the Battle of the Camel during which he was killed. (*See* **'Ā'isha bint Abī Bakr**; **Camel, Battle of the**; **al-Zubayr b. al-'Awwām**.)

Tamburlaine *See* **Tīmūr-i Lang**.

Tamerlane *See* **Tīmūr-i Lang**.

Tamīm Major Arab tribe in Eastern Arabia in early Islamic history. The clans of Tamīm maintained close links with **Quraysh** (q.v.) in pre-Islamic times. (*See* **Sūrat al-Ḥujurāt**.)

Tanzīh (Ar.) Considering or declaring God to be above and beyond anthropomorphic elements or description. *Tanzīh* stresses the remote and transcendent aspect of God, while its opposite, **tashbīh** (q.v.), emphasizes, sometimes overmuch in the view of some Islamic theologians, the immanent aspect of God. These two Qur'ānic concepts are neatly summarized in the Qur'ānic assertion, on the one hand, that God has no like and, on the other, the statement that God is nearer to man than his own jugular vein. (*See* **Allāh**.)

Tanzīl (Ar.) Revelation, i.e. of the **Qur'ān**.

Tanẓīmāt (Ar.) Reforms promulgated by the **Ottomans** (q.v.) from 1255/1839 to 1298/1880 which promised to guarantee the basic rights of all subjects regardless of their religion. These reforms did not prevent the break-up of the Ottoman empire. (*See* **Ahl al-Kitāb**; **Dhimmī**; **Mawlā**.)

Taqdīr (Ar.) Predestination. The **Qur'ān** contains verses which may be interpreted in favour of both free will and predestination. An example of the latter is v.27 of **Sūrat al-Ra'd** (q.v.): 'God leads astray whomsoever He wishes, and guides to Him whoever repents'. (*See* **Kasb**; **Qadar**; **Qadariyya**.)

Taqiyya (Ar.) Dissimulation of one's religion, especially in time of persecution or danger. The practice was permitted by **Shī'ism** (q.v.) and also by the **Druze** (q.v.) religion.

Taqlīd (Ar.) Literally, 'imitation'. The word acquired the more technical legal sense of uncritical dependence on past precedent and law as expounded by the law Schools (**madhāhib** (q.v.)). In this sense it may be compared with the concept of 'case law'. *Taqlīd* may also be contrasted with **ijtihād** (q.v.).

Tarāwīḥ (Ar.) Extra prayers undertaken on a voluntary basis during the nights of the month of fasting, **Ramaḍān** (q.v.). The *ṣalāt al-tarāwīḥ* (literally, 'the prayer of pauses') can comprise as many as forty *raka'āt*, with a pause after every four. (*See* **Rak'a**; **Ṣalāt**.)

al-Ṭāriq (Ar.) The title of the 86th **sūra** of the **Qur'ān**; it means 'The Night Star'. The *sūra* belongs to the Meccan period and contains 17 verses. Its title is drawn from the oath in v.1: 'By the heaven and the night star'. The *sūra* refers to God's power to raise man from the dead on Judgement Day, and counsels patience with the unbelievers.

Ṭarīqa (Ar.) [pl. *ṭuruq*] The word is very frequently used to designate a **ṣūfī** (q.v.) order. Technically speaking, however, in

Taṣawwuf (q.v.) it has the primary sense of a mystical way or path. Compare **Ṭā'ifa**.

Taṣawwuf Ṣūfism, the mysticism of Islam. This is the inner dimension of Islam and has been neatly described as 'the Science of the Heart'. There is no such thing as a Ṣūfism apart from Islam though there are, of course, many religions with their own mystical dimension. The *word* 'ṣūfism' is, however, exclusively Islamic since the *ṣūfī*s sought - and seek - to found their spirituality in and upon the **Qur'ān**. Although a variety of etymologies for the word **ṣūfī** (q.v.) have been put forward, the most likely expanation is that it derives from the Arabic word *ṣūf* meaning 'wool' in reference to the garments worn by the early *ṣūfī*s. The *ṣūfī*s often tried to be above sect, accepting the one which ruled in the country where they lived. Many aspects of *taṣawwuf* are covered in this *Dictionary*. *See* for example, **Baqā'**; **Dhikr**; **Fanā'**; **Khānagāh**; **Ribāṭ**; **Sajjāda**; **Tekkē**; **Zāwiya**. For some of the *ṣūfī* orders, *see* **Aḥmadiyya** (2); **Burhāniyya**; **Naqshabandiyya**; **Ni'matullāhiyya**; **Qādiriyya**; **Rifā'iyya**; **Sanūsiyya**; **Shādhiliyya**; **Tijāniyya**.

Tasbīḥ (Ar.) Glorification, praising of God i.e. by saying the Arabic phrase *Subḥāna Allāh* which means 'Praise be to God!'

Tashbīh (Ar.) Anthropomorphism, describing God in human terms. The whole problem of how God should be described and the nature of His attributes precipitated much debate in mediaeval Islam. (*See* **'Arsh**; **al-Ash'arī**; **Istawā**; **Mu'tazila**; **Ṣifāt Allāh**; **Tanzīh**.)

Tasnīm (Ar.) Nectar. This is the name of a spring (*'ayn*) in Paradise. Its waters will be drunk by those 'brought near' (i.e. to God). This is mentioned in the **Qur'ān** in vv.27–28 of **Sūrat al-Muṭaffifīn** (q.v.). Some traditions view Tasnīm more as a river than a spring. (*See* **al-Janna**; **Kāfūr**; **al-Kawthar**; **Salsabīl**.)

Taste (Mystical sense) *See* **Dhawq**.

Ta'ṭīl (Ar.) Stripping God of all attributes; the opposite of **tashbīh** (q.v.). (*See* **al-Ash'arī**; **Istawā**; **Mu'tazila**; **Ṣifāt Allāh**.)

Ṭawāf (Ar.) Circumambulation, i.e. of the **Ka'ba** (q.v.) seven times at the start of the **Ḥajj** (q.v.). At the end of the pilgrimage, before departing from **Mecca** (q.v.), 'the circumambulation of farewell' (*ṭawāf al-wadā'*) may be performed but this is not compulsory. (*See* **Muṭawwif**.)

Tawassul (Ar.) Entreaty, intercession, especially that which is sung during a **ṣūfī** (q.v.) **ḥaḍra** (q.v.). (*See* **Ḥizb**.)

Tawātur (Ar.) Technical term used in **ḥadīth** (q.v.) criticism denoting the consideration that a tradition is **mutawātir** (q.v.).

Tawba (Ar.) Repentance. The Arabic verb *tāba*, said of a man, indicates 'to repent'; when it is said of God it means 'to forgive'. Thus *tawwāb* means both 'repentant' (a man) and 'Forgiving' (God). Polytheism (**Shirk** (q.v.)) is the only sin which will not be forgiven. Otherwise those who turn to God in repentance *will* be forgiven. *See*, for example, v.25 of **Sūrat al-Shūrā** (q.v.) in the **Qur'ān**.

al-Tawba (Ar.) The title of the 9th **sūra** of the **Qur'ān**; it means 'The Repentance'. The *sūra* belongs to the Medinan period and has 129 verses. Uniquely in the Qur'ān it lacks the **Basmala** (q.v.) at the beginning. The *sūra* draws its name from v.104 which refers to God accepting repentance from His servants. The *sūra* distances the Muslims from the polytheists, refers to various peoples to whom God has sent messengers, counsels the Prophet **Muḥammad** to fight unbelievers and hypocrites (who are both destined for Hell), and contains a number of references to war and fighting. Towards the end of the *sūra*, the asking for forgiveness for his idolatrous father by **Ibrāhīm** (q.v.) is noted. (*See* **Āzar**; **al-Nār**.)

Tawḥīd (Ar.) Declaration of the Oneness (**Waḥda** (q.v.)) of God, belief in that Oneness or Unity, monotheism. This is one of the most fundamental Islamic doctrines.

Ta'wīl (Ar.) Interpretation, allegorical interpretation of the **Qur'ān**. (*See* **Ismā'īlīs**; **Tafsīr**.)

Tax, Taxation *See* **Jizya**; **Kharāj**; **Ṣadaqa**; **'Ushr**; **Zakāt**.

Tayammum (Ar.) The substitution (for reasons of availability, health etc.) of sand, stone, or even snow for the usual purification by water and the ritual ablution therewith. (*See* **Ghusl**; **Wuḍū'**.)

Taym One of the clans of the tribe of **Quraysh** (q.v.). **Abū Bakr** (q.v.), the successor of **Muḥammad**, belonged to this clan as did **Ṭalḥa b. 'Ubaydullāh al-Taymī** (q.v.).

Ta'ziya (Ar.) Literally, 'Consolation'. More technically, the word has the sense of a Shī'ite 'passion play' in commemoration of the sufferings of **al-Ḥusayn b. 'Alī** (q.v.) performed in **al-Muḥarram** (q.v.). There are also associated street processions. (*See* **'Āshūrā'**; **Ithnā 'Asharīs**; **Karbalā'**.)

Tekkē (Turk.) The Turkish equivalent of a **zāwiya** (q.v.) or **khānagāh** (q.v.). (*See* **Ribāṭ**; **Taṣawwuf**.)

Temporary Marriage *See* **Mut'a**.

Thamūd Pre-Islamic Arabian tribe mentioned in the **Qur'ān** to whom God sent the prophet **Ṣāliḥ** (q.v.). (*See* **Shu'ayb**; **Sūrat al-A'rāf**; **Sūrat Fuṣṣilat**; **Sūrat al-Ḥāqqa**; **Sūrat Hūd**.)

Thaqīf Major Arabian tribe to which the people of **al-Ṭā'if** (q.v.) belonged. (*See* **Ḥunayn, Battle of**)

Tha'r *See* **Qiṣāṣ**.

Theft *See* **Sariqa**.

Theology *See* **Kalām**.

Throne *See* **'Arsh; Istawā**.

Throne Verse *See* **Āyat al-Kursī**.

Tijāniyya Major **ṣūfī** (q.v.) order named after its founder Aḥmad al-Tijānī (1150/1737-8–1230/1815) who was born in Southern Algeria. He made the pilgrimage to **Mecca** (q.v.) and settled eventually in **Fez** (q.v.). The order began in 1196/1782 when Aḥmad announced that he had seen a vision of the Prophet **Muḥammad** who bade him begin his *ṣūfī* work. The early order did not stress **zuhd** (q.v.) and the ownership of wealth was accepted. A particular characteristic of the order is its stress on thanksgiving to God. The order gained popularity in North Africa as well as the Western Sudan, Senegal and elsewhere in West Africa.

Tīmūrids *See* **Tīmūr-i Lang.**

Tīmūr-i Lang (*c.* 738/1337–807/1405) Tamburlaine, Tamerlane, Tīmūr the Lame. He made himself ruler in **Samarqand** (q.v.) in 771/1369 and began a series of destructive and bloodthirsty campaigns across Persia, Caucasia and, indeed, much of the Middle East, building pyramids out of his enemies' skulls. Ostensibly a **Sunnī** (q.v.) Muslim, he exhibited no tolerance for the **Ahl al-Kitāb** (q.v.), killing many of the Christians of Mesopotamia. One of his few saving graces, from an Islamic architectural point of view, was his building programme in Samarqand where he lies buried. The dynasty of the Tīmūrids descended from him. (*See* **Ankara, Battle of**)

al-Tīn (Ar.) The title of the 95th **sūra** of the **Qur'ān**; it means 'The Fig'. The *sūra* belongs to the Meccan period and contains 8 verses. Its title is drawn from the 1st verse which has the oath 'By the fig and the olive'. The *sūra* goes on to warn of what awaits the unbeliever and concludes by stressing the greatness of God's justice.

al-Tirmidhī, Abū 'Īsā Muḥammad (209/824–died between 270/883-4 and 279/892-3) One of the six major compilers of **ḥadīth** (q.v.) for **Sunnī** (q.v.) Islam. Little is known of his actual life but he is said to have been blind. This did not inhibit much travel in search of traditions. His compilation is variously characterized by the title *The Sound* (*al-Ṣaḥīḥ*) and *The Comprehensive* (*al-Jāmi'*).

Tithe *See* **'Ushr**.

Tours, Battle of *See* **Poitiers, Battle of**

Tradition *See* **Ḥadīth**; **Ḥadīth Qudsī**.

Transcendence *See* **Allāh**; **Tanzīh**.

Travel *See* **Ibn Baṭṭūṭa**; **Maḥfūẓ**; **Riḥla**.

Trench, Siege and Battle of the *See* **al-Khandaq, Siege and Battle of**

Truth, The *See* **al-Ḥaqq**.

Tūlūnids *See* **Ibn Ṭūlūn, Aḥmad**.

Tūnis or Tūnus (Ar.) Tunis, capital city of Tunisia, established as an Arab capital from 79/698; it lies near the ruins of Carthage which the Arabs captured. The city of Tunis has frequently occupied a pivotal role in the history of the **Maghrib** (q.v.). It was a centre for one of the most important dynasties to flourish in the *Maghrib*, the **Ḥafṣids** (q.v.), from the 7th/13th century until the capture of Tunis by the **Ottomans** (q.v.) in 982/1574. From an intellectual and cultural point of view, the rule of the Ḥafṣids marked the golden age of Tunis. (*See* **Aghlabids**; **al-Zaytūna**.)

al-Ṭūr (Ar.) The title of the 52nd **sūra** of the **Qur'ān**; it means 'The Mountain' but has also been considered as a proper name indicating the mountain in Sinai where **Mūsā** (q.v.) conversed with God. The *sūra* belongs to the Meccan period and has 49 verses. Its title is drawn from the 1st verse which reads 'By the Mountain'. The *sūra* refers to the fires of Hell and the joys of Paradise and challenges disbelievers to produce the like of the Qur'ān. The Prophet **Muḥammad** is reassured that he is neither a soothsayer nor mad. (*See* **Houris**; **al-Janna**; **al-Nār**.)

Turban Item of headgear worn by Muslims and others in the Middle East. The Turks became famous for the massive turbans worn by some of their dignitaries in the days of the Ottoman empire. (*See* **Ḥijāb**; **Ottomans**).

Twelvers *See* **Ithnā 'Asharīs**.

Uḥud, Battle of Second major battle fought between the Prophet **Muḥammad** supported by the Medinans, and the Meccans. It took place in 3/625 at Uḥud, a hill to the West of **Medina** (q.v.). The Meccans were led by **Abū Sufyān** (q.v.). In strictly military terms the result of the battle was a draw: it is true that Muḥammad was wounded and his uncle **Ḥamza b. 'Abd al-Muṭṭalib** (q.v.) killed together with more than seventy Muslims. But Muḥammad and his Muslim community still remained in Medina. (*See* **Khālid b. al-Walīd**; **Mecca**; **Sūrat al-Nisā'**.)

'Ukāẓ Town South-East of **Mecca** (q.v.) where an annual fair was held in pre-Islamic times, for several weeks. Much poetry was recited during the fair which was, however, abolished by the Prophet **Muḥammad**.

'Ulamā' (Ar.) [sing. *'ālim*] Religious scholars, jurists (loosely), learned men, imāms, judges, Āyatullāhs and similar people. The *'ulamā'* were, and are, often referred to as if they formed a coherent professional *monolithic group* of intellectuals and academics. While there were, and are, such groups, the 'group ethic' should not be overstressed. The *'ulamā'* were often regarded as custodians of 'orthodoxy'. The Arabic word should never be translated as 'clergy' of which there are none in Islam. (*See* **Āyatullāh**; **Faqīh**; **Imām**; **Qāḍī**.)

'Umar b. 'Abd al-'Azīz called **'Umar II** (died 101/720) Alone among the **Umayyads** (q.v.) 'Umar II, who succeeded Sulaymān in 99/717, was regarded as a pious and righteous caliph by later Islamic historians. He is famous for his *Fiscal Rescript* which attempted to ensure equality of taxation between converts to Islam and the Arab Muslims. (*See* **Ahl al-Kitāb**; **Dhimmī**; **Mawlā**; **Tax, Taxation**.)

'Umar b. al-Khaṭṭāb (*c.* AD 591-23/644) Father of **Ḥafṣa** (q.v.), and the 2nd **khalīfa** (q.v.), after the death of **Abū Bakr** (q.v.) in 13/634. He belonged to the clan of 'Adī b. Ka'b of the tribe of **Quraysh** (q.v.). He fought at the Battles of Badr and Uḥud and his rule saw a continuation of the age of conquests inaugurated by Abū Bakr. 'Umar was assassinated by a Persian slave in 23/644. (*See* **Badr, Battle of**; **Rāshidūn**; **Shūrā**; **Uḥud, Battle of**)

Umayya The family of Umayya was part of the clan of **'Abd Shams** (q.v.) of the tribe of **Quraysh** (q.v.). Umayya passed on their name to an entire dynasty with the accession of **Mu'āwiya b. Abī Sufyān** (q.v.). (*See* **Umayyads**.)

Umayyads First major dynasty in mediaeval Islamic history, which established itself in **Damascus** (q.v.) after the death of **'Alī b. Abī Ṭālib** (q.v.) who was the last of the **Rāshidūn** (q.v.). The Umayyads ruled a growing empire from 41/661 until 132/750. Their dynastic name derived ultimately from the grandfather of **Abū Sufyān** (q.v.) whose name was Umayya b. 'Abd Shams.

The Umayyad caliphs, who have frequently been accused of being kings rather than caliphs, because of their perceived secularism, were ultimately overthrown by the **'Abbāsids** (q.v.). Shaban has shown that discontent by some of the Arabs in the Eastern corners of the Arab empire was one major factor which helped a movement culminating in that overthrow. An Umayyad Kingdom was also later founded in Spain. (**'Abd al-Malik b. Marwān**; **al-Andalus**; **Hishām**; **Khalīfa**; **Mu'āwiya b. Abī Sufyān**; **'Umar b. 'Abd al-'Azīz**; **Umayya**; **Zāb, Battle of the Greater**)

Umma (Ar.) Community, people, nation. This was a highly emotive word in early Islamic history in the time of the Prophet **Muḥammad**, and remains so among the Arabs today, many of whom dream of, or regard themselves as, a single Arab *umma*.

Umm Ḥabība Widowed daughter of **Abū Sufyān** (q.v.) who later married the Prophet **Muḥammad**.

Ummī (Ar.) Illiterate, unlettered. The Prophet **Muḥammad** in the **Qur'ān**, in vv.157 and 158 of **Sūrat al-A'rāf** (q.v.) is described as *al-Nabī al-Ummī*: the phrase is usually translated by Muslims as 'the illiterate Prophet', 'the unlettered Prophet'.

Umm Kulthūm Daughter of the Prophet **Muḥammad** from his marriage to **Khadīja bint Khuwaylid** (q.v.). Umm Kulthūm married **'Uthmān b. 'Affān** (q.v.). She died at the time of the expedition to **Tabūk** (q.v.) in 9/630.

Umm Salama (Hind.) Widow of Abū Salama, who married the Prophet **Muḥammad** in 4/626. She belonged to the clan of **Makhzūm** (q.v.) of the tribe of **Quraysh** (q.v.).

'Umra *See under* **Ḥajj**.

Unbelief *See* **Kufr**.

Unbeliever *See* **Kāfir**.

Union of Muslim Organizations of U.K. and Eire [UMO] Established in London in 1390/1970, the UMO aims to co-ordinate the activities of the various Muslim groups and organizations in the U.K. and Eire. It has a cultural, social and educational function and also strives to establish good relations between Muslims and non-Muslims.

Unity of God *See* **Tawḥīd**.

Unlettered (of Muḥammad) *See* **Ummī**.

'Ushr (Ar.) [pl. *'ushūr*] Tithe. The Arabic word as such is not Qur'ānic. However, v.141 of **Sūrat al-An'ām** (q.v.) in the **Qur'ān** has been interpreted as referring to tithing. *'Ushr* was a tithing tax on *Muslim*-owned property and land and, as such, is to be distinguished from **kharāj** (q.v.) and **jizya** (q.v.), both taxes on *non-Muslims*. With time, the real distinction between such taxes as *'ushr* and *kharāj* often became confused. (*See also* **Dhimmī**; **Ṣadaqa**; **Zakāt**.)

Uṣūl al-Fiqh (Ar.) The roots or sources of jurisprudence (**fiqh** (q.v.)). Following **al-Shāfi'ī** (q.v.), these may be listed as: the **Qur'ān**, the **Sunna** (q.v.), **ijmā'** (q.v.) and **qiyās** (q.v.).

Usury *See* **Ribā**.

'Uthmān b. 'Affān (died 35/656) 3rd **khalīfa** (q.v.) who assumed power after the death of **'Umar b. al-Khaṭṭāb** (q.v.) in 23/644. He was a member of the **Umayya** (q.v.) family and was among the earliest to convert to Islam. Arabic sources see his reign in terms of six good and six bad years. His rule is of particular importance for the history of the **Qur'ān**, for it was under 'Uthmān that Islamic tradition holds that the Sacred Text was put together in its final form. 'Uthman was assassinated in

Medina (q.v.) in 35/656. He was, at various times, married to two of the daughters of the Prophet **Muḥammad**: **Ruqayya** (q.v.) and **Umm Kulthūm** (q.v.). (*See* **Rāshidūn**; **Shūrā**; **Zayd b. Thābit**.)

'Uthmān dan Fodio (1167/1754–1232/1817) Born in Gobir, West Africa, and initiated into the **Qādiriyya** (q.v.), he began to preach and write in early adulthood and incurred the displeasure of the King of Gobir. 'Uthmān and his followers made a **hijra** (q.v.) to the borders of Gobir. The former waged a **jihād** (q.v.), the Gobir capital fell and a reformed Islam spread through the lands of the Hausa. However, it was an Islam characterized by adherence to the legalism of the **Mālikīs** (q.v.). Theologically, 'Uthmān's views sometimes have something in common with the **Murji'a** (q.v.). (*See* **Wahhābīs**.)

'Uzayr Ezra. He is mentioned once in the **Qur'ān** in v.30 of **Sūrat al-Tawba** (q.v.), the beginning of which reads: 'The Jews said " 'Uzayr is the son of God" and the Christians said "The Messiah is the son of God". That is what they say with their mouths.'

al-'Uzzā (Ar.) Pre-Islamic goddess of Arabia, who has been identified with the Venus star, with a main shrine between **al-Ṭā'if** (q.v.) and **Mecca** (q.v.). Her name meant 'the Mighty'. She was worshipped in pre-Islamic times not only by such Arabian tribes as **Thaqīf** (q.v.) and **Quraysh** (q.v.) but also by the Lakhmids of Ḥīra. She is mentioned, and disparaged, in the **Qur'ān** together with **al-Lāt** (q.v.) and **Manāt** (q.v.). (*See* vv.19–23 of **Sūrat al-Najm**.) (*See also* **Jāhiliyya**; **Satanic Verses, The**)

Veil, Veiling *See* **Burqu'**; **Chādor**; **Ḥijāb**; **Purdah**.

Verse (of the Qur'ān) *See* **Āya**.

Verse of the Stoning *See* **Āyat al-Rajm**.

Vezier *See* **Wazīr**.

Vilāyat-i Faqīh *See* **Khumaynī**.

Vision of God *See* **Ru'yat Allāh**.

Vizier *See* **Wazīr**.

al-Wa'd wa 'l-Wa'īd (Ar.) Literally, 'The Promise and the Threat(s)'. This was one of the principles or catch phrases of the **Mu'tazila**. Basically, it encapsulated the Mu'tazilite idea that God had to reward the virtuous in Paradise, according to His promise, and punish the wicked in Hell according to His threat. (*See* **al-Amr bi 'l-Ma'rūf**; **al-Janna**; **al-Nār**.)

Waḥda *See* **Ibn al-'Arabī**; **Tawḥīd**.

Wahhābīs (Wahhābiyya) Followers of the strict puritanical teachings of **Ibn 'Abd al-Wahhāb** (q.v.). They are sometimes called 'Unitarians' (*Muwaḥḥidūn*) and so should not be confused with the **Almohads** (q.v.). The Wahhābīs embraced a strict fundamentalism in the spirit of **Aḥmad b. Ḥanbal** (q.v.) and some of their ethos still pervades Saudi Arabia today. Among the various things forbidden by the Wahhābīs were intercession of the saints, use of the rosary, use of **ijmā'** (q.v.) in law (except that of the Prophet **Muḥammad**'s companions), visiting the tombs of saints, and tobacco. (*See* **Fundamentalism, Islamic**; **Ḥanbalīs**; **Hijra**; **Ṣaḥāba**.)

Waiting Period *See* **'Idda**; **Ṭalāq**.

Walī (Ar.) [pl. *awliyā'*] Saint, holy man. While **taṣawwuf** (q.v.) acknowledges a whole hierarchy of saints and ordinary Muslims the world over pay popular devotion to, and intercede at, saints' tombs and shrines, many Muslim theologians have regarded such practices and intercession with suspicion and disquiet. This is particularly the case with those influenced by the **Wahhābīs** (q.v.). (*See* **Quṭb**; **Rābi'a al-'Adawiyya**; **Shafā'a**.)

Waqf (Ar.) [pl. *awqāf*] In Islamic law, the legal creation of a pious foundation or endowment whereby the owner relinquishes his right of disposal provided that the usufruct is for charitable purposes. Popularly the word *waqf* has been applied to the endowment itself. This endowment once made is perpetual and irretrievable. Many Middle Eastern countries have, or had, a Ministry of *Awqāf* for the management of such endowments. In North Africa the preferred Arabic term for *waqf* is *ḥubs* or *ḥubus* [pl. *aḥbās*] which is transliterated as the French 'habous'.

al-Wāqi'a (Ar.) The title of the 56th **sūra** of the **Qur'ān**; it means 'The Happening'. The *sūra* belongs to the Meccan period and has 96 verses. It draws its title from the 1st verse. The *sūra* contains descriptions of the delights of Paradise which await the just, and the pains of Hell for the wicked. God's creative powers are stressed as a signal that man should believe, thank God and glorify Him. In v.77, in a famous line, the Qur'ān is described as 'a noble Qur'ān' (*Qur'ān karīm*). (*See* **al-Janna**; **al-Nār**.)

al-Wāqidī, Abū 'Abd Allāh Muḥammad (130/747–207/823) Early Muslim historian and judge, patronized by **Hārūn al-Rashīd** (q.v.). His major work, *The Book of Campaigns* (*Kitāb al-Maghāzī*), is an important source for early Islamic history and the life of **Muḥammad**, though some accused al-Wāqidī of unreliability.

Waraqa b. Nawfal Christian, or **ḥanīf** (q.v.), cousin of **Khadīja bint Khuwaylid**, the first wife of the Prophet **Muḥammad**. When Waraqa's advice was sought about Muḥammad's mission and revelations, Waraqa confirmed their truth. (*See* **Asad**.)

Wāṣil b. 'Aṭā' (80/699-700–131/748-9) Notable leader and theologian of the **Mu'tazila** (q.v.) in **al-Baṣra** (q.v.). He was originally one of the group which congregated round **al-Ḥasan al-Baṣrī** (q.v.).

Wazīr (Ar.) [pl. *wuzarā'*] Vezier, vizier, minister. The office of minister or adviser to the **Khalīfa** (q.v.) developed in power, especially in the period of the **'Abbāsids** (q.v.) under the **Barmakids** (q.v.). The Arabic word today has the sense of a minister in a government.

Whirling Dervishes *See* **Mawlawiyya**.

Wilāyat al-Faqīh *See* **Khumaynī**.

William of Rubruck, Friar (*c*. 612-29/1215-30–died after 655/1257) Franciscan friar who, following the example of St. Francis of Assisi (died 623/1226) (and the latter's visit to Egypt during the Fifth Crusade), made a journey to the court of the Great Mongol Khān Möngke, between 651/1253 and 653/1255. He reported back on his journey in a lengthy letter to King Louis IX of France, and Friar William is thus a very valuable source for the early history of the **Mongols** (q.v.) before they converted in large numbers to Islam. The Mongols seem to have been very interested in theological debate and permitted Friar William to debate his beliefs publicly with Muslims, Nestorians and Buddhists.

Wine *See* **Khamr**; **Nabīdh**.

Wird (Ar.) [pl. *awrād*] Time used for extra worship; or part of the **Qur'ān** recited at such a time; or a **ṣūfī** (q.v.) litany comprising Qur'ānic excerpts recited many times, as a kind of 'daily office' of various ṣūfī *ṭarīqas*. (*See* **Dhikr**; **Ṣalāt**; **Tarāwīḥ**; **Ṭarīqa**.)

Witr (Ar.) Literally, 'uneven', 'odd'. Voluntary prayer comprising an *odd* number of *raka'āt* said between the **'ishā'** (q.v.)

and **ṣubḥ** (q.v.) prayers. A **ḥadīth** (q.v.) describes God as being and loving *witr*. (*See* **Rak'a**; **Ṣalāt**.)

Worship *See* **Dhikr**; **'Ibāda**; **Rak'a**; **Ṣalāt**; **Tarāwīḥ**; **Wird**; **Witr**.

Wuḍū' (Ar.) Minor ritual washing of parts of the body before prayer. It assumes that **ghusl** (q.v.) has already taken place. Sand may be used if water is scarce or unavailable. (*See* **Mīḍa'a**; **Ṣalāt**; **Tayammum**.)

Wuqūf (Ar.) Standing, i.e. at **'Arafa** (q.v.) as one of the rites of the **ḥajj** (q.v.). This is undertaken on the 9th day of the Muslim month of **Dhū 'l-Ḥijja** (q.v.).

Yaḥyā (Ar.) John. He is the Qur'ānic counterpart of the New Testament Baptist, and appears in the **Qur'ān** with prophetic status as the longed-for child of **Zakariyyā** (q.v.). (*See* **Sūrat Maryam**.)

Ya'qūb (Ar.) Jacob, the father of **Yūsuf** (q.v.). He appears (for the most part unnamed) in **Sūrat Yūsuf** (q.v.) as part of the famous Joseph story; and also in **Sūrat al-Baqara** (q.v.) beside such figures as **Ibrāhīm** (q.v.), **Ismā'īl** (q.v.) and **Isḥāq** (q.v.). In **Sūrat Maryam** (q.v.) Ya'qūb is named as one whom God has made a prophet (*see* v.49).

Yarmūk, Battle of Battle fought South of **Damascus** (q.v.) at the River Yarmūk, a tributary of the River Jordan, between the invading Arab armies and the Byzantines, in 16/637. The Arab forces were led by **Abu 'Ubayda b. al-Jarrāḥ** (q.v.) while Sacellarius Theodorus commanded the Byzantines. The Arabs won the battle which provided the key to the conquest of Syria. (*See* **Khālid b. al-Walīd**.)

Yāsīn [Yā' Sīn] (Ar.) The title of the 36th **sūra** of the **Qur'ān**; it consists of two letters of the Arabic alphabet Y and S. The *sūra* belongs to the Meccan period and contains 83 verses. Its title is drawn from the 1st verse which comprises just these two letters. This *sūra* is often recited at times of distress and approaching death. It contains a parable of a village to which delegates are sent (vv.13 ff), describes some of the signs of God's power, and refers to the Last Day with the joys of Paradise which the righteous will enjoy and the fires of Hell prepared for the unbelievers. It is stressed in v.79 that the body will be raised from the dead. (*See* **al-Janna**; **Mysterious Letters of the Qur'ān**; **al-Nār**.)

Yathrib Original name borne by the city of **Medina** (q.v.).

Yawm al-Dīn (Ar.) Literally, 'the Day of Faith'. This is one of the names in Arabic given to the Day of Resurrection. (*See below*.)

Yawm al-Jum'a (Ar.) Friday. This is the day of the week when Muslims gather, if at all possible, to perform congregationally the Midday Prayer in the mosque, and listen to a sermon there from an **Imām** (q.v.) or a prayer leader. Business transactions are suspended during this prayer time. (*See* **Khuṭba**; **Ṣalāt**; **Sūrat al-Jum'a**.)

Yawm al-Qiyāma (Ar.) The Day of Resurrection, the Day of Judgement, the Last Day. The cataclysmic events and upheavals of this Day are frequently and graphically described in the **Qur'ān**. This Day has many other names in Arabic. One of the more common is *Yawm al-Dīn* (*see* entry above). (*See also* **al-Ba'th**; **al-Ḥisāb**; **Ishārāt al-Sā'a**; **Isrāfīl**.)

Yūnus (1) (Ar.) Jonah, also called **Dhū 'l-Nūn** (q.v.). He was a messenger (*rasūl*) sent to warn a people (the inhabitants of the city of Nineveh). Exceptionally, they listen to his warning. The **Qur'ān** also portrays Yūnus as swallowed by a great fish. (*See* **Rasūl**; **Sūrat Yūnus**.)

Yūnus (2) (Ar.) Jonah: the title of the 10th **sūra** of the **Qur'ān**. The *sūra* belongs mainly to the late Meccan period and has 109 verses. It takes its title from the reference to Yūnus in v.98. (In fact, there is more about Yūnus in **Sūrat al-Ṣāffāt** (q.v.) than in *Sūrat Yūnus*.) The latter begins with three of the **Mysterious Letters of the Qur'ān** (q.v.) and stresses God's creative power. The righteous will be rewarded in Paradise while the wicked will suffer in Hell. Later, man is challenged to produce a *sūra* like one of those in the Qur'ān. Towards the end of *Sūrat Yūnus* reference is made to **Mūsā** (q.v.) and **Hārūn** (q.v.) before **Fir'awn** (q.v.), and the ultimate drowning of the latter. (*See* **al-Janna**; **al-Nār**; **Yūnus** (1).)

Yūsuf (1) (Ar.) Joseph. For the life of Joseph, see the following entry.

Yūsuf (2) (Ar.) The title of the 12th **sūra** of the **Qur'ān**; Yūsuf is a proper name, the Arabic for Joseph. The *sūra* belongs mainly to the late Meccan period and contains 111 verses. It takes its title from the entire *sūra* which, as the longest piece of extended narrative in the whole Qur'ān, gives the story of Yūsuf. The latter, who bears the title of **al-Ṣiddīq** (q.v.), ranks as one of the prophets of the Qur'ān. The *sūra* named after him (in which many of the leading characters apart from Yūsuf, incidentally, are unnamed) tells how Yūsuf relates his dream of eleven stars, the sun and the moon to his father, incurs the jealousy and wrath of his brothers and is eventually sold into Egypt. Here the wife of **Qiṭfīr** (q.v.), called **Zulaykhā** (q.v.), attempts to seduce him. Having been cast into prison, Yūsuf interprets the dreams of his fellow prisoners, and is eventually summoned by Pharaoh to interpret the latter's dreams. Pharaoh appoints Yūsuf to a position of power in Egypt and he deals, at first incognito, with his brothers who visit Egypt for food, eventually revealing himself to them. The *sūra* moves towards its conclusion with Yūsuf taking his father and his mother in his arms, and placing them on the throne, and finally ends with a panegyric on God, thus tying up the didactic threads of the whole story. Noteworthy, from the literary point of view, in this *sūra* are the function of the dream as one of the motors which moves the story along, the motif of the garment, and the special knowledge possessed by Yūsuf which leads him to final power and freedom. For an excellent, and very readable, introduction to the Joseph story, see the article by M. A. S. Abdel Haleem entitled 'The Story of Joseph in the Qur'ān and the Old Testament' (See back of the *Dictionary* for full bibliographical details). (*See also* **Fir'awn**; **al-Sā'a**; **Ya'qūb**.)

Zāb, Battle of the Greater Major battle fought on the banks of the Greater Zāb River (a tributary of the Tigris) between the army of the last Umayyad caliph Marwān II (*reg*. 127/744–132/750) and 'Abbāsid rebels in 132/750. The 'Abbāsid army was commanded by 'Abd Allāh b. 'Alı, uncle of the first 'Abbāsid caliph **al-Saffāḥ** (q.v.). The Umayyad forces were defeated and Marwān fled to Syria; this defeat heralded the end of the **Umayyads** (q.v.) as a dynasty in the Middle East (though a branch survived to rule in Spain) and the rise of the **'Abbāsids** as a major imperial power based on **Baghdād** (q.v.).

al-Zabāniyya Principal angelic guardians of Hell who appear in the **Qur'ān** in v.18 of **Sūrat al-'Alaq** (q.v.); elsewhere, in v.30 of **Sūrat al-Muddathir** (q.v.), their number is given as 19. The Arabic name *al-Zabāniyya* means 'those who thrust violently'. **Mālik** (q.v.), the chief of the *Zabāniyya*, will command them to cast people into the Fire. (*See* **Angel**; **Daqyā'īl**; **al-Nār**.)

Ẓāhir (Ar.) Exoteric, outer. That which is *ẓāhir* in Islam is that which is external, on the surface or obvious. The word had particular connotations in the Qur'ānic exegesis of the **Ismā'īlīs** (q.v.). Its opposite was **bāṭin** (q.v.). (*See* **Ibn Ḥazm**; **Tafsīr**; **Ẓāhirīs**.)

Ẓāhirīs Adherents of a School of Islamic Law, now long defunct, which stressed an entirely literal or explicit (**ẓāhir** (q.v.)) interpretation of both the **Qur'ān** (q.v.) and the **Sunna**

(q.v.). Although not founded by **Ibn Ḥazm** (q.v.), he was its most famous exponent.

Zaitouna *See* **al-Zaytūna, Jāmiʻ**.

Zakariyyā or **Zakāriyyā'** (Ar.) Zachary, Zachariah, the father of **Yaḥyā** (q.v.). Zakariyyā figures in the **Qur'ān** primarily in **Sūrat Maryam** (q.v.). At the beginning of this *sūra* he prays for, and is given, a son, Yaḥyā, despite his old age and his wife's barrenness. As a sign of the pending birth, Zakariyyā becomes dumb for a period of three days.

Zakāt (Ar.) often transliterated *Zakāh* [pl. *zakawāt*] Obligatory alms tax which constitutes one of the five pillars of Islam. Compare **Ṣadaqa** (q.v.). (*See* **Arkān**.)

al-Zalzala (Ar.) The title of the 99th **sūra** of the **Qur'ān**; it means 'The Earthquake'. The *sūra* belongs to the Medinan period and has 8 verses. Its title comes from the reference to earthquake (on the Last Day) in the 1st verse. The 2nd verse makes indirect reference to the doctrine of the resurrection of the body from the dead and concludes that on the Day of Judgement man will see (the record of) his good and bad deeds. (*See* **al-Ḥisāb**; **Yawm al-Qiyāma**.)

al-Zamakhsharī, Abū 'l-Qāsim Maḥmūd (467/1075-538/1144) Major exegete of the **Qur'ān** and Arabic scholar. Born in Persia, he visited **Mecca** (q.v.) and **Baghdād** (q.v.) and was an enthusiastic devotee of the Arabic language. His Muʻtazilite leanings are apparent in his great commentary on the Qur'ān called *The Unveiler* (*al-Kashshāf*). (*See* **al-Bayḍāwī**; **Muʻtazila**; **al-Ṭabarī**; **Tafsīr**.)

Zamzam, Well of Well within the precincts of the Great Mosque of **Mecca** (q.v.). For its origins, *see* **Ismāʻīl** (1). The name of the Well in Arabic represents the sound of the water as it rushed out when it was discovered. Pilgrims to Mecca drink the water of Zamzam which they believe has a special sacredness; some believe that it has healing properties. (*See* **Ḥajj**; **al-Masjid al-Ḥarām**.)

al-Zaqqūm, The Tree of Bitter smelling and fearsome tree in the pit of Hell with flowers which resemble demonic heads. The stomachs of sinners obliged to eat from this tree in Hell will be badly burned. The tree is mentioned in the **Qur'ān**, for example in v.43 of **Sūrat al-Dukhān** (q.v.) and v.62 of **Sūrat al-Ṣāffāt** (q.v.). The Zaqqūm tree with its bitter fruit and foul smell was not only associated with the infernal regions of Hell but also with Arabia. (*See* **al-Nār**.)

Zāwiya (Ar.) [pl. *zawāyā*] Literally, 'a corner'. In the technical terminology of **taṣawwuf** (q.v.) the *zāwiya* has been defined as a small **khānagāh** (q.v.). However, the *zāwiya* was usually attached to a specific **ṭarīqa** (q.v.). In North African usage the *zāwiya* implied a small **ṣūfī** (q.v.) teaching mosque established over a saint's tomb. (*See* **Ribāṭ**; **Tekkē**.)

Zayd b. 'Alī *See* **Zaydīs**.

Zayd b. Ḥāritha (died 8/630) Originally a slave of **Khadīja bint Khuwaylid** (q.v.), he was later freed and adopted by **Muḥammad**. He was married to **Zaynab** (q.v.) bint Jahsh, and is mentioned in the **Qur'ān** in **Sūrat al-Aḥzāb** (q.v.).

Zayd b. Thābit (died *c*. 34-5/655) Secretary to the Prophet **Muḥammad** and, later, copyist and editor of the **Qur'ān**. (*See* **Ḥafṣa bint 'Umar**.)

Zaydīs (Zaydiyya) Third of the three major branches of **Shī'ism** (q.v.) after the **Ithnā 'Asharīs** (q.v.) and the **Ismā'īlīs** (q.v.). The Zaydīs are named after a grandson of **al-Ḥusayn b. 'Alī** (q.v.), whom they followed as **Imām** (q.v.), called Zayd b.

'Alī (died *c.* 122/740). Zaydī theology has a Mu'tazilī orientation but from the point of view of law, the Zaydīs are close to the four **Sunnī** (q.v.) **madhāhib** (q.v.). In mediaeval times the Zaydīs achieved political power in a state to the South of the Caspian Sea, and also in the Yemen, the latter lasting into modern times until 1382/1962. Today Zaydīs are still to be found mainly in the Yemen. (*See* **Mu'tazila**.)

Zaynab The name of three women associated with the Prophet **Muḥammad**: (1) Zaynab bint Jaḥsh, one of Muḥammad's cousins, was first married to **Zayd b. Ḥāritha** (q.v.) and later, after her divorce, to Muḥammad. (2) Zaynab bint Khuzayma was a widow later married by Muḥammad. (3) Zaynab bint Muḥammad was a daughter of the Prophet and **Khadīja bint Khuwaylid** (q.v.). Other 'Zaynabs' whom the reader may encounter are the sister of **al-Ḥusayn b. 'Alī** (q.v.), believed to be buried in the Mosque of al-Sayyida Zaynab in **Cairo** (q.v.); and the cousin and companion of al-Sayyida **Nafīsa** (q.v.).

al-Zaytūna, Jāmi' Literally, 'the Mosque of the Olive Tree'. What became Tunis's most famous Mosque-University was first founded in *c.* 114/732 and later rebuilt in the 3rd/9th century. The cultural and educational prestige of this Mosque in **Tūnis** (q.v.) paralleled that of **al-Azhar** (q.v.) in **Cairo** (q.v.). In modern times the teaching function of this Mosque was absorbed into the University of Tunis and al-Zaytūna became a constituent institution of that University as 'Ez Zitouna' Faculty of Theology and Religious Science.

Zikr *See* **Dhikr**.

Zinā' (Ar.) The Arabic word means both adultery and fornication, sins strongly condemned in the **Qur'ān**. (*See* **Ḥadd**.)

Zindīq (Ar.) [pl. *zanādiqa*] Term of opprobrium in mediaeval Islamic history, often rendered as 'free-thinker', 'unbeliever', 'heretic', 'dualist'. The word derives from Persian.

Ziyāra (Ar.) Visit, visiting, pilgrimage. Specifically, this meant the practice of visiting holy places and the tombs of saints, a practice much disliked by the **Wahhābīs** (q.v.). (*See* **Baraka**; **Ḥajj**; **Marabout**; **Taṣawwuf**.)

al-Zubayr b. al-'Awwām (died 36/656) Early convert to Islam and one of the nephews of **Khadīja bint Khuwaylid** (q.v.). He opposed **'Alī b. Abī Ṭālib** (q.v.) at the Battle of the Camel, very soon after which he was killed. (*See* **'Ā'isha bint Abī Bakr**; **Camel, Battle of the**; **Ṭalḥa b. 'Ubaydullāh al-Taymī**.)

Zuhd (Ar.) Asceticism, renunciation of worldly and material things. This is often associated with **taṣawwuf** (q.v.) though it was by no means characteristic of every **ṭarīqa** (q.v.) or **ṣūfī** (q.v.) individual. (*See* **Tijāniyya**.)

al-Ẓuhr, Ṣalāt (Ar.) The Midday Prayer. (*See* **Ṣalāt**.)

al-Zukhruf (Ar.) The title of the 43rd **sūra** of the **Qur'ān**; it means 'The Ornament' or 'The Gold'. The *sūra* belongs to the Meccan period and contains 89 verses. It takes its title from the reference to gold or ornament in v.35. The *sūra* begins with two of the **Mysterious Letters of the Qur'ān** (q.v.) and goes on to survey details of God's creation. Aspects of the missions of **Ibrāhīm** (q.v.), **Mūsā** (q.v.) and **'Īsā** (q.v.) follow, and the *sūra* concludes with references to God's power and omniscience. (*See* **Mālik**.)

Zulaykhā Potiphar's wife who attempts to seduce **Yūsuf** (q.v.) in **Sūrat Yūsuf** (q.v.) in the **Qur'ān**. The commentator **al-Bayḍāwī** (q.v.) also supplies the name Rā'īl as an alternative for Zulaykhā. (*See* **Qiṭfīr**.)

al-Zumar (Ar.) The title of the 39th **sūra** of the **Qur'ān**; it means 'The Crowds'. The *sūra* belongs to the Meccan period and has 75 verses. Its title is drawn from v.71 and v.73 in which the unbelievers will be driven into Hell in crowds or droves, and, similarly, the pious will be driven towards Paradise in crowds. The *sūra* begins with reference to the revelation of the Qur'ān and goes on to survey God's benefits to man, as well as His divine power. Reference is later made to the Last Day and the Judgement. Those who enter Paradise will see angels circling the throne of God whom they praise. (*See* **Angel**; **al-Ḥisāb**; **al-Janna**; **al-Nār**; **Yawm al-Qiyāma**.)

GUIDE TO FURTHER READING

There is a huge, and often bewildering, array of books in numerous languages today dealing with Islam and its many facets. The list which follows is of secondary sources which have actually been consulted in the compilation of this *Dictionary* and to which grateful acknowledgement is herewith made. It is directed mainly but not exclusively at the reader of English. The reader of other relevant languages, notably Arabic, is directed to the main body of the *Dictionary* where a variety of Arabic and other texts, also relevant to this *Dictionary*, are cited. Most are readily available in a variety of editions. (In the alphabetization of what follows, 'al' and 'el' are ignored *at the beginning of the entry*.)

Abdalati, Hammudah, *Islam in Focus*, (Salimiah-Kuwait: International Islamic Federation of Student Organizations, 1981).

Abu-Izzeddin, Nejla M., *The Druzes: A New Study of their History, Faith and Society*, (Leiden: E. J. Brill, 1984).

Abu Laylah, M, *In Pursuit of Virtue: The Moral Theology and Psychology of Ibn Hazm al-Andalusi*, (London: TaHa, 1990).

Abun-Nasr, Jamil M., *The Tijaniyya: A Sufi Order in the Modern World*, (London: O.U.P., 1965).

Ahmad, Aziz, *An Intellectual History of Islam in India*, Islamic Surveys 7 (Edinburgh: Edinburgh University Press, 1969).

Ally, Muhammad Mashuq, *The Growth and Organization of the Muslim Community in Britain*, Research Papers no. 1, (Birmingham: Centre for the Study of Islam and Christian-Muslim Relations, Selly Oak Colleges, March, 1979).

Ashtiany, Julia, Johnstone, T. M., Latham, J. D., Serjeant, R. B. and Smith, G. Rex (eds.), *'Abbasid Belles-Lettres*, The Cambridge History of Arabic Literature, vol. 2, (Cambridge: C.U.P., 1990).

Attar, Farid ud-Din, *The Conference of the Birds*, trans. by C. S. Nott, (London: Routledge and Kegan Paul, 1961).

al-Azmeh, Aziz, *Ibn Khaldūn: An Essay in Reinterpretation*, (London: Frank Cass, 1982).

al-Baidawi, *'The Light of Inspiration and Secret of Interpretation', Being a Translation of the Chapter of Joseph (Sūrat Yūsuf) With the Commentary of Nasir Id-Din al-Baidāwī*, trans. by E. F. F. Bishop and M. Kaddal. (Glasgow: Jackson, 1957).

Baldick, Julian. *Mystical Islam: An Introduction to Sufism*, (London: Tauris, 1989).

Balyuzi, H. M. *The Báb: The Herald of the Day of Days*, (Oxford: George Ronald, 1973).

el-Batrik, Younes A. (ed.), *The World of Naguib Mahfouz*, (London: Egyptian Education Bureau, 1989).

Beeston, A. F. L., Johnstone, T. M., Serjeant, R. B., and Smith, G. R. (eds.), *Arabic Literature to the End of the Umayyad Period*, The Cambridge History of Arabic Literature, vol. 1, (Cambridge: C.U.P., 1983).

Behrens-Abouseif, Doris, *The Minarets of Cairo*, (Cairo: American University in Cairo Press, 1985).

Bell, Richard and Watt, W. M., *Bell's Introduction to the Qur'ān*, rev. and enlarged by W. M. Watt, Islamic Surveys 8, (Edinburgh: Edinburgh University Press, 1970).

Betts, Robert Brenton, *The Druze*, (New Haven & London: Yale University Press, 1988).

Binder, Leonard, *Religion and Politics in Pakistan*, (Berkeley & Los Angeles: University of California Press, 1963).

Birge, John Kingsley, *The Bektashi Order of Dervishes*, (London: Luzac, 1965).

Bloom, Jonathan, *Minaret, Symbol of Islam*, Oxford Studies in Islamic Art VII, (Oxford: O.U.P., 1989).

Bosworth, C. E., *The Islamic Dynasties: A Chronological and Genealogical Handbook*, Islamic Surveys 5, (Edinburgh: Edinburgh University Press, 1967).

Brine, Alan, *Religions Through Festivals: Islam*, (Harlow: Longman, 1989).

Burton, J., 'Those are the High-Flying Cranes', *Journal of Semitic Studies*, vol. 15 (1970), pp. 246–265.

Butt, Gerald, *The Arab World: A Personal View*, (London: B.B.C., 1987).

Cachia, Pierre, *Ṭāhā Ḥusayn: His Place in the Egyptian Literary Renaissance*, (London: Luzac, 1956).

Cambridge History of Arabic Literature see Ashtiany; Beeston; Young.

Central Office of Information, *Aspects of Islam in Britain*, (London: HMSO, 1990).

Chesterton, G. K., *The Collected Poems*, 6th edn., (London: Methuen, 1937).

Choueiri, Youssef M., *Islamic Fundamentalism*, (London: Pinter/Boston: Twayne, 1990).

Coulson, N. J., *A History of Islamic Law*, Islamic Surveys 2, (Edinburgh: Edinburgh University Press, 1964).

Davies, Philip, *The Penguin Guide to the Monuments of India: Volume Two: Islamic, Rajput, European*, (London: Penguin, 1989).

Dunlop, D. M., *Arab Civilization to A.D. 1500*, (London: Longman/Beirut: Librairie du Liban, 1971).

el-Enany, Rasheed, *see* Mahfouz.

Encyclopaedia of Islam, New Edition, ed. H. A. R. Gibb *et al.*, 6 vols. cont., (Leiden: E. J. Brill/London: Luzac, 1960–).

Ernst, Carl W., *Words of Ecstasy in Sufism*, (Albany, New York: State University of New York Press, 1985).

Ettinghausen, Richard and Grabar, Oleg, *The Art and Architecture of Islam: 650–1250*, The Pelican History of Art, (Harmondsworth: Penguin, 1987).

Fakhry, Majid, *A History of Islamic Philosophy*, 2nd edn., (London: Longman/New York: Columbia University Press, 1983).

—— *Islamic Occasionalism and its Critique by Averroës and Aquinas*, (London: Allen & Unwin, 1958).

Fernandes, Leonor, *The Evolution of a Sufi Institution in Mamluk Egypt:* The Khanqah, (Berlin: Klaus Schwarz Verlag, 1988).

Fitzgerald, Edward, *see* Khayyam.

Frank, Richard M., *The Metaphysics of Created Being according to Abû l-Hudhayl al-'Allâf: A Philosophical Study of the Earliest Kalâm*, (Istanbul: Nederlands Historisch-Archaeologisch Instituut in het Nabije Oosten, 1966).

Friedlander, Ira, *The Whirling Dervishes*, (London: Wildwood House, 1975).

Fyzee, Asaf A. A., *Outlines of Muhammadan Law*, 3rd edn., (London: O.U.P., 1964).

Gascoigne, Bamber, *The Great Moghuls*, (London: Cape, 1971).

Gätje, Helmut, *The Qur'ān and its Exegesis: Selected Texts with Classical and Modern Muslim Interpretations*, (London: Routledge & Kegan Paul, 1976).

Gaudefroy-Demombynes, Maurice, *Muslim Institutions*, (London: Allen & Unwin, 1950).

al-Ghitani, Gamal, *Zayni Barakat*, trans. by Farouk Abdel Wahab, (London: Penguin, 1990).

Gibb, H. A. R., *Arabic Literature: An Introduction*, 2nd rev. edn., (Oxford: Clarendon Press, 1963).

Gibbon, Edward, *The History of the Decline and Fall of the Roman Empire*, ed. J. B. Bury, vol. VI, (London: Methuen, 1898).

Glassé, Cyril, *The Concise Encyclopaedia of Islam*, (London: Stacey International, 1989).

Grabar, Oleg, *The Alhambra*, (London: Allen Lane, 1978).

—— *The Formation of Islamic Art*, (New Haven & London: Yale University Press, 1973).

—— *The Great Mosque of Isfahan*, (London: Tauris, 1990).

Graham, Robert, *Iran: The Illusion of Power*, rev. edn., (London: Croom Helm, 1979).

Guillaume, Alfred, *The Traditions of Islam: An Introduction to the Study of the Hadith Literature*, (Beirut: Khayats, 1966).

Haeri, Shahla, *Law of Desire: Temporary Marriage in Iran*, (London: Tauris, 1989).

Haleem, M. A. S. Abdel, 'The Story of Joseph in the Qur'ān and the Old Testament', *Islam and Christian-Muslim Relations*, vol. 1:2 (December 1990), pp. 171–191.

Haq, M. Anwarul, *The Faith Movement of Mawlānā Muḥammad Ilyās*, (London: Allen & Unwin, 1972).

Haslip, Joan, *The Sultan: The Life of Abdul Hamid II*, (London: Cassell, 1958).

Hava, J. G., *Al-Farā'id Arabic-English Dictionary*, (Beirut: Dār al-Mashriq, 1970).

Haywood, John A., *Modern Arabic Literature 1800–1970: An Introduction with Extracts in Translation*, (London: Lund Humphries, 1971).

Hinds, Martin and Badawi, El-Said, *A Dictionary of Egyptian Arabic: Arabic-English*, (Beirut: Librairie du Liban, 1986).

Hiro, Dilip, *Islamic Fundamentalism*, (London: Collins, Grafton Books, 1988).

Holt, P. M., *The Age of the Crusades: The Near East from the Eleventh Century to 1517*, A History of the Near East, (London and New York: Longman, 1986).

—— *Egypt and the Fertile Crescent 1516–1922: A Political History*, (London: Longman, 1966).

Holt, P. M., Lambton, A. K. S. & Lewis, B. (eds.), *The Cambridge History of Islam*, 2 vols., (Cambridge: C.U.P., 1970).

Horrie, Chris and Chippindale, Peter, *What is Islam?* (London: W. H. Allen, Star, 1990).

Hourani, Albert, *Arabic Thought in the Liberal Age 1798–1939*, (Cambridge: C.U.P., repr. 1988).

Hourani, George F., *Islamic Rationalism: The Ethics of 'Abd al-Jabbār*, (Oxford: Clarendon Press, 1971).

Ibn Battuta, *The Travels of Ibn Baṭṭūṭa AD 1325–1354*, trans. by H. A. R. Gibb, 3 vols., (Cambridge: C.U.P. for the Hakluyt Society, 1958–71).

Ibn Ishaq, *The Life of Muhammad: A Translation of Isḥāq's* Sīrat Rasūl Allāh, with introd. and notes by A. Guillaume, (Karachi: O.U.P., 1955, 1980).

Irwin, Robert, *The Middle East in the Middle Ages: The Early Mamluk Sultanate 1250–1382*, (London: Croom Helm, 1986).

Islamic Conference Organisation, *Charter and Regulations of the Organisation of the Islamic Conference* [bound with other ICO documents, all typescript].

Islamic Conference Organisation, Al-Quds Committee, *Al-Quds Document*, (ICO, n.d.).

Juynboll, G. H. A., *Muslim Tradition: Studies in Chronology, Provenance and Authorship of Early Ḥadīth*, (Cambridge: C.U.P., 1983).

Kassis, Hanna E., *A Concordance of the Qur'an*, (Berkeley, Los Angeles and London: University of California Press, 1983).

Keddie, Nikki R., *An Islamic Response to Imperialism: Political and Religious Writings of Sayyid Jamal ad-Din 'al-Afghani'*, including a translation of the 'Refutation of the Materialists' from the original Persian by Nikki R. Keddie and Hamid Algar. New edn., (Berkeley: University of California Press, 1983).

Kendrick, Rosalyn, *Examining Religions: Islam*, (Oxford: Heinemann Educational Books, 1989).

Kennedy, Hugh, *The Prophet and the Age of the Caliphates: The Islamic Near East from the Sixth to the Eleventh Century*, A History of the Near East, (London and New York: Longman, 1986).

Khayyam, Omar, *The Rubaiyat of Omar Khayyam*, The first version of Edward Fitzgerald, (London: The Folio Society, 1970).

Lane, Edward William, *An Account of the Manners and Customs of the Modern Egyptians*, 2nd edn., (London: Ward, Lock & Co., 1890).

Lawrence, Bruce B., *Shahrastānī on the Indian Religions*, (The Hague/Paris: Mouton Publishers, 1976).

Lewis, Bernard, *The Arabs in History*, (London: Hutchinson, 1968).

—— *The Assassins: A Radical Sect in Islam*, (London: Weidenfeld & Nicolson, 1967).

Lewis, Geoffrey (Trans.), *The Book of Dede Korkut*, (Harmondsworth: Penguin, 1974).

Lings, Martin, *Muhammad: His Life Based on the Earliest Sources*, (London: Allen & Unwin/Islamic Texts Society, 1983).

Mahfouz, Naguib, *Children of Gebelawi*, trans. by Philip Stewart, (London: Heinemann, 1981).

—— *Respected Sir*, trans. by Rasheed El-Enany, (London: Quartet Books, 1986).

Malik Ibn Anas, *Al-Muwatta of Imam Malik ibn Anas: The First Formulation of Islamic Law*, trans. by A. A. Bewley, (London & New York: Kegan Paul International, 1989).

Marsot, Afaf Lutfi al-Sayyid, *Egypt in the Reign of Muhammad Ali*, (Cambridge: C.U.P., 1984).

al-Mas'udi, *The Meadows of Gold: The Abbasids*, trans. & ed. by Paul Lunde and Caroline Stone, (London & New York: Kegan Paul International, 1989).

Metcalf, Barbara Daly, *Islamic Revival in British India: Deoband, 1860–1900*, (Princeton, New Jersey: Princeton University Press, 1982).

Momen, Moojan, *An Introduction to Shi'i Islam: The History and Doctrines of Twelver Shi'ism*, (New Haven & London: Yale University Press, 1985).

al-Nawawi, *Forty Hadith*, trans. by Ezzeddin Ibraham and Denys Johnson-Davies, (Damascus: Holy Koran Publishing House, 1977).

Netton, Ian Richard, *Allāh Transcendent: Studies in the Structure and Semiotics of Islamic Philosophy, Theology and Cosmology*, (London and New York: Routledge, 1989).

—— 'Arabia and the Pilgrim Paradigm of Ibn Baṭṭūṭa: A Braudelian Approach' in I. R. Netton (ed.), *Arabia and the Gulf: From Traditional Society to Modern States*, (London: Croom Helm, 1986).

—— 'Basic Structures and Signs of Alienation in the *Riḥla* of Ibn Jubayr', *Journal of Arabic Literature*, vol. XXII:1 (1991).

—— *Al-Fārābī and his School*, (London: Routledge, 1992).

—— 'Foreign Influences and Recurring Ismā'īlī Motifs in the *Rasā'il* of the Brethren of Purity' in Alessandro Bausani (ed.), *Convegno Sugli Ikhwān Aṣ-Ṣafā' (Roma, 25–26 Ottobre 1979)*, (Rome: Accademia Nazionale dei Lincei, 1981).

—— *Muslim Neoplatonists: An Introduction to the Thought of the Brethren of Purity (Ikhwān al-Ṣafā')*, (London: Allen & Unwin, 1982/Edinburgh: Edinburgh University Press, 1991, Islamic Surveys 19).

—— 'The Mysteries of Islam' in G. S. Rousseau and Roy Porter (eds.), *Exoticism in the Enlightenment*, (Manchester: Manchester University Press, 1990).

—— 'Myth, Miracle and Magic in the *Riḥla* of Ibn Baṭṭūṭa', *Journal of Semitic Studies*, vol. 29:1 (1984), pp. 131–140.

Nicholson, R. A., *A Literary History of the Arabs*, (Cambridge: C.U.P., repr. 1969).

Nielsen, Jorgen S., *Muslim Immigration and Settlement in Britain*, Research Papers no. 21, (Birmingham: Centre for the Study of Islam and Christian-Muslim Relations, Selly Oak Colleges, March 1984).

Parker, Richard B., Sabin, Robin, and Williams, Caroline, *Islamic Monuments in Cairo: A Practical Guide*, 3rd rev. and enlarged edn., (Cairo: American University in Cairo Press, 1985, 1988).

Parrinder, Geoffrey, *Jesus in the Qur'ān*, London: Sheldon Press, 1977).

Pellat, Charles, *The Life and Works of Jāḥiẓ: Translations of Selected Texts*, (London: Routledge & Kegan Paul, 1969).

Peters, F. E., *Aristotle and the Arabs: The Aristotelian Tradition in Islam*, (New York: New York University Press/London: University of London Press, 1968).

Peters, J. R. T. M., *God's Created Speech: A Study in the Speculative Theology of the Mu'tazilî Qâḍî l-Quḍât Abû l-Ḥasan 'Abd al-Jabbâr bn Aḥmad al-Hamaḏânî*, (Leiden: E. J. Brill, 1976.

Piscatori, James P., *Islam in the Political Process*, (Cambridge: C.U.P., 1983).

al-Qadi, Imam 'Abd ar-Rahim ibn Ahmad, *Islamic Book of the Dead: A Collection of Hadiths on the Fire and the Garden*, (Wood Dalling, Norwich: Diwan Press, 1977).

Qur'ān, The Holy [Ali:] *The Holy Qur'an*, Text, Translation and Commentary by Abdullah Yusuf Ali, (Kuwait: Dhāt al-Salāsil, 1984) [Bilingual Arabic-English text].

Qur'ān, The Holy [Arberry:] *The Koran Interpreted*, by Arthur J. Arberry, 2 vols., (London: Allen & Unwin/New York: The Macmillan Company, 1955, 1971). [English translation of Qur'ān only].

Qur'ān, The Holy [Dawood:] *The Koran*, A Translation by N. J. Dawood, 4th rev. edn., (London: Allen Lane, 1978). [English translation of Qur'ān only, with colour illustrations of mosques and 're-arrangement' of order of chapters (*sūras*)].

Qur'ān, The Holy [Khatib:] *The Bounteous Koran*, a Translation of Meaning and Commentary by M. M. Khatib, (London: Macmillan Press, 1986). [Bilingual Arabic-English text. The Arabic text printed is that of The Royal Cairo Edition and the whole work was 'Authorized by Al-Azhar' in 1984].

Rabi', Muhammad Mahmoud, *The Political Theory of Ibn Khaldūn*, (Leiden: E. J. Brill, 1967).

Rice, David Talbot, *Islamic Art*, rev. edn., (London: Thames & Hudson, 1975).

Rodinson, Maxime, *Mohammed*, (Harmondsworth: Penguin, 1973).

Rosenthal, Franz, *Knowledge Triumphant: The Concept of Knowledge in Medieval Islam*, (Leiden: E. J. Brill, 1970).

Schimmel, Annemarie, *Mystical Dimensions of Islam*, (Chapel Hill, North Carolina: University of North Carolina Press, 1978).

Seale, Morris S., *Muslim Theology: A Study of Origins with Reference to the Church Fathers*, (London: Luzac, 1964).

—— *Qur'an and Bible: Studies in Interpretation and Dialogue*, (London: Croom Helm, 1978).

Shaban, M. A., *The 'Abbāsid Revolution*, (Cambridge: C.U.P., 1970).

—— *Islamic History A.D. 600–750 (A.H. 132): A New Interpretation*, (Cambridge: C.U.P., 1971).

—— *Islamic History: A New Interpretation 2: A.D. 750–1055 (A.H. 132–448)*, (Cambridge: C.U.P., 1976).

Shaw, Stanford, *History of the Ottoman Empire and Modern Turkey: Volume I: Empire of the Gazis: The Rise and Decline of the Ottoman Empire, 1280–1808*, (Cambridge: C.U.P., 1976).

Shorter Encyclopaedia of Islam, ed. H. A. R. Gibb and J. H. Kramers, (Leiden: E. J. Brill/London: Luzac, 1961).

Sivan, Emmanuel, *Radical Islam: Medieval Theology and Modern Politics*, (New Haven & London: Yale University Press, 1985).

Smart, J. R., *Teach Yourself Arabic*, (Dunton Green: Hodder & Stoughton, 1986).

Smith, Jane Idleman and Haddad, Yvonne Yazbeck, *The Islamic Understanding of Death and Resurrection*, (Albany, New York: State University of New York Press, 1981).

al-Tabari, *The Commentary on the Qur'ān*, vol. I, Trans., Introd., and Notes by J. Cooper, (Oxford: O.U.P., 1987)

Tibawi, A. L., *Islamic Education: Its Traditions and Modernization into the Arab National Systems*, (London: Luzac, 1972).

Trevelyan, Raleigh, *Shades of the Alhambra*, (London: The Folio Society, 1984).

Trimingham, J. Spencer, *The Sufi Orders in Islam*, (Oxford: Clarendon Press, 1971).

Ünsal, Behçet, *Turkish Islamic Architecture in Seljuk and Ottoman Times 1071–1923*, (London: Academy Editions/New York: St Martin's Press, 1973).

Watt, W. Montgomery, *Companion to the Qur'ān, Based on the Arberry Translation*, (London: Allen & Unwin, 1967).

—— *The Formative Period of Islamic Thought*, (Edinburgh: Edinburgh University Press, 1973).

—— *Islamic Philosophy and Theology: An Extended Survey*, 2nd edn., Islamic Surveys, (Edinburgh: Edinburgh University Press, 1985).

—— *Muhammad at Mecca*, (Oxford: Clarendon Press, 1953, 1972).
—— *Muhammad at Medina*, (Oxford: Clarendon Press, 1956, 1968).
—— *Muhammad, Prophet and Statesman*, (London: O.U.P., 1961, 1967).
—— *Muslim Intellectual: A Study of al-Ghazali*, (Edinburgh: Edinburgh University Press, 1963, 1971).
Watt, W. Montgomery and Cachia, Pierre, *A History of Islamic Spain*, Islamic Surveys 4, (Edinburgh: Edinburgh University Press, 1965).
Wehr, Hans, *A Dictionary of Modern Written Arabic*, ed. J. Milton Cowan, 2nd printing, (Wiesbaden: Otto Harrassowitz/ London: Allen & Unwin, 1966).
Wensinck, A. J., Jomier, J. & Lewis, B., art. 'Ḥadjdj' in *The Encyclopaedia of Islam, New Edition*, vol. 3, (Leiden: E. J. Brill/London: Luzac, 1986), pp. 31–38.
William of Rubruck, Friar, *The Mission of Friar William of Rubruck: His Journey to the Court of the Great Khan Möngke 1253–1255*, trans. by Peter Jackson, (London: Hakluyt Society, 1990).
Young, M. J. L., Latham, J. D. and Sergeant, R. B. (eds.), *Religion, Learning and Science in the 'Abbasid Period*, The Cambridge History of Arabic Literature, vol. 3, (Cambridge: C.U.P., 1990).
Ziadeh, Nicola A., *Sanūsīya: A Study of a Revivalist Movement in Islam*, (Leiden: E. J. Brill, 1968).

Other Books by Ian Richard Netton

Allāh Transcendent: Studies in the Structure and Semiotics of Islamic Philosophy, Theology and Cosmology

Arabia and the Gulf: From Traditional Society to Modern States (editor)

Al-Fārābī and His School

Golden Roads: Migration, Pilgrimage and Travel in Mediaeval and Modern Islam (editor)

Middle East Materials in United Kingdom and Irish Libraries: A Directory

Muslim Neoplatonists: An Introduction to the Thought of the Brethren of Purity (*Ikhwān al-Ṣafā'*)